Carnival of Repetition

PENN STUDIES IN CONTEMPORARY AMERICAN FICTION

A Series Edited by Emory Elliott, University of California at Riverside

A complete listing of the books in this series appears at the back of this volume

Carnival of Repetition

Gaddis's *The Recognitions* and
Postmodern Theory

JOHN JOHNSTON

upp

University of Pennsylvania Press/PHILADELPHIA

813
G123j

Library of Congress Cataloging-in-Publication Data

Johnston, John (John H.)
    Carnival of repetition: Gaddis's The recognitions and postmodern
theory / John Johnston.
        p.   cm. — (Penn studies in contemporary American fiction)
    Includes bibliographical references.
    ISBN 0-8122-8179-9
        1. Gaddis, William, 1922–   Recognitions.   2. Postmodernism
(Literature)—United States.   3. Repetition in literature.
    I. Title.   II. Series.
    PS3557.A28R434   1989
    813'.54—dc20   89-40397
                                                        CIP

Contents

Introduction

Most first novels are too imitative, either of the "life" they seek to capture or of the writers and conventions that serve as their models. William Gaddis's first novel, *The Recognitions,* problematizes these twin pitfalls by making imitation itself its theme—imitation, that is, in the sense of both copy and counterfeit. Gaddis pursues this theme on many levels and registers—aesthetic, social, and religious—through the activities of myriads of characters across several continents, as well as into mazes of arcane knowledge and bogus scholarship; it even enters reflexively into the novel's structure through the doubling and repetition of prior texts, and the interplay between literal and disguised quotation.

Yet, despite its obvious high achievement, critical recognition of the novel's interest and complexity has been very slow in coming. From its publication in 1955 until Gaddis published his second novel, *JR,* in 1975, *The Recognitions* received scant critical attention; in fact, except for a few sympathetic reviews and scattered essays, it was completely ignored. Only when *JR* received the National Book Award in 1976 did it look as though Gaddis's small cult following was beginning to expand to larger, more respectable proportions. Still, it was not until the publication in 1985 of Gaddis's third novel, *Carpenter's Gothic,* a shorter and more accessible work greeted by Cynthia Ozick's front-page rave review in the *New York Times Book Review,* that the name William Gaddis began to be ranked among America's foremost contemporary writers. Even with this growing recognition, however, very little extended analysis of Gaddis's fiction has been forthcoming.[1] No doubt readers and critics alike have been deterred by its great length, perhaps even put off by its blend of extreme erudition with bald satire. Nevertheless, the neglect seems egregious now, given the large number of books and essays devoted to contemporary American writers of lesser talent and ambition.

This slighting of *The Recognitions* in particular seems all the more unjustified in light of the history of post–World War II American fiction, since Gaddis's first novel so clearly heralds what was to come. If the dominant impulse among writers during the 1950s was to deploy the novel in its more traditional, realist form to explore the existential dilemmas of the individual in the new postwar "mass society," the 1960s witnessed a shift in interest from the psychological complexities of individual character to a more experimental and self-conscious concern with different narrative forms, and realism was continually shading off into fantasy, the grotesque, black humor, and the absurd. This turn, moreover, found parallels in the new fiction of France, Germany, and Latin America.

Within this perspective, *The Recognitions* can be quite easily located. Both formally and thematically, direct lines of continuity stem from Gaddis's novel to the many variations of Menippean satire, prose fiction anatomy, and encyclopedic narrative written by William Burroughs, John Barth, Thomas Pynchon, Robert Coover, Joseph McElroy, Don DeLillo, and others who attained eminence in the 1960s and early 1970s. Only Ralph Ellison's *Invisible Man,* published in 1952, presents a rival precursor of this new fictional strain, and its wide attention was due mainly to its treatment of a black man's experience in a dominant white society. Many critics, moreover, saw important connections between the new fiction and the "classics" of high modernism.[2] Yet surely, more than any other contemporary American novel, *The Recognitions* harks back to these latter, to the extent that no serious discussion of it can ignore its relationship to the novels of James Joyce, Thomas Mann, and André Gide. Indeed, in looking both forward to a fiction that it may be said to inaugurate or prefigure and back at a fiction that it extends and modifies, Gaddis's first novel is truly Janus-faced, and thus occupies an especially significant transitional position in the evolution of modern American fiction.

One might even say "strategic" position, insofar as the novel seems to sit on the cusp between modernism and what is increasingly being referred to as postmodernism. Admittedly, the latter is a confusing and problematic term. Yet, what makes postmodernism attractive as a provisional period concept is that it not only forces a comparison with earlier works of modernism (in order that continuities and departures may be marked out), but it also may be linked to the total reshaping of literary criticism that occurred in the late 1960s and 1970s, mainly as a consequence of a large wave of theoretical writing from the Continent.[3] Anglo-American empiricism, whether it issued in a formalist or historical criticism, found its basic assumptions and methodology challenged on every front as a whole new range of critical practices—semiotics, structuralism, psychoanalysis, Marxism, feminism, deconstruction—rather than simply vying with the older styles of criticism, as myth study and the early kind of Freudian analysis had done, reconceived the work of literature as a "text" and consequently posed new questions about it. Meanwhile, the first works of high modernism began to look, if not antiquated and conventional, at least diminished in their difficulty and subversive force as their basic assumptions and effects became all too familiar through university acculturation and mass-media absorption.[+] Possibly the same fate lies in wait for the openly textual, discontinuous, and "schizophrenic" kind of writing that is currently being labeled post-modern, of which Beckett's *Watt,* Burroughs's *Naked Lunch,* Barthelme's *City Life,* Pynchon's *Gravity's Rainbow,* and Ashbery's poetry may serve as examples.

In this second, more recent perspective, *The Recognitions* commands a new interest, for it is now possible to see that it anticipated, if sometimes only symptomatically, much of what will come to be at issue theoretically. For example, as it persistently worries the opposition between original and imitation, genuine and counterfeit, Gaddis's novel pushes toward its own kind of deconstruction *avant la lettre.* Moreover, in its collaging and superimposition of narrative upon narrative and voice upon voice, the novel creates a multiplicity of references, allusions, textual transformations and metamorphoses; for Gaddis, evidently, "intertextuality" was a compositional procedure from the outset. Indeed, the tension or oscillation within *The Recognitions* between a logic of representation and a logic of the text makes it a prime focus for current textual theories, especially since its own textuality is implicitly linked with the new effects of mass-media reproduction. This feature alone would seem to establish Gaddis's novel as a privileged locus for investigating the historical conditions of possibility for the emergence of "textuality."

Perhaps most important, explicitly textual interests in *The Recognitions* are linked to the dissolution of the subject, or to what is referred to in Critical Theory as the loss of the individual or bourgeois subject. Certainly Gaddis's depiction of character is postindividual and post-Freudian in the sense that his characters are not fully autonomous and intelligible in the terms of bourgeois psychology, and do not develop in self-awareness and moral perception. Instead, they often seem like personae in a psychodrama or partial crystallizations out of a social multiplicity. Furthermore, the novel itself, as a heterogeneously styled and multivoiced composition, questions the assumption of a unified authorial subject whose vision it might be said "to express." More than anything else, this anticipation of postmodernist themes and fictional assumptions demands the kind of theoretical approach to *The Recognitions* that will be elaborated in the pages that follow.

These, then, are the coordinates within which this study has been conceived: an important and relatively unknown work of contemporary fiction, a new and in many ways yet-to-be-defined literary and cultural context into which this work must somehow be inserted, and a new set of "speculative instruments" providing new tools of analysis. What remains to be specified here are the means by which these coordinates become a critical framework and how *The Recognitions* itself dictates the choice of terms.

Mikhail Bakhtin's theory of the dialogic or polyphonic novel provides the overall theoretical orientation. Indeed, a guiding intention of this study has been to situate *The Recognitions* in what must now be seen, thanks to Bakhtin's work on the novel, as a distinctive subtradition of modern fiction. I shall be much less concerned therefore with Bakhtin's position as a postformalist Russian critic or with his writings published under the name of (or conjointly with) V. N. Volosinov or P. N. Medvedev—although these are of great theoretical importance—than with his entirely new approach to prose fiction. So, throughout what follows, I draw upon his *Problems in Dostoevsky's Poetics, Rabelais and His World,* and the theoretical essays on the novel in *The Dialogic Imagination* for concepts that Bakhtin developed specifically for analyzing the kind of fiction that *The Recognitions* exemplifies. Whether we call it contemporary Menippean satire or carnivalesque fiction, the important point is that Bakhtin's theory accounts for the distinctive features and formal unity not only of *The Recognitions* but also of much of the most innovative and ambitious American fiction since *Invisible Man,* a list of which would include, besides *The Recognitions,* Burroughs's *Naked Lunch,* Barth's *The Sot-Weed Factor,* Pynchon's *Gravity's Rainbow,* Coover's *The Public Burning,* and DeLillo's *Ratner's Star.*

Among Bakhtin's many ideas about literature, his concept of a "dialogic" or a dialogical structure is the most essential for our analysis. It should be noted, however, that Bakhtin's concept, like several of his critical formulations, is susceptible to several different interpretations and uses. By dialogic Bakhtin initially meant a new principle of literary composition based on the open-ended, internal dialogues that resound throughout Dostoevsky's fiction. This fiction, Bakhtin wrote, contains a "plurality of independent and unmerged voices and consciousnesses" that are never objectified and given "finalizable" definition by a larger, more englobing authorial discourse or consciousness.[5] This interaction among consciousnesses staged by Dostoevsky means that no discourse, including the author's, is ever privileged. For this reason, Michael Holquist, in his glossary entry for "dialogue" in *The Dialogic Imagination,* states that "a word, discourse, language or culture undergoes 'dialogization' when it becomes relativized, deprivileged, aware of competing definitions for the same things."[6] However, another theorist, Julia Kristeva, argues in her essay "Word, Dialogue, and Novel" that Bakhtin's notion of the dialogic entails a "semic complex" implying "the double, language and another logic," most notably in narratives where a symbolic logic of distance, substitution, and relationship vies with a logic of linear continuity, cause/effect, substance, and identity.[7] In understanding the dialogic as the entwinement of two different logics, Kristeva provides a stepping stone from Bakhtin to semiotic and textual approaches to modern fiction and thereby extends the concept's usefulness. Thus I assume, following Kristeva, that in Dostoevsky's fiction the dialogic remains for the most part "at a representational, fictional level," whereas in later polyphonic fiction like Gaddis's it becomes "interior to language."

However, in order to describe the specific dialogic at work in *The Recognitions,* I press into service a body of work from another contemporary French thinker, Gilles Deleuze. In *Différence et répétition* and *Logique du sens,* Deleuze develops an anti-Hegelian philosophy that draws upon linguistics, physics, biology, literature, and psychoanalysis, all in order to propose an aesthetic grounded no longer in representation but rather on a "new image of thought."[8] More specifically, Deleuze's concept of the simulacrum and general project of "overthrowing Platonism" provide the terms for analyzing the dialogic that emerges within *The Recognitions* as the novel's basic thematic and structural opposition between the counterfeit and authentic is eroded and thrown into question, and a logic of the model and copy begins to give way to a logic of the simulacrum and phantasm. It is this "reversal," I demonstrate in Chapter One, that constitutes the novel's central event. Chapter Two provides a summary of the novel's multifarious plots and carnivalesque themes as a necessary preliminary to the detailed analysis of the repercussions of this reversal, first in relation to the novel's postindividual conception of human identity in Chapter Three and then, in Chapter Four, to the heterogeneous, "double-voiced" and hybrid nature of its narrative form. Finally, in the last chapter, I move toward a discussion of *The Recognitions* in relation to postmodernism, both as theory and fictional practice, and then conclude with analyses of *JR* and *Carpenter's Gothic* as postmodern novels.

Chapter 1

Repetition and Difference

> As you know, I am working on the assumption that our
> psychical mechanism has come about by a process of strati-
> fication: the material present-at-hand as memory traces is
> from time to time subjected to a restructuring in accordance
> with fresh circumstances—it undergoes, as it were, a re-
> transcription. Thus what is essentially new in my theory is
> the thesis that memory is present-at-hand not once, but sev-
> eral times over, that it is registered or deposited in various
> species of signs.
>
> —Sigmund Freud, Letter to Wilhem Fliess, June 12, 1896

Copies and Counterfeits

Every act of recognition implies a repetition, for we can only "recognize" what we have seen or experienced before: such is the central
informing principle of William Gaddis's *The Recognitions*, where as idea
and technique it is developed in all its manifold possibility and partic-
ularity. Characters, situations, catch phrases, and allusions—everything
occurs and recurs in some grosser or more refined version, in both serious
and parodied formulations, and Gaddis plays continuously on our "recognitions" of their similarity and difference. The larger question posed
by the novel is how this difference is to be taken and understood: as a
perversion or deviation from some pre-established norm or essence, or
as the production of a new event?

Hence the emphasis above should fall on the word "version." For if
it is clear that *The Recognitions* is primarily concerned, as one critic has
put it,[1] with "the multiple and paradoxical relations between recognition
and forgery"—of paintings, money, ideas, social identity, and sexual roles,
even words, a series of items that are somehow not the "real" thing, that
harbor some difference—it is equally clear that these same counterfeit
items have come in large part to make up the very fabric of contemporary
American life. But beyond comprising a thorough, even unremitting,
anatomy of such suspect representations, *The Recognitions* goes so far as
to throw into question even the existence of some founding first or
authentic version and to suggest that all human identities and actions

alike may indeed constitute only items in a series for which there is no original or true model.

On the most general level, Gaddis's novel is a modern retelling of the *Clementine Recognitions,* in a manner similar to James Joyce's retelling of Homer's *Odyssey* in *Ulysses.* Significantly, the *Clementine Recognitions* has been the object of some controversy concerning its date of composition, authorship, and textual authenticity and was often erroneously attributed to Clement of Rome. (It is now generally thought to have been written anonymously early in the third century A.D.) The status of this "source" text is ambiguous in other respects as well. For one, the author seems to have had no intention of presenting his material as a factual account. Instead, choosing the disciples of Christ and their followers as the principal characters, he incorporated their most important beliefs into dialogue and wove the whole together with a thread of fictitious narrative. The result is a theological romance centered on the quest of a young man named Clement for the true religion and the salvation of his soul. It recounts his meeting with Saint Peter and conversion to Christianity and then his journey with Peter from Rome to cities in the Middle East where the latter preached the gospel. Embedded in the narrative are long debates with Simon Magus, who tempts Peter by offering him magic powers as an alternative to Christ's promises of everlasting life. As a consequence of these features, the *Clementine Recognitions* has been taken to be a saint's life—much of its material, in fact, was later incorporated into the *Legenda aurea*—even though Clement was not a "real" saint (the frequent confusion of Clement with Clement of Rome no doubt contributed to this mistake). But more important, because of the temptation scenes and the figure of Simon Magus, scholars generally regard the *Clementine Recognitions* as a precursor or first version of the Faust legend.[2]

Not surprisingly, then, in addition to presenting a modern-day version of Clement's quest, Gaddis's *The Recognitions* also repeats the Faust story, albeit in a truncated form. But like Clement's quest, the Faust legend only surfaces intermittently—enough to give the narrative a multileveled resonance—and mostly in reference to the life of the protagonist, Wyatt Gwyon, who is tempted by a shady entrepreneur and con man named Recktall Brown into forging paintings by old masters of the Northern Renaissance. The role of these two mythic narratives in the novel will later be examined in some detail, but here I should stress two salient consequences of their "repetition": first, the sense in which *The Recog-*

nitions thereby becomes a palimpsest written over and "in between" narrative fragments taken from earlier moments in Western cultural history, while at the same time unlayering or de-sedimenting these fragments, and secondly, the fact that these precursor narratives exist in many versions, and their originality and authenticity are not easily established. Thus, if *The Recognitions* can be said to foreground the problem of its own intertextuality and to elicit an "archeological perspective" by repeating an apparently originary narrative, the status and significance of this "original" is also thrown into question by the very fact that it only exists as a series of multiple versions and transformations.[3]

Such narrative layerings may also suggest that Gaddis has adopted Joyce's "mythical method" as an organizational device; in fact, as Bernard Benstock has convincingly demonstrated, Gaddis is profoundly indebted to Joyce for both textual and thematic borrowings.[4] At the conclusion of *A Portrait of the Artist as a Young Man,* Stephen Dedalus sets out to "forge in the smithy of [his] soul the uncreated conscience of [his] race." What appears to interest Gaddis is the ambiguity of the verb "to forge," and the paradox by which a forgery can yield "recognitions" of reality. Such recognitions confront us with the textual nature of perception, since they make us conscious, through the play of repetition and difference, of the differential nature of perception and language. For it is only when one is confronted with multiple forgeries and imitations that the "original" becomes a problem—as if in a peculiar way the forgery calls up the original, which didn't exist beforehand *as* an original.

Moreover, in the case of visual art, the copy of an original work had its own value well into the nineteenth century, when copying was still considered an acceptable practice. Only in our own time has the copy become illegitimate, and the hallmark of the inauthentic. As soon as the work of art can no longer be said to represent an objective order (of God, nature, society, or discourse) that both transcends and guarantees the art's validity, all art becomes "original," but only as a sign of the artist's subjectivity as it is revealed by his or her mark, gesture, or style. Thus, it is often said that modern art no longer represents a *content* (which can now be reproduced mechanically), but instead constitutes an act of pictorial invention that draws upon the past for its inspiration, forms, and motifs. According to this logic, what had been a form of representation now becomes a repetition of forms, and the distinction between forgery and copy no longer matters—except, of course, in the art market at the moment the object assumes exchange value.[5]

The Recognitions takes up this entire problematic through its interest in the counterfeiting and forgery of art. Let us consider, in this regard, the role of Hieronymus Bosch's painting *The Seven Deadly Sins* in the life of the novel's protagonist Wyatt Gwyon. His father had purchased the "original," we learn, from the estate of the Conte di Brescia while in Italy but had brought it through customs "disguised" as a copy. (That the painting *is* indeed a copy is intimated by the fact that the Conte di Brescia's name evokes Dante's archcounterfeiter Adamo da Brescia in the Malebolge section of the *Inferno*.) Years later, in order to obtain money for art school, Wyatt himself copies the painting and substitutes his copy for the "original," which he then sells. Later, when the "original" turns up in the collection of the corrupt art dealer Recktall Brown, Wyatt realizes that it was only a copy after all that his father had bought and that he had copied. But then Basil Valentine, a sophistical art connoisseur in league with Brown, explains that the same trick that Wyatt had played on his father has also been played on Brown and that the painting he had copied was indeed the "original." "Thank God there was gold to forge," Wyatt exclaims in relief. As we'll see in a moment, the phrase carries considerable thematic import, since it makes explicit a whole system of analogies essential to the novel's economy of representation. Just as gold, the "origin" of wealth, sign of authenticity, and embodiment of value, guarantees—even forms the basis of—a system of monetary exchange, so the existence of the original guarantees the meaning and efficacy of an aesthetic economy. Yet, in a final reversal, Wyatt discovers the painting he has taken to be the "original" was indeed only a copy:

> —Copying a copy? Is that where I started? All my life I've sworn it was real, year after year, that damned table top [painting] floating in the bottom of the tank, I've sworn it was real, and today? A child could tell it's a copy [. . .] — Now, if there was no gold? . . . continuing an effort to assemble a pattern from breakage where features had failed.—And if what I've been forging does not exist? And if I . . . if I, I. . . . (381)

Wyatt's anguished realization that at his own "origins" there was no founding original to forge leads to a delirious breakdown that spells the end of the counterfeiting ring he has formed with Brown and Valentine. It also heightens the reader's own deepening suspicion that every supposed original in *The Recognitions* may turn out to be an imitation or counterfeit. In fact, in the increasingly manifest absence of anything true and authentic in the novel, the very proliferation of forgeries, counterfeits, imposters, and sham items of every sort and description augurs a possible dissolution of the basis on which the difference is grounded. In the novel, this "event" seems both anticipated and presumed, as the narrative moves toward a point where the distinction between original and copy ceases to matter for Wyatt (and perhaps the reader as well).

Another series of paintings—in parallel as it were—illustrates this same process through another series of reversals. While still an art student, Wyatt had painted a portrait of Emperor Valerian in the style of Hans Memling, a fifteenth-century Flemish painter whose pious portraits are done mostly in the style of his teacher, Rogier van der Weyden. Without his knowledge, Wyatt's own art teacher, Herr Koppel, secretly sold the painting as an "undiscovered Memling." Later, the painting was purchased by Brown, who assumed it to be an original. Valentine then had it copied, substituted the copy for what he too thought was the original, and sent the latter "back to Europe where it belongs"—thereby removing it from an economy corrupted by the circulation of counterfeits.

Ironically, Valentine himself is partly responsible for this proliferation of forgeries, since he is a member of Brown's counterfeiting ring. As the art expert in the ring, his role is to raise doubts about a newly discovered "original," and then, by reversing himself, to establish the painting's credibility on more secure grounds. In the case of Wyatt's Memling imitation, his attempt to restore the original to its provenance in Europe makes sense or can be justified only if he can reliably distinguish between the original and a copy. That he should mistake an imitation for an undiscovered Memling, however, attests to his inability to do so. In his attempt to reverse what amounts to a kind of Gresham's law operating in the aesthetic domain, Valentine thus unwittingly reveals the loss of distinction between a "genuine" imitation and a counterfeit.

Yet, as we gradually come to see, this is not exactly accurate either, for Wyatt's painting is neither an imitation nor an original but a simulation of a Memling or a simulacrum. It is not an imitation or copy because there is (was) no original, but it is not an original either since it was not painted by Memling himself. Nor, as Wyatt explains at some length, is it a painting done simply in the style of Memling, for such a superficial forgery is quickly spotted by the experts. Instead, it is an attempt to (re)produce, using exactly the same materials and under the same "spiritual" conditions in which Memling worked—conditions established and maintained by the art guild—a genuine and authentic work of art, as if Memling himself had painted it. In this respect, Wyatt's attempt to fabricate or simulate a Memling is very similar to Pierre Menard's attempt to rewrite *Don Quixote* in Borges's famous story. As a simulation or simulacrum, his painting eludes the very opposition between an original and a copy.[6]

In *The Recognitions,* what holds true for paintings also applies to human identity. A young friend of Wyatt's, Otto Pivner, is trying to write a play, which he knocks together from the bits and pieces of dialogue that he hears around him, but most of it is taken from his exchanges with Wyatt, with the result that the main character of the play, Gordon, becomes a pale reflection or imitation of Wyatt. But since Otto himself, we soon realize, is a watered-down version of Wyatt, his efforts yield both a "real" and a "fictional" double of the main character. Moreover, because Wyatt is gradually identified with a whole series of cultural and mythic figures (Faust, Clement, John Huss, Raymond Lully, and Prester John), it becomes increasingly problematic to speak of him as an "original" in any meaningful sense. Finally, this series of doublings is brought to a comic resolution when Otto, who is obsessed with his identity and forever peering at his mirror image, abandons his "real" identity completely and becomes a version of Gordon, his own fictitious creation. Since these reflections and identity changes occur across hundreds of pages of quasi-naturalistic fiction, the effect is unsettling yet undeniably humorous. But whatever the effect, the important point is that the entire constellation of mirror reflections and doublings serves to illustrate comically how the dicta that art imitates life and life imitates art are both true and, therefore, reversible. In other words, in *The Recognitions* life and art cannot be held separate and do not form a stable opposition. As one critic has put it: in *The Recognitions* reality and art become interchangeable metaphors for each other.[7]

Otto's phantasmic identity is "recognized" in various ways by other characters, one of whom even refers to him as "part of a series of an original that never existed." But Otto is by no means the only character who attempts to forge an identity by imitating what he thinks is a more authentic or interesting version of himself. In fact, the entire novel is crowded with fakes and counterfeits of every imaginable sort: characters not only fabricate identities or disguise and misrepresent themselves (both consciously and unconsciously) but also engage in every form of fakery and imitation, from plagiarism and journalistic hackwork to the forging of passports, the counterfeiting of money, and the production and advertising of sham consumer items.

In addition to its thematic importance in the aesthetic and social realms, imitation—again in the twofold sense of copy and counterfeit—is also "anatomized" in the religious realm. Recalling the novel's Clementine "original" leads us to expect that *The Recognitions* will be concerned in some way with the possibility of sainthood and religious belief in the modern world. Thomas à Kempis's *Imitatio Christi*, mentioned several times in the novel, provides one obvious connection, for it argues that a saint's life must be the reenactment (that is, an imitation or repetition) of Christ's life. Within *The Recognitions,* the doctrine is broadly parodied in several ways, as when one character, "quoting" an unnamed friend, asserts that "the saints were counterfeits of Christ, and that Christ was a counterfeit of God" (483). More significantly, one strand of the plot culminates in the canonization of an eleven-year-old girl, whose only saintly act was to be raped by a madly deluded man who thinks that only intercourse with a virgin will cure him of a fatal disease, and whose penitence initiates a series of suspect "miracles." Yet while his penitence, which seems genuine, is soon followed by remission of the disease, evidence also accumulates which suggests that the entire affair is a conspiracy organized to bring money to a Spanish monastery. Thus, in a double reversal typical of the novel, the miracle and canonization are both discredited and oddly justified in one and the same movement.

Although counterfeiting is hardly an original theme in modern fiction, in *The Recognitions* the very excess of the counterfeit and the reversals that often ensue from this excess make Gaddis's treatment of it completely unique. Turning briefly to André Gide's novel *The Counterfeiters,* which is also structured by the copy/counterfeit opposition, we can obtain a preliminary measure of Gaddis's innovations. The major difference is that Gide's novel, though it also plays out the same opposition between the genuine and the false, the authentic and the counterfeit, never questions or destabilizes this founding opposition itself. The central character, Bernard, who is obsessed with both his own sincerity and that of others, explains how the metaphor of the true and false coin is to be extended to the evaluation of feelings as well as to other people. And though he admits that "these feelings ring as false as counters, but they pass for good coin," there is never any doubt that the counterfeit will finally be revealed as the false. Hence, we discover, along with Bernard, that Edouard is the authentic novelist—the true author surrogate, as it were—and the Comte de Passavant, the false one. Furthermore, the distinction is to be applied to the novel itself: because *The Counterfeiters* investigates the conditions and limitations of its own artistic conventions, it must be taken as a more genuine or authentic representation than the naturalistic novel it criticizes, which is seen as "false" to life, a degraded copy of a copy.

Within *The Counterfeiters* we can also observe a system of homologies between sexual, monetary, and literary exchanges which are framed or anchored through a relation to the father. After passing through a circuit of literary and homosexual father figures, Bernard forgets the problem of his bastardy and returns at last to the haven of his "true" (nominal, but not biological) father, Profitendieu, whose very name suggests a "profit in God," thus reinforcing the realignment and containment of the analogies. In simple terms, Bernard, having wandered or erred through a realm of counterfeits, returns to the father and his true home. Though not directly thematized as such, this Christian framework never-theless guarantees the stability and coherence of the novel as an artistic representation.

Initially, *The Recognitions* seems to proceed according to a similar fic-tional logic, though here the central character, Wyatt Gwyon, is himself a counterfeiter. As in *The Counterfeiters,* this central character encounters many inauthentic artists. One in particular, a novelist named Ludy, pro-vides the public with just what it wants: writing that, like a Hallmark card, exactly fulfills its every conventional expectation. Yet it is always clear that while Wyatt's paintings are indeed "forgeries" of past art, they are still far more interesting and even authentic than anything Ludy or the other self-proclaimed artists in the novel can conceive or produce. Moreover, in *The Recognitions,* as in *The Counterfeiters,* a system of anal-ogies between art, money, identity, and fatherhood is similarly implied. But here, the differences between Gide's novel and Gaddis's become especially significant. When Wyatt attempts to return to the father, he discovers that no such return is possible. Not only does his father turn out *not* to be the Protestant reverend he appears to be, the latter being merely a disguise to cover his "reversion" to Mithraism, but Wyatt also discovers that there is no possible escape from this world of proliferating counterfeits, which increasingly takes on the appearance of a mad carnival.

For the reader, this very excess of false and suspect versions may begin to erode the stability and firmness of the novel's sustaining thematic opposition, especially as it becomes evident that the counterfeit theme has been internalized textually. For example, the layering of mythic narratives seems to indicate that the novel's plot is only a degraded echo or copy of the Faust legend, itself an echo of Clement's story. While reading *The Recognitions* we may even experience the pressure of an imminent reversal, as an overwhelming imbalance between the counterfeit and the authentic threatens to undermine a qualitative distinction, and the novel's constitutive and most fundamental opposition appears more and more unstable and commutable.

The differences between the *The Counterfeiters* and *The Recognitions* are thus both quantitative and qualitative: in Gaddis's novel, the circulation of counterfeits or simulacra—whether of paintings, money, religious relics, or social and sexual identity—is much more extensive, to the point where the distinction between the "real" and the "counterfeit" begins to blur and the "difference" is increasingly thrown into question. Yet, ironically enough, this blurring of distinctions does not inhibit the process of exchange, which still functions smoothly, perhaps even more fluidly, thereby implying that "recognition" of the authentic may not be a requisite condition but only a secondary effect.

More important than the loss of the distinction between the true and the counterfeit, however, is the loss of the homologies as they are articulated and finally realigned in Gide's novel. While these homologies may seem to have only metaphorical significance, they actually reflect, because they depend upon and reproduce, a whole system of value equivalences. In *Économie et symbolique*, Jean-Joseph Goux has analyzed how such a system of equivalences and the consequent hierarchy of values are constituted. First, there is the imposition of:

> a principle of order and subordination according to which the great (complex and multiform) majority of "signs" (products, acts and gestures, subjects, objects) are assigned a place under the sacred authority of several from among their number. At certain points of condensation [for Goux these are: gold, the father, the phallus, and the Word] value seems to be stored up, capitalized, centralized, investing certain elements with a privileged representativity, indeed, with the monopoly of representativity within the diversified collection

of which they are elements. The enigmatic genesis of this promotion is then effaced, rendering their monopoly absolute (detached and unlimited) in their transcendental role as a standard and measure of values.[8]

Goux's analysis allows us to specify the breakdown of a structure of homologies in *The Recognitions* more precisely and to recognize a simultaneous loosening up, if not a dissolution, of exactly those points of condensation where value is centralized. I have already mentioned the absent or ineffectual father, the counterfeiting of money and art, and later we shall see how the novel plays with the sexual identity of the characters. In fact, money and sexual identity are often humorously conflated in *The Recognitions,* as both characters and currency are often suspected of being "queer." As to the power and central authority of the Word or *logos,* it is obvious from the novel's onset that we have entered an "infinitely proliferating, cross-referenced encyclopedic world [of words] which is eminently profane, deceitful and double-crossing."[9] In this regard, it should be recalled that the insidious power of words once detached from the *logos* has been of paramount concern in the Western tradition at least since Plato, who instituted a hierarchical system of analogies similar to the one Goux describes. More specifically, Plato suggests a precise analogy between the model, the "good" (or true) copy, and the "bad" copy in relation to the father of the *logos,* the *logos* itself, and writing. Furthermore, Jacques Derrida has shown that for Plato writing itself becomes a simulacrum (a bad copy of a copy) or a "false claimant" (*un faux prétendant*), insofar as it presumes to seize upon the *logos* by violence or by ruse, or even to supercede it completely by not passing through the father.[10] In either case, the rebel son, the deceitful word, and writing are all for Plato analogous instances of subversion.

In contrast to *The Counterfeiters,* then, *The Recognitions* seems to be neither governed nor supported by a harmonious system of homologies that can be recentered and realigned through the resolution of the narrative: in the plot, the return to the father is tried and found to be no longer possible; in fact, as we shall later see, Gaddis even parodies another possibility—the Joycean "symbolic" solution. This raises the question of whether the delirious proliferation of forgeries, counterfeits, imposters, and sham items encountered in *The Recognitions* finally erodes or subverts the foundational analogies Goux pinpoints, and thus dissolves the basis on which oppositional "difference" in the classical sense is grounded. For it should be clear from the examples offered thus far that the surfeit of the fake and counterfeit in the novel tends not only to destabilize a basic thematic opposition but also to augur a possible mutation of the symbolic order that sustains representation itself. In order to explore more fully this erosion of the copy/counterfeit opposition and the consequences for the novel's structure as a whole, the moment when this opposition was founded and the "difference" installed must be re-examined. In short, we must reread Plato.

The Return of the Simulacra

Among the many oppositions Plato bequeathed to Western culture—essence and appearance, the intelligible and the sensible, the Idea and the image, the model and the copy—the most germane to our discussion is the division established in *The Sophist* between the copy and the simulacrum (or counterfeit). There, in the course of his attempt to define the sophist, the Eleatic Stranger distinguishes between two kinds of imitation or image-making (*eidolon*): one that produces an appearance or effect of similarity but is not a true likeness (and is therefore designated as a phantasm), and one that produces a true likeness (an icon)." As in other dialogues where the objective is to choose between the true and the false (or between the pure and the impure, the authentic and the inauthentic), the philosophical task is to distinguish between good and bad copies, or rather between copies (icons) that are well founded and simulacra (phantasms) that are not. As images, both true copies and simulacra produce the effect of likeness, but whereas the true copies perpetuate likeness, the simulacra only dissemble or simulate it. Instead of communicating the essence of the Idea by representing internally its relations and proportions as the good copies do, the simulacra harbor a difference or disparity. Unlike the good copies, which are anchored or grounded in their likeness to the Ideas, the simulacra are ground*less:* they arise from the abyss and exist only as degraded and imperfect copies of a copy. Now, Platonism as a whole depends on the triumph of the good copies over the simulacra, which, because of their demoniac character, must be repressed and prevented from "rising to the surface" and insinuating themselves into social life. Truth itself is at stake, for if copies remain true to the model, by reproducing its likeness (and thereby participating in the Idea), the simulacra have no true model. In fact, the overwhelming presence of simulacra would displace all true models or, more radically, imply their nonexistence; in either case, the very possibility of truth would be destroyed.

Just as there are two kinds of imitation, the copies and the simulacra, so there are two kinds of teachers: the philosophers who base their teaching on true knowledge of the Ideas and the sophists who teach the rhetorical manipulation of opinion, who deny or dissemble the truth. For Plato, therefore, the sophist is the creature of the simulacrum, the satyr or Proteus who insinuates himself everywhere. He is also the rebel son, the insurgent who seeks to destabilize and subvert the Platonic order of knowledge and truth. Yet this potential for instability and subversion is already present within Plato's dialogue. As Gilles Deleuze demonstrates, at several points in the text Plato allows his own ironic method to carry him to the very threshold of the abyss opened up by the possibility of no longer being able to distinguish the true from the false copy, or more centrally, the true philosopher from the dissembling sophist. One step further, Deleuze asserts, and Plato himself would have initiated the reversal or overthrow of Platonism, thereby inaugurating a new era in philosophy, heralded by the "return of the simulacra" and the end of truth.[12]

For one strand of modern philosphy, represented most forcefully by Heidegger, Derrida, and other French poststructuralists, this is indeed the aim of the "philosophy of the future" announced by Nietzsche. For Nietzsche, such a project entails the abolition of both the world of essences *and* the world of appearances—in other words, of the very logic that allows them to be opposed. Deleuze's contribution is to have shown that the difference between these two philosophies—that of Plato and that of Nietzsche—hinges on two radically different conceptions of difference, which in turn imply two ways of conceiving repetition. In "Platon et le simulacre" Deleuze distinguishes between these two conceptions of difference as follows:

> Let us consider two formulations: "only that which resembles itself differs," and "only differences resemble one another." It is a question of two readings of the world insofar as the one urges us to think of difference starting from a pre-established similitude or identity, whereas the other invites us on the contrary to think of similitude and even identity as the product of a fundamental disparity. The first defines exactly the world of copies or of representations; it establishes the world as icon. The second, against the first, defines the world of simulacra. It establishes the world itself as phantasm.[13]

In this perspective, Platonic repetition appears as the repetition of pre-established essences or archetypal forms, that is, as an "essentializing" mode of thought that can only think of "difference" as secondary and negative. By means of the Platonic notion of participation and the principle of self-identity, it gives rise to a correspondence theory of truth and to the conception of art as mimesis. (The doctrine of representation based on these assumptions was of course later developed by Aristotle.) In opposition to this philosophy of the Same, the Nietzschean mode of repetition posits a world articulated in terms of difference, where every object is intrinsically unique and similarities appear only against a background of differential relationships. The "same" returns, but as a disguise or displacement of "difference."[4]

It was the Platonic conception, however, taken up by Christianity and then reformulated in transcendental philosophy, that came to assume a normative status in Western culture. Yet there has always been this "other" philosophical tradition, evident in such thinkers as Lucretius and Spinoza. In *Différence et répétition,* Deleuze draws upon Kierkegaard, Nietzsche, and Heidegger—all philosophers of "difference"—in order to show that the "overthrow of Platonism" is essential to the generalized anti-Hegelianism characteristic of modern philosophy and that difference and repetition have taken the place of the identical and the negative, of identity and contradiction:

> The primacy of identity, in whatever manner it is conceived, defines the world of representation. But modern thought is born from the bankruptcy of representation, as from the loss of identities, and from the discovery of all the forces which act beneath the representation of identity. The modern world is one of simulacra. There man does not outlive God; the identity of the subject does not outlive that of substance. All identities are only simulated, produced like an "optical effect" by a deeper play which is that of difference and repetition."[5]

Now that the transcendental realm that formerly provided the guarantee and support of truth, representation, and identity is no longer possible, Deleuze argues, the philosophy of the future must be a philosophy of immanence and multiplicity, with no dialectic subsuming the One and the Many, with no grand Totality unifying all the parts.

Deleuze's reading of *The Sophist* and his formulation of the two ways of conceiving difference enable us to see the extent to which *The Recognitions* constitutes a modern fictional gloss on Plato's text and a working out of the theological, aesthetic, and social consequences of "overturning Platonism."[6] While, at first, *The Recognitions* may seem to be advocating a Platonic "recognition of reality" through the power of art, as several of the major characters' musings on the "origin of design" might suggest, Gaddis's novel is actually haunted by a strong sense that those Platonic assumptions are now exhausted. The constant reversal and eventual erosion of the authentic/counterfeit opposition is, of course, one highly symptomatic instance of the Platonic paradigm's instability. More generally, as simulacra and phantasms proliferate in a mad delirium, the Platonic notion that the world is an "icon" and that "recognition" (*anagnoresis*) the mode by which we apprehend its reality cannot be seriously sustained.[17]

Yet, in one sense, this formulation already goes too far, or is not yet precise enough. For dramatically figured in *The Recognitions* is a movement or reversal that approximates in fictional terms what Deleuze describes as the "overturning" of Platonism: "in the infinite movement of degraded resemblance, from copy to copy, we reach this point where everything changes nature, where the copy itself reverses into a simulacrum, where finally resemblance and spiritual imitation give place to repetition."[18] This turning point or point of reversal is the conceptual fulcrum upon which *The Recognitions* turns. More precisely, the central "event" pervading *The Recognitions* must be envisioned as a reversal from the Platonic paradigm of model and copy (or original and imitation) to the Deleuzian (or Nietzschean) one of the simulacrum and phantasm. Of course, it is not an "event" in the ordinary sense of the word, for it is never reducible to a specific state of things. Instead, it takes place according to what Deleuze calls the "time of Aion," a time, that is, in which the "event" has always already just happened or is always just about to happen, but never occurs in the present moment.[19] In more ordinary language, *The Recognitions* at once presumes and anticipates this reversal, even though it does not literally occur.

Gaddis's novel is therefore "ambivalent" in a very strong sense: it both looks back at Platonic recognition and forward to Deleuzian repetition, and articulates this Janus-like state in a series of reversible images of which the copy/counterfeit series is the most obvious. This reversibility stems from an underlying structural ambivalence revealed in the co-existence of two antagonistic logics at work within *The Recognitions*. According to the first or Platonic "logic," an originary essence provides the guarantee of truth, authenticity, and identity. A true recognition will always have this essence (or its lack) as its content, which in turn can only be conveyed by a true model or copy. In contrast, the second or

Nietzschean "logic" implies a series without a founding original or true version. It might be formulated as follows: since there is no original, the model for the copy is itself a copy, and the copy is the copy of a copy. There can be no true recognition but only creative misrecognitions, since every representation is always a displacement and a disguise. Behind the mask covering the face, there is only another mask; underneath interpretations covering over the facts, there are only other interpretations; there is no proper or literal meaning to words, only figurative meanings which have lost their sensuous power, and concepts are only dissembled metaphors. Finally, there is no authentic version of a text, only translations; no truth, only pastiche and parody, misquotation and dissemination.[20]

In the terms of this second logic, Plato's distinction between the simulacrum and the "good" copy no longer holds, for there can be no pre-existent model for the copy to be true to. Instead, the "model" must now be understood as having been established in an act of belated induction from the copy that is purportedly true to it, produced as an aftereffect so to speak, and then hypostatized as the origin. As a fabricator of paintings that are actually simulacra, Wyatt creates or invents "models" which are based on the copies he is trying to emulate. In other words, the model comes into being as the absent origin to which the copy refers, with this act of reference really the consequence of an originary difference opened up by the notion of the copy itself.[21]

In *The Recognitions,* these two opposed "logics" or understandings of the model-copy relationship are intricated in what Mikhail Bakhtin calls a "dialogic," which allows both to operate simultaneously. More precisely, *The Recognitions* is constituted according to a dialogic founded on the Platonic model-copy paradigm and its simultaneous subversion or overturning. In this double perspective, each "bad" copy or counterfeit must be read as a simulacrum, but either in the Platonic or the Deleuzian sense, depending on the context. Similarly, the narrative as a whole must be read as re-enacting the fragmentation and loss of some primal authoritative center or agency predicated on Platonic distinctions *and* as a reversal into an emergent multiplicity brought about through the resurfacing and proliferation of simulacra. In this latter perspective, however, such a loss can be seen only as an illusion. The points to be emphasized are that the novel oscillates between these two irreconcilable articulations and that no synthesis is possible.

Repetition in Two Modes

At some point in the course of reading *The Recognitions,* surely every reader must begin to feel that almost every reported detail is something heard or overheard, seen or recognized from somewhere before, as if the novel were functioning as a vast echo chamber or a textual machine producing a constant sense of déjà vu. In relation to the cultural past, the text establishes a network of cultural references, echoes, and allusions—that is, historical signposts and repeated motifs—which invite "recognition" at the level of cultural memory and historical consciousness. At the same time, through a process of internal repetition and variation, details and situations echo each other in a movement intended to make the accidental seem pertinent and the detail significant. But if everything in the novel doubles, mimics, or echoes something from somewhere else (whether from outside or inside the world of the novel), we must ask ourselves how these repetitions are related: are they versions of the "same" or do they articulate a "difference" by being only disguises and simulations of the same? In other words, are these repetitions all of the same kind or are we dealing with different *modes* of repetition? If *The Recognitions* is indeed structured dialogically, according to two opposed conceptions of "difference," then we should expect to find that repetition also operates in the novel according to two distinct modes. But how are they to be distinguished?

In a first mode, or what I shall call "simple" repetition, situations, scenes, catchphrases, and allusions appear and reappear in serious and satiric (or parodic) reprise. Consider, for example, the story Otto tells in the wake of his fumbling attempt to catch hold of a strange and fleeting intuition:

> Like a story I heard once, a friend of mine told me, somebody I used to know, a story about a forged painting. It was a forged Titian that somebody has painted over another old painting, when they scraped the forged Titian away they found some worthless old painting underneath it, the forger had used it because it was an old canvas. But then there was something under that worthless painting, and they scraped it off and underneath that they found a Titian, a real Titian that had been there all the time. It was as though when the forger was working, and he didn't know the original was underneath, I mean he didn't know he knew it, but it knew, I mean something knew. I mean, do you see what I mean? That underneath that the original is there, that the real . . . thing is there, and on the surface you . . . if you can only . . . see what I mean? (480)

The passage's significance arises from the fact that it obviously echoes the examples of paintings cited earlier, where a painting's status oscillates between original and copy or gives way to a series of reversals; in fact, the passage seems to contain in miniature the entire thematic of art as original and/or counterfeit as it is developed in the novel. Thus, it might even be said to constitute a *mise en abyme* for *The Recognitions* as a whole, insofar as it indicates the novel's overall compositional principle by pointing self-reflexively to a layered series of "versions" that imitate and/or conceal an original.[22] And of course there is a deflationary irony generated by having Otto of all characters pronounce such an important idea, since Otto himself fails to wonder about the "original" behind his own faked identity. The passage will also acquire a further significance retrospectively when the reader later discovers Wyatt "scraping off" the details of an old painting in a Spanish monastery while talking about Titian. Nevertheless, despite these interpretive possibilities, the passage still functions as a simple thematic repetition—simple because it repeats a previously established pattern or theme without calling into question the opposition upon which it is based, in this case the difference between an original and copy.

Recurring words and catchphrases provide another important instance of repetition. Indeed, the importance of social discourse as a medium of exchange registering recognitions or failures of recognition is paramount in *The Recognitions,* and Gaddis displays a truly uncanny capacity to reproduce and organize speech patterns that identify characters and delineate attitudes, even though many characters are no more than isolated fragments of speech, unidentified and anonymous voices that become audible at parties and cafés. In such instances Gaddis does more however than simply mimic their gossip and cocktail chatter: he creates a veritable acoustic collage out of speech fragments and repeated phrases, so that as phrases like "the solids of Uccello" or "Whhhhassamatter, you queer or somemhmm?" float in and out of different conversations they establish an air of false familiarity. And there is another, closely related effect: the prying loose of words from any particular reference. The phrase "the solids of Uccello," for example, after being used in a proper and meaningful way, gradually loses its "original" meaning after many repetitions and becomes merely a sign or index (usually false) of the speaker's knowledge and sensitivity to art. In another, seemingly similar instance, a character named Herschel explains how he uses a certain word:

> —Chavenet. It really doesn't mean anything, but it's familiar to everybody if you say it quickly. They mention a painter's style, you nod and say, Rather . . . chavenet, or, He's rather derivative of, Chavenet wouldn't you say? Spending the summer? Yes, in the south of France, a little villa near Chavenet. Poets, movie stars, perfume . . . shavenay, Herschel brayed becomingly. (558)

In contrast to "the solids of Uccello," the word "Chavenet" is actually one of the many verbal simulacra that appear in the novel. That is, though the two expressions are used for the same purpose, "chavenet" has no "original" meaning, although it does eventually acquire meaning as it begins to recur in encounters between characters at various social gatherings and gradually assumes a certain value as currency of social exchange. In this way, it produces a kind of recognition, or a "recognition-effect," since the reference is at best floating or changing from context to context and designates no essential content.

These two different kinds of verbal repetition produce two correspondingly different effects on the reader. As the phrase "the solids Uccello" is degraded in use from context to context until it finally reaches the point of being virtually meaningless, the effect is one of irony. The irony results from our perception of the discrepancy between its "original" meaningful use and its subsequent abuse and misappropriation. We are witness, in short, to a phrase's decline and fall. In a more significant context, such a decline might even produce a certain nostalgia for an earlier and "more meaningful" instance. The use of "chavenet," on the other hand, can only produce the effect of humor. Having "no past" or earlier and more meaningful use, its precise reference floats in an eternal and reiterated present. In contrast to the degradation enacted by the first mode of repetition, here a sort of "meaning" is produced simply through repetition itself.

Another kind of verbal repetition, similarly "free-floating" like this last example, has a more peculiar and interesting effect. When Otto encounters a young poet named Esme, she shows him a sample of her writing, a poem containing the word "crotch," which Otto finds deeply shocking. Later, in a heroin-induced trance, Esme unaccountably writes the line on a sheet of paper: "An ant going home who does not live anywhere" (297). Next, at a big party occurring hundreds of pages later, a character turns up whose name is Mr. Crotcher, and who is writing a book about ant life.

One possible explanation of this kind of repetition and the pleasure it affords is that we are dealing with a species of *Witz* as Freud defined it.[23] That the referents, though relatively insignificant in themselves, have overt sexual connotations would lend weight to such a hypothesis. As would the fact that many of the characters' names—like Don Bildow or Mr. Feddle—pun on or form aural distortions of recognizable objects. In fact, *The Recognitions* contains many examples of such networks of connected signifiers whose signifieds have no ascertainably important denotative meaning or that pervert recognizable analogies. This raises the possibility that the entire text may be structured, at least in part, by this almost subliminal network formed by recurrent phonemes, buried puns, and nonsense words.

Such a network would suggest that Gaddis's novel has organizational strands of connection that operate on levels other than those of traditional plot and character interest or even thematic repetition, these interests being supplemented and in some instances even replaced by an attention directed toward textual cross-referencing and chains of association. The paradigmatic exposition of this kind of over-determined ordering of material is, of course, Freud's *The Interpretation of Dreams*. Applying Freud's explanation of the workings of the unconscious as a principle of textual organization, we could say that the authorial unconscious, pressured by a kind of compulsion for order in the psychic economy, multiplies an untold number of secondary connections and cross-references among the various narrative episodes—connections which, from the point of view of the narrative, appear completely gratuitous. The result is an elaborate network of associations leading back and forth—in synchronic reticulation, so to speak—which thereby produces a haunting aura of familiarity without any precisely definable "objective correlative" that would explain it.

In *The Recognitions,* this widespread effect is directly linked to the presence of simulacra. For the moment, let's simply note that the Crotcher episode functions as the simulacrum of a mini-narrative, in that its repetitions articulate a line of connection that produces sense out of nonsense but without any appeal to an "original" version, archetypal form, or prior representation. In other words, the "episode" is comprised of a heterogeneous series of items or signs connected not by analogy, as in the case of a mimetic representation and which would mean that the series reflects or embodies a previously constituted meaning as a particular instance, but rather by pure repetition, in such a way that the series itself produces meaning as a "textual event." This kind of event presents a striking contrast with the more conventional narrative episodes and acts of the characters which do depend on priorly constituted patterns or archetypes in order to make or receive their sense. Furthermore, in the Crotcher example, where there is no appeal to any previous pattern or analogue and therefore no implied comparison, the effect is not of ironic "re-cognition" but of humor, as unexpected meaning suddenly erupts on a surface of nonsense constituted by pure signifiers. Through sheer repe-tition of heterogeneous items an immanent and virtual "logic of the text" realizes itself in a wholly unforeseeable manner.

In sum, these examples may be taken to illustrate the novel's two modes of repetition. In the first mode, repetition of the same or the similar (theme, character, expression, or whatever) produces recognition, and, in the case of a falling away from or loss of the original, any "difference" between versions is "recognized" as a discrepancy which evokes or implies some form of irony. In this first mode, therefore, the basis for recognition itself is never thrown into question. For this reason, I call this mode of repetition "simple." In contrast, the Bosch painting series, by producing reversal upon reversal and hence a fundamental state of reversibility, constitutes a repetition of a different order, which I shall call "complex."[24] By throwing into question the very basis of the original/copy opposition, complex repetition raises the whole problematic of "difference" in the Nietzschean sense elaborated earlier. Thus, Wyatt's Memling painting, the word "chavenet," and the Crotcher episode are all instances of com-plex repetition where identity becomes a form of self-difference; that is, identity no longer rests on some previously established model, essence, or analogy but instead institutes differential systems that are mutually resonant but remain distinct from each other. Consequently, these ex-amples do not depend upon "recognition" for their functioning but produce a kind of recognition-effect. Simply put, complex repetition allows no reduction to a simple "repetition of the same," but allows "difference" in itself to emerge in the constant interplay it initiates be-tween identity and difference. Finally, this second mode of repetition defines or constitutes a space in which simulacra must be understood in and for themselves, and not as degraded copies of copies as in the Platonic perspective.

Yet another example, the incident of Anselm's self-castration, will il-lustrate how these two modes of repetition are sometimes entwined in a hybrid form that partakes of both. Because of the circumstances—Anselm's act is immediately preceded by his entry into the New York subway system on all fours and his refusal to "recognize" or acknowledge his mother—the scene seems intended to be read as a "psychotic" episode. Moreover, an earlier textual digression makes it likely that the reader will recall Origen's act of sacrificial self-emasculation. In this perspective, Anselm's act will likely appear as a degraded repetition of what was once a spiritually meaningful one and hence another ironic contrast, although the act is too gruesome and excessive to appear simply as ironic.

When examined closely, however, the episode also appears to function as a "textual event" in a manner similar to the Crotcher example. Anselm, as we shall later see in some detail, is a composite figure who functions both as a character in his own right and as a "switchword" for various textual chains of association. For example, his name obviously recalls Saint Anselm, known primarily for his ontological proof of God's existence. Furthermore, his act of self-emasculation immediately follows his prolonged but finally unsuccessful attack on his friend Stanley's religious beliefs, all at a party where other characters discuss Somerset Maugham's *The Razor's Edge* and where, in the apartment bathroom, Anselm finds the razor that formerly belonged to Wyatt's father, a Protestant minister who has lost his belief in the Christian God. Given this set of complicated cross-referents, Anselm's self-castration can be read as a "crossing" of two modes of repetition. According to a logic of analogy, his act repeats a cultural archetype, but here it is drained of meaning and religious significance, especially since it occurs without psychological preparation. On the other hand, the elements of the narrative situation seem linked primarily by a textual logic of repetition and association, in such a way that the narrative appears literally produced on a surface of connected signifiers. Origen's act of self-emasculation is mentioned early in *The Recognitions,* on the same page in fact on which Anselm is first introduced but with no implied connection between the two. Through Anselm's act, the two references are enchained in a "representation." The effect of this cross-over is some sort of syncretism of recognition and black humor; it forms, one might say, an instance of the grotesque, since it blends or collages at the level of representation "events" which, because they operate according to entirely different logics, cannot be synthesized.

Many of the textual anomalies evident in *The Recognitions* work in a similar manner. Let's look at a more important example. When Wyatt returns home to his father's parsonage after several years' absence, the seemingly simpleminded family serving girl, Janet, becomes very excited. At first, she takes Wyatt for Prester John and then for Christ returning from the tomb. But when she unaccountably decides that he is a "false Christ," she rushes to the barn and tries, like Pasiphaë, to give herself to a bull. Our first inclination may be to explain such behavior as another "psychotic" confusion of the literal and the symbolic, but an alternative "textual" reading is also hinted at. According to Greek myth, Poseidon caused Pasiphë to conceive a lustful passion for a bull because Minos had refused to sacrifice a white bull to him. In this episode, Wyatt has returned home to take up the ministry and thus fulfill his filial obligation, but he soon discovers that his father has reverted to Mithraism and demands his own sacrifice before entry into "the brotherhood." Wyatt's panicked refusal and escape occur just before Janet attempts to give herself to the bull.

In a curious way, then, the episode constitutes another kind of "crossing" or telescoping from one textual determination to another, as if at the level of representation two different narrative fragments had been confusedly set together. In this jamming together or monstrous coupling of a textual logic and an analogical one, meaning is short-circuited and the effect, once again, is neither irony nor humor but a form of the grotesque.

In the examples of simple and complex repetition considered above, the crucial distinction was between effects of recognition (of a form or idea), as opposed to some kind of "textual difference" producing "events" that escape the logic of representation. Furthermore, in the case of simple repetition, some form of irony tends to be the chief effect, whereas in complex repetition it is one of "intensity," or difference registered as a pure effect (we shall return momentarily to this notion). These observations may be summarized schematically as follows:

Simple repetition	*Complex repetition*
an archetypal form, model, or representational analogue	a configuration of signifiers
icon (good copies)	phantasms (simulacra)
recognition	encounter with "difference"
irony	intensity

But if each mode of repetition corresponds to or operates according to a its own specific, irreducible logic (even though, as we have seen, these two different "logics" are entwined in a "dialogic"), it must now be determined how each of these two logics signifies and thereby bestows significance on fictional material. In the case of the simple repetition, the answer is exactly what we should expect: through the repetition of a previously established essence, meaning, or form. Thus signification depends upon a formal or iconic "recognition," even when there is discrepancy or deviation, in which case the text produces irony. But what about the second logic, where there can be no "recognition" since there is no previously established essence or identity? We cannot say that we "recognize a divergence," since our very terms would indicate that we were still in the grip of the first logic. In the Crotcher episode and use of the word "chavenet," the repetition of signifiers freed from signifieds creates a sort of "meaning" even though the series of displacements and substitutions, because of the heterogeneity of the constituent elements, follows no recognizable pattern. The problem would appear to be that any combination can unexpectedly become significant, but signifying what exactly?

Intensity and the Recognition-Effect

The question of how (and what) simulacra signify brings us up against a paradox formulated in different ways by Claude Lévi-Strauss, Jacques Lacan, and Gilles Deleuze, but it is a paradox intrinsic to literature. As the hero of Witold Gombrowicz's novel *Cosmos* says, there are too many signifying signs, and it's not clear to him (or the reader) what they mean. Gombrowicz's novel creates a situation which Deleuze describes as follows:

> The fact is, the primordial signifier is of the order of language; yet however it is acquired, the elements of language had to have been given all together, in one fell swoop, since they don't exist independently of their possible differential relationships. But the signified in general is of the order of the known; yet the known is constrained to the law of a progressive movement which goes from part to part, *partes extra partes*.[25]

When language came into being, the whole world took on meaning all at once, but before anyone could know *what* "meaning." This dissymmetry (or "inadequation," as Lévi-Strauss calls it) between the synchronic signifying system and the diachronic nature of the known is manifested at the level of language in an "overabundance of signifiers in relation to the signifieds to which they might apply." Lévi-Strauss postulates that this contradiction is resolved through the existence of "floating" signifiers and signifieds, "whose role is to allow symbolic thought to operate despite the contradiction inherent in it." He gives a number of examples (words like *truc, machin, quelque chose,* and *aliquid* as well as the more familiar notion of *mana*) for which we could give English equivalents (thinga-majig, doodad, and so on). According to Lévi-Strauss, the "floating" signifier, itself empty of meaning and therefore capable of receiving a variety of meanings, functions to fill the gap in signification.

For Deleuze, however, these floating signifiers and signifieds are only examples of the *instance paradoxal* by which heterogeneous series communicate in any structure in general. Given at least two heterogeneous series—of words, objects, events, divergent propositions, meanings, and expressions—which never assume the same or equal value, one series can be considered as "signifying" and the other as "signified." Moreover, there is always an inevitable "excess" in the signifying series and a cor-responding "lack" in the signified series. In other words, the two series will always be marked simultaneously, one by excess, the other by lack, with the two determinations changing places without ever balancing each other. As Deleuze explains:

> What is in excess in the signifying series is literally an empty slot (*une case vide*), a place without an occupant that is always displaced, and what is lacking in the signified series is a given and unplaced supernumerary, an unknown, an occupant without a place and hence displaced. They are the two faces of the same thing, but two odd faces or an odd couple through which the series communicate without losing their difference.[26]

Such serial structures, formed by the disequilibrium between different series, pervade modern literature. Deleuze himself analyzes the series in Lewis Carroll's *Sylvie and Bruno* and the Alice books, and points out others in *Finnegans Wake,* the novels of Gombrowicz, Alain Robbe-Grillet, and Pierre Klossowski. For the American reader, Samuel Beckett's *Watt,* Rudolph Wurlitzer's *Flats,* and Thomas Pynchon's *V.* may provide more familiar illustrations. In Pynchon's novel, for example, as Herbert Stencil's search for the ever elusive "V" unfolds, *v*'s begin to proliferate throughout the novel: Victoria, Vera, Valletta, Vesuvius, Venezuela, the V-note Bar, and Botticelli's *Venus* as well as the *v* formed by the receding line of lights in a street or by spread thighs, the mons veneris, or a pattern of migratory birds. The perpetual displacement from one signifier to another in a movement that never arrives at a stable signified which would be the cause or meaning of this disruption constitutes the fictional structure.

The Recognitions contains many instances of such heterogeneous series. The main character, Wyatt Gwyon, is associated with a whole series of names or signifiers—Clement, Faust, Raymond Lully, John Huss, Hugo van der Goes, and so on—whose signified is never actualized in his own person in a series of corresponding acts, so that his identity is defined through an "excess" in a signifying series and a "lack" or nonactualization at the level of the signified. Similarly, there are series of objects—paintings, counterfeit money, numerous human limbs and body parts, religious relics, a Mickey Mouse watch, a griffin's egg, a coconut, a golden bull—set circulating through the novel that as a series of signifiers appear excessive and yet whose exact signifieds or significance remain "unknown," displaced or suspended. And, as we have seen, there are series of words—such as "chavenet" or "the solids of Uccello" —that function in a similar way. (In Lévi-Strauss's terms, the first is a "floating signifier," the second a "floating signified.") Paradoxically, these various "gaps" in signification account for the novel's semantic richness, for only because of such gaps can it appear both excessively full and surfeited with every conceivable thing that could fill a novel and yet incomplete and indeterminant in meaning.

But here it is necessary to distinguish between series that combine items from the most diverse groups and thereby frustrate any attempt to read their interrelationships analogically—like the series formed by the word "crotch," ants, and Mr. Crotcher—from those that do not. For it is always possible, by a process of metaphorical substitution in the series of objects cited above, to read the coconut as a parody or disguised repetition of the griffin's egg mentioned earlier in the novel or the human limbs as desacralized or "profane" versions of holy relics. Similarly, metonymic links can be established with the characters: thus, the Mickey Mouse watch signifies its owner Agnes Deigh, the exclamation "Chrast!" identifies Ed Feasley, and so forth. On the other hand, in instances where the items form series that remain disparate and divergent, the representational basis appears "nonsensical," or the product of an arbitrary linkage of signifiers. This second type of series, of which there are many striking examples, must be conceived as simulacra, since they are not merely random series of items. While frustrating the kind of reading and attribution of meaning based on recognition, they nevertheless produce internal resonances or "meaning" effects.

When this happens, such heterogeneous and disparate series make up what Deleuze calls an "intensive system." As he explains:

> If we suppose that the series (two or more, each defined by the differences between the terms that define it) enter into communication as a result of the action of some force, it appears that this communication relates the differences to other differences, or constitutes differences in a system of differences: these second degree differences play the role of a "differentiator," that is, relate the differences of the first degree to each other. This state of things is adequately expressed in certain physical concepts: a *coupling* between heterogeneous series, from which derives an *internal resonance* in the system, from which derives a *forced movement* whose amplitude spills over the base series itself.[27]

When communication is thus established between the heterogeneous series, events begin to occur within the system which Deleuze describes in these terms: "Spatiotemporal dynamisms fill the system, expressing at once both the resonance of the coupled series and the amplitude of forced movement which flows over them."[28] In a word, the system produces "intensities." By "intensity" Deleuze means an effect produced or constituted by a difference that refers only to other differences; that is to say, a difference perceived or experienced in and of itself. Difference, in this sense, cannot be "re-cognized"—it can only be encountered as an effect. An "intensive system" is therefore not a representational system, although it is not incompatible with representation. Rather, one might say that representation always presupposes and suppresses such systems in order to eliminate what can only be perceived in representational terms as a set of arbitrary or nonsensical relationships.

The proliferation of simulacra in *The Recognitions* tends to produce just such an "intensive system," as more and more of the series forming the simulacra are brought into a state of resonance.[29] Later we shall see how this system is set into motion in the novel. For the moment I simply want to underscore the principal effect of its internal resonance, namely the recurrence of "intensities" that punctuates *The Recognitions* and which even the unassuming reader is unlikely to miss. Perhaps the most important example in the narrative occurs when Wyatt returns home to his father's parsonage and quickly discovers that "None of them knows who I am." This realization is immediately followed by another disorienting perception:

But even before these words were out, something else had assailed him. He began looking wildly around the room, where shapes refused to identify themselves, and endured only in terms of the others, each a presence made possible only by what everything else was not, each suffering the space it filled to bear it only as a part of a whole which, with a part standing forth to identify itself, would perish. (439)

This moment of intensity—of differential perception accompanying his loss of recognition—signals an imminent turning point in the novel, for soon afterward Wyatt plummets into a world of simulacra, a carnival world, he suddenly discovers, that will never be set right again. Although in one sense lost, Wyatt has also entered upon what might be called a voyage of " intensities," one that will set rippling through the novel resonant echoes and reflections, in the manner of a Deleuzian "intensive system." But in fact, many such moments of "intensity" occur throughout *The Recognitions,* and they are not confined solely to Wyatt's experience. These moments provide a visible contrast to moments of "recognition," which also proliferate, in "dialogic" counterpoint, to the moments of intensity. Together the two articulate an alternating rhythm of structuration.

Let's look therefore at an equally significant moment of "recognition." Wyatt has just been to the Museum of Modern Art, where he has seen Picasso's *Night Fishing at Antibes.* He is so moved by the painting that he walks right by his wife Esther, who came with a friend, without seeing or "recognizing" her. As he later explains:

—Yes but, when I saw it, it was one of those moments of reality, of near-recognition of reality. I'd been...I've been worn out in this piece of work, and when I finished it I was free, free all of a sudden out in the world. In the street everything was unfamiliar, everything and everyone I saw was unreal, I felt like I was going to lose my balance out there, this feeling was getting all knotted up inside me and I went in there just to stop for a minute. And then I saw this thing. When I saw it all of a sudden everything was freed into one recognition, really freed into reality that we never see, you never see it. You don't see it in paintings because most of the time you can't see beyond a painting. Most paintings, the instant you see them they become familiar, and then it's too late. Listen, do you see what I mean? (91–92)

The passage moves from a feeling of reality loss and unfamiliarity to being freed into a recognition of "reality," a reality however that "we never see," presumably because of a certain overfamiliarity that obscures it. Both the dramatic situation and play of terms suggest a continual reversibility between oppositions (real/unreal, familiar/unfamiliar) that can never be stabilized. When we try to pin down the exact reference of the phrase "recognition of reality," we are immediately caught up in a network of internal differentiations without positive terms. If the larger context of the novel is taken into account, Wyatt's assertion (that we can't see reality in most paintings because we can't see "beyond" them) may be interpreted to refer to the Platonic recognition of ideal forms, which we can never "see" but must intuit. But he could also mean (or be taken to mean) "beyond" the surface in another sense altogether. Many passages in the novel (such as Otto's story cited earlier) evince a concern with layerings and laminations, surfaces that both obscure and reveal, so that "reality" here could refer to multiple or manifold patterns embedded in the more familiar surface details of everyday life.

If we move "beyond" the surface of Gaddis's text and look at Picasso's painting, we shall notice that its blending of the sea and night sky as well as its concern with fishing as a metaphysical conceit echo or resonate with Wyatt's theological obsession that the sky is a celestial sea and that maybe "we are fished for." And the painting's relevance hardly stops there. One of Picasso's commentators, Timothy Hilton, sets its imagery in a more "familiar" light:

> *Night Fishing* has a queer mixture of descriptive reportage and thematic dignity, of the old and the contemporary, of the quotidian but ancient professional activity of the fishermen and the vacation-sportif mode in the girls, gaily dressed, licking at an ice cream cone. Much in the painting is whimsical; and yet the central motif is the killing of animals. It is a decorative painting—it even reminds one of those mosaic murals in primary schools—yet fairly significant things are being done to the organization of pictorial space and the idea of a wall-size painting.[10]

Hilton goes on to note the importance of the painting's "submarine connotations" in the contemporary art historical context and the fluidity of its composition. The importance of the latter resides in the way it allows "associated but not locked forms" to be placed together. The result is a flattened, "all-over" structure rather than a cubist one. This is also evident in the painting's use of color: the olive greens, muted reds, and purples, and particularly the blacks, are used to connect areas of the canvas and to punctuate the repetition and echo of shapes.

For all their obvious differences, Picasso's painting and Gaddis's novel resonate through a series of echoings and repeated motifs, for the novel also offers a "queer mixture" of the thematically dignified and the trivial, of the whimsical and the deeply serious. Gaddis's choice of Picasso—the modernist master of pastiche, imitation, and parody, the painter who could never confine himself to a single style—is also significant here. Both play out the twin images or roles of the artist: as divine creator mimicking God's handiwork through cosmic analogies and the artist as con man and fraud, the magician who produces spellbinding illusions with his magic. Important too is the sense in which the painting, like Gaddis's novel, projects a Janus-like stance that both looks back at the stylizations and symbolizing language of earlier synthetic cubism and looks forward to the big murals of abstract expressionism with their large-scale, "all-over" compositions. In short, Picasso's painting manipulates complexly orchestrated recognitions in order to produce entirely new effects.

Yet the relationship of *The Recognitions* to the Picasso painting is not, for all these correspondences, one of analogy; the painting, rather, forms only one item in a whole series of paintings and works of art which assume multiple functions in the novel.[31] It is mentioned here merely as one instance of how "recognition" is treated in a key scene, and how it opens out onto both existential and intertextual concerns. Of course, this inevitably transfers the process of recognition to the reader, but now "recognition" becomes a misleading term, insofar as the reader is often participating in the production of meanings that do not preexist the working of the text but are activated during the reading process.

The example also serves to indicate how recognition and intensity are not so easily separable. Actually, such moments often tend to shade into one another, particularly when an incipient recognition is cut short by a denial of any complicity or "intimacy" with the subject of the recognition, as when Otto happens upon the sight of a volcano: "It stood out of space, in time like a thing seen in memory. Not to be touched or known in any way, it ignored him, beauty which would admit of no tampering, to be lost in the horror of intimacy. With every effort of his eyes it grew less real" (725). Or when Wyatt is confronted with the moon's sudden appearance:

He was stopped in his tracks by the horned hulk of the old moon hung alone in the sky, and this seemed to upset him a good deal, for he shivered and tried to leave it but could not, listened, and heard nothing, finally there was nothing for it but to sit bound in this intimacy which refused him, waiting, until the light came at last and obliterated it. (53)

When Wyatt refuses the pathetic pseudonovelist Ludy a look of recognition and complicity, the latter also experiences an intense moment of disorientation: "He stared; and found himself trying to find something to fix his eyes upon, but every line led him to another, every shape gave way to some even more transient possibility. And he stood there trapped" (892). Such recurrent moments of intensity are often charged with the suddenly unfamiliar and uncanny, and frequently come when a character suddenly loses his bearings. Mr. Yak, returning to this hotel room in Madrid, experiences just such a sudden anxiety:

> The outside shutters were almost closed on the narrow balcony, but sounds came up from Alphonso del Gato, the sound of voices and a barrel organ somewhere in the lame joy of some indistinguishable tune, through the shutters and the imposition of joy in the red-figured drapes that hung there motionless. Before him the mirrors, from the one tall and narrow mounted in the armoire to the small square one over the one-spigot washstand, and back, embraced one another's images, as the rain took up against the shutters, and reached the glass, and he stood there, chilled, his memory frantic for something precious left out in the rain, or a window left open, the rain pounding in, in the dark, engulfing a consciousness alert now in all the sudden perspicacity of terror, deepening round it so that it seems to have been falling all the time: sounds came from a great distance, a strange city, in a foreign land, and the sense he'd just been put down here this instant alone, and for the first time, engulfed in the sense of something lost. (821)

With increasing intensity, the oscillations between the inside and the outside, the familiar and the strange, force into consciousness an undefinable sense of loss.

Something else, moreover, is involved in this last example, for it amounts to an uncanny repetition of a situation that occurs early in the novel. When Wyatt's father, also staying in a hotel in Madrid, is drawn to an open window, he too experiences a similar moment of intensity:

> Through that open window he was awakened by lightning, and not to the lightning itself but the sudden absence of it, when the flash had awakened him to an eternal instant of half-consciousness and left him fully awake, chilled, alone and astonished at the sudden darkness where all had been light a moment before, chilled so thoroughly that the consciousness of it seemed to extend to every faintly seen object in the room, chilled with dread as the rain pounding against the will pounded into his consciousness as though to engulf and drown it.—Did I close the study window? . . . The door to the carriage barn? Anything . . . did I leave anything out in the rain? Polly? . . . a doll he had had forty years

before, mistress of a house under the birch trees in the afternoon sun, and those trees now, supple in the gale of wind charged inexhaustibly with water and darkness, the rest mud: the sense of something lost. (12)

In addition to the repeated inside/outside oppositions, what is central to both passages is the depiction of a consciousness about to be "engulfed" suddenly in a "sense of something lost." The repetition of this phrase alone, which recurs in varying contexts throughout the novel, is enough to bring the passages into resonance. Furthermore, in both passages attention is drawn to lost objects or displaced images, though apparently they are not what motivate this feeling of loss. Whether we want to consider them "floating" signifiers or not, in both cases clearly some kind of absent symbolic object remains *unnamed*. But if this is true, then these characters are here being depicted in the terms of a Platonic logic, since there can be no lost objects in a field or space of simulacra but only substitutions and displacements in series without originals. This Platonic perspective, I shall suggest, accounts for the fact that these moments of intensity only come as a negative experience, as an experience of something missing or lost. And indeed, throughout the novel, such moments often occur to minor characters who seem pushed toward the edge of hysteria when "differences" suddenly accumulate and intensify, causing sudden drops in the level of consciousness, as in a "rush" or fall or sense of engulfment. Even such seemingly innocent passages as the following flicker at the edges with this potential: "The sky was perfectly clear. It was a rare, explicit clarity, to sanction revelation. People looked up; finding nothing, they rescued their sense from exile, and looked down again" (542).

In contrast, Wyatt's most typical moments of intensity reveal a rather striking difference. While the two passages cited above are still fresh in mind, let's look at just such a moment in another passage which renders a comparable experience from Wyatt's perspective. The passage occurs in a scene that becomes a brief but expanded "spot of time" at the breakfast table on the morning after Wyatt's return home to his father's parsonage. At this point, Wyatt thinks he has escaped from counterfeiting and the counterfeit world of New York, so his mind is clear and his thoughts coherent (at least compared to what comes later).

The sun was high enough now to fill the dining room with its light, over the dark dining table, and the low table under the window, and warm on the back of his neck when he woke moving nothing but his eyelids, opened the bowl of cold oatmeal before him, and nothing else but a spoon. He did stare at the bowl and the spoon for a moment, or a minute, in that waking suspension of time when co-ordination is impossible, when every fragment of reality intrudes on its own terms, separately, clattering in and the mind tries to grasp each one as it passes, sensing that these things could be understood one by one and unrelated, if the stream could be stopped before it grows into a torrent, and the mind is engulfed in the totality of consciousness. Al-Shira-al-jamanija, consider the Dog Star: death? or Islam. Then perfect diamonds, and so across that brink of unbearable loneliness, and fully awake, startled only with the quiet, and the sunlight bearing flecks of silent motion. If there had been a dream, it was gone back where it came from, to refurbish its props, to be recast probably, possibly rewritten, given a new twist to put it across, make it memorable to the audience and acceptable to the censor, all that, but the same old director, same producer, waiting to dissemble the same obscenities before the same captive audience, waiting, again, the first curtain of sleep. He smiled, looking at the oatmeal, and as he did so reached up a hand as though to feel the smile on his face, and fix it there; it was gone when he looked up to the end of the table and saw it empty, and as immediately occupied it from memory but memory which, so suddenly assailed, leaped too far back, and brought forth the Emperor Valerian blinded, in taut agony, flayed under the hand of Sapor, the Persian emperor who battled Christianity in the name of the sun prophet Zoroaster, whose god, Ormazd, lord of light and goodness, wars ceaselessly against Ahriman, and the hosts of evil. (404–405)

By the end of the second sentence we are reminded of the other passages and the imminent "engulfment of consciousness." *Al-Shira-al-jamanija,* the Arabic word for Sirius or the Dog star, is often on Wyatt's mind, as is the choice ("death? or Islam") offered Shabbetai Zebi. The "perfect diamonds" refer to minutes, in an oblique reference to one of his grandfather's sermons ("Lost: one golden hour, set with sixty diamond minutes . . .") quoted earlier in the novel (13). The sentence concerning the missing or forgotten dream is something of an authorial intrusion, since Wyatt evinces no interest in Freud. Dreams are important in the novel and often prefigure events, but here the statement merely draws attention to the problem of representation in relation to repetition and the unconscious. The important moment comes when Wyatt looks down toward the end of the table where he expects to see his father sitting, and the latter's absence causes him to "flash" immediately onto the blind Emperor Valerian, whom, as he says a few pages later, his father resembles. Actually, he is thinking, he later explains (421), of Valerian as depicted in the painting by Memling. However, the alert reader knows that Memling painted no such dramatic scene, that in fact Wyatt is referring, perhaps unconsciously, to his first student "imitation" of Memling, which was sold as an "original" by his teacher Herr Koppel and purchased by Brown as such. In Wyatt's mind, then, his "absent" father has already been replaced by a counterfeit image or simulacrum. Furthermore, this image of the blinded father defeated by a Persian emperor fighting for a later avatar of Mithras is symbolically proleptic, since Wyatt does not yet know that Gwyon has already reverted to Mithraism and is not the father he thinks him to be. Thus, through this rather complex series of substitutions, the text anticipates and even presumes the "reversal" that will later send Wyatt into a delirium when he discovers that he has always been "counterfeiting" copies of copies. Finally, it is significant that the passage does not culminate in a "sense of something lost." Wyatt, in fact, will never have that experience—not only because he "flips" into a world of simulacra where there are no lost objects, but because, in a sense yet to be clarified, he *is* that lost symbolic object.

At this point in our reading, however, we risk confusing phenomenological and structural perspectives. In the preceding examples, where we saw how various characters experience a moment of intensity, we were still positioned "on this side" of the reversal the novel stages or brings about. But at the textual (or structural) level, this reversal has "always already" happened. In dramatic, representational terms, it only becomes fully apparent in Wyatt's disoriented experiences, not only in relation to his moments of "intensity" but above all in his "fall" into a world of simulacra. To register the ensuing effects of this fall, which are dramatized in various ways, even rendered directly in stream-of-consciousness sections, will turn out to be the narrative's central function. Moreover, as we shall see, Wyatt's "descent" into a world bereft of authenticity will also assume a positive value, as it becomes a means for registering "intensities" that no longer assumes the Platonic understanding of "difference." In this way, Wyatt's experience of "difference" will precipitate the reversal of perspective that becomes the novel's central event. Wyatt, in short, is the central character because he is the focal point for this reversal.

Needless to say, this "event" will have profound repercussions on our reading of *The Recognitions*. For the moment, we need only consider its effect on the formation of various series of items or signs encountered in the novel. Implicitly, these series constitute not only a manner of representing the world but also articulate a specific kind of ambivalent structure. Simply stated, this structure can be conceived in either of two ways, depending on how the series are perceived. On the one hand, they may yield a system of analogies and, on the other, a concatenation of divergent but resonant series. That is, in accordance with Platonism, perversions or deviations in social and sexual identity, the counterfeiting of money, art, and so on are semantically parallel in that they all constitute an analogous falling away from the true, the authentic, the original. But in the "reversed Platonic" or Deleuzian perspective, where we start from their differences, these items can be related only through their differences, that is through differentials that establish the basis for comparison. These differentials differ from one series to another, and proliferate in a concatenation. Thus there is no way to unify or totalize the series of series as a whole. However, inasmuch as these disparate series all subvert or maintain a difference from iconic relationships, they also form simulacra or phantasms. When these simulacra, in turn, begin to resonate by echoing and crossing one another, they form what Deleuze calls an "intensive system." So, in the terms set forth earlier, we can now say that the novel encompasses a tendency to form two entirely different kinds of systems: on the one hand, an iconic system based on analogy and, on the other, a field of simulacra formed by a concatenation of resonant but divergent series, which in turn make up a novelistic "intensive system."

Finally, Goux's analysis indicates how these two systems are related: since the privileging of the father, the phallus, gold, and the word (as points of condensation of value) underlies and supports the system of analogies, the concerted erosion of these points by the massive and overwhelming return or "re-surfacing" of simulacra allows an indefinite proliferation of series without beginning or end. The first case constitutes a contained or bounded homogeneous series; the second, an open heterogeneous series. It would seem that the first defines a cosmos and the second, at least potentially, a chaos. For if the first marks a clear hierarchical separation between what has order, structure, value, essence—all else falling into the realm of the accidental, the random, the discrete, the contingent—this is clearly not the case for the second: it is always possible that a seemingly isolated or random item, no matter how small or insignificant, forms an element in some series, or series within a series. Obviously, the possibilities are infinite; even so, the total aggregate is not a chaos, but perhaps what James Joyce (in *Finnegans Wake*) meant by a "chaosmos," or a state in which it is no longer possible to distinguish between the two.

I am proposing that Gaddis's novel forms just such an incipient novelistic "chaosmos." This tendency, however, is held in check by the Platonism it "overturns," with the result that the novel's structure is dialogic and ambivalent, pulling between two different kinds of systems, each sustained by a different "logic": on the one hand, a system of iconic analogies ultimately Platonic in inspiration and, on the other, a Deleuzian "intensive system" for which the simulacrum is the constituent element. Ultimately, I shall argue, the novel's surface complexity, great heterogeneity, and above all its carnivalesque character derive from this basic and unresolvable tension and the ambivalent structure that underlies it. This structural ambivalence accounts for the fact that while the novel's central event is a reversal from the first system to the second, a reversal to a certain extent dramatized in the main character's experience, it never takes place in an actual event and continues to allow both perspectives to remain operative. But before the full consequences of this reversal can be explored, I must first describe the novel's surface complexity.

Chapter 2

Masquerades and Dispersions

The schizophrenic voyage is the only kind there is. Later this will be the American meaning of frontiers: something to go beyond, limits to cross over, flows to set in motion, non-coded spaces to enter.

—Gilles Deleuze and Félix Guattari,
Anti-Oedipus

According to Bakhtin, reversibility and inversion are the essential strategies of carnivalesque fiction, with inversions of social, physical, and semantic hierarchies (king/clown, face/ass, sacred/profane) generating the most common carnival images and expressions.[1] So far I have concentrated only on a philosophico-aesthetic inversion, which does not mean however that *The Recognitions* does not employ these more familiar carnival inversions. In fact, the energy and spirit of carnival pervade the novel. For in depicting New York in the late 1940s as a world "turned upside down," in which social and aesthetic hierarchies are overturned and the restraints of "good taste" lifted, the novel adopts the "jolly relativity" (Bakhtin) and semiotic riot of carnival as its creative principle. In accord with carnival, it is a world in which the substance of social identity has been dissolved in travesty and masquerade, and everyone mixes in free and overly familiar contact. Not surprisingly, those usually considered to be the socially marginal and the excluded—counterfeiters, drug addicts, homosexuals, schizophrenics, bohemian intellectuals, hack writers, and con men—are here found at the center. The antics and black humor of these characters, like the clowns, jesters, fools, and mimes in carnival performances, invert and mock the normalizing assumptions of modern society. And, in a further carnivalizing reversal, all that is "high" and privileged in the culture is shown to be subject to repetition, perceived now as the degrading mechanism of consumer capitalism and mass culture, which also produces "copies without originals."

As a prose fictional narrative, therefore, *The Recognitions* proposes a mimesis different from the kind consecrated by George Lukács and Erich Auerbach, one that reaches back to Menippean satire and Socratic dialogue, to Lucian, Petronius, and Apuleius, to a form which can allow different languages, styles, and values to mix together, and "philosophy [to be] decked out in the many-colored garb of hetaera," as Bion Borysthenes, an early practitioner of Menippean satire, is reported to have put it. Indeed, in the perspective provided by Bakhtin's theory of carnivalesque fiction, *The Recognitions* connects to a different conception of the novel altogether: an antihierarchical and antiepical genre whose "origin" lies in popular, basically oral literature, in "laughter" and excess rather than in "reason" and restraint. In this respect, Rabelais must be included among Gaddis's "sources," whether a direct influence or not. In *The Recognitions,* as in *Gargantua* and *Pantagruel,* Western culture is plundered to form an encyclopedic collection of themes, quotations, anecdotes, examples, and comparisons. Every rendered scene, every exchange between characters, calls up an array of allusions. At the same time, there is no apparent aesthetic standard: the crudest jokes jostle with sophistication and literary high seriousness; erudition, psychological and philosophical enlightenment flow from and mix with obscene expressions and stories, as ordinary reality threatens to disappear into the maw of madness, obsession, and "tasteless" fantasy. At one point in the novel, Anselm, who is its "Diogenes," complains that he has sycosis—"Not psychosis, like these other crazy bastards. Plain sycosis. Scabs" (523). Many characters are afflicted with some illness or disease (a minor motif running through the novel), but the pun is startling and leaves us wondering if indeed Anselm is psychotic, especially after he castrates himself. But like the novel's "underworld naturalism," such extreme acts and states of mind are basic features of carnivalesque fiction.

In order to see how the novel's carnivalesque themes and strategies operate on a large scale and finally form a fictional whole, its multifarious plots must now be examined in some detail. *The Recognitions* is divided into three major parts, with each part subdivided into Roman-numbered chapters of varying length, and concludes with an unnumbered "epilogue." The central action roughly follows the life of Wyatt Gwyon, a young painter who becomes a forger of paintings by old masters of the early Northern Renaissance in the years just following World War II. The "roughly" is to be taken in two ways. First, chronologically: Part I is concerned with events from Wyatt's New England childhood, then jumps ahead to scenes in Paris where he is an indigent and unsuccessful artist and then to New York where his marriage falls apart and he becomes a forger; in Part II, after threatening to expose his forgeries, Wyatt returns briefly to his New England home, then, soon after his arrival back in New York, the counterfeiting ring is dissolved when Brown falls fatally from the stairhead at his own party; in Part III, Wyatt appears in Spain but, after several episodes, vanishes from the narrative; the novel then concludes in Italy with the deaths and dispersal of several minor characters. Second, in the scenic or spatial sense: much of this action is presented obliquely, in the background or off to the side of a vast panorama of activities pursued by scores of minor characters. In addition to the difficulties occasioned by the digressive and discontinuous narrative, the potential for confusion is compounded by the fact that, early on in the novel and for most of its length, Wyatt ceases to be referred to by name.

Because of the novel's great length (956 pages) and the complexity of its interwoven events, which are presented amidst many rapid shifts and digressions in the narrative, a plot synopsis or scene-by-scene account would be difficult and probably ineffectual. I have opted instead for a combination of summary, analysis, and commentary which, while essentially following the novel's main lines of development, also allows for digressions of my own where they seem necessary or helpful. Given the manner in which narrative sequentiality in *The Recognitions* is constantly disrupted by juggernaut structures of ideas, capsule histories and asides, intellectual harangues and colloquies, this procedure seemed the most appropriate.

A Portrait of the Artist as Forger: *The Recognitions,* Part I

The Recognitions opens with a flashback account of the trip to Spain taken by Reverend Gwyon, Wyatt's father, who is a Protestant minister in a small, unnamed New England town. During the Atlantic crossing, Camilla, Wyatt's mother, who is accompanying the Reverend, is struck with appendicitis and dies as a result of the incompetency of the ship's doctor, Frank Sinisterra. Actually, the latter is not a real doctor at all but rather a professional counterfeiter on the run who will turn up hundreds of pages later and become an important character. The novel's first sentence, which begins an account of Camilla's funeral procession and burial near a Franciscan monastery in San Zwingli, Spain, strikes a thematically central motif: "Even Camilla had enjoyed masquerades, of the safe sort where the mask may be dropped at that critical moment it presumes itself as reality" (3). The burial procession, we later discover, is a masquerade in two senses: Camilla is taken to be and buried a Catholic, whereas in fact she is a Protestant, like her husband, and the white funeral carriage which bears her to the cemetery is ordained for infants and virgins. Thus, "Camilla had borne Gwyon a son and gone, virginal, to earth: virginal in the sight of man, at any rate" (4). Furthermore, since she dies on All Saints' Day, her burial procession occurs during a festival in San Zwingli. And in another confusion, occurring many years later, her body is mistaken for that of an 11-year-old who had been assaulted and murdered. After the rapist confesses, the Church decides that the young virgin is to be canonized and made patron saint of the monastery, but it is Camilla's body that is mistakenly exhumed and enshrined. A further dimension of Camilla's identity is also intimated when textual clues nudge the reader to see her as an incarnation of the White Goddess described by Robert Graves.[2] And finally, having dispersed Camilla's clothes among the townspeople, Gwyon is "hailed in the streets by sundry extremes of his wife's wardrobe, worn with sportive and occasionally necessitous disregard for the original design" (17), a detail that initiates two related themes: dispersion of identity and travesty, in the literal sense. As a whole, the incident of Camilla's death thus inaugurates one of the many series of confusions, reversals, mistaken identities, and recognitions that gives the novel its multilayered and richly allusive texture, and that transfers the process of recognition to the reading activity itself.

Camilla's death produces a feeling of liberation within Gwyon: "whether it was release from something, or into something, he could not tell. He felt that a decision had been made somewhere beyond his own consciousness: that he must follow its bent now, and discover its import later" (15). At first, the import seems to be a movement toward Roman Catholicism, as he is left alone seeking solace in Spain's Catholic monasteries and collecting holy relics, the latter, however, often "pagan in the variety of his choice" (16). When he returns home, he resumes his former studies:

In his loneliness, Gwyon found himself studying again. With the loss of Camilla he returned to the times before he had known her, among the Zuni and Mojave, the Plains Indians and the Kwakiutl. He strayed far from his continent, and spent late hours of the night participating in dark practices from Borneo to Assam. On the desk before him, piled and spread broadcast about his study, lay Euripides and Saint Teresa of Avila, Denys the Carthusian, Plutarch, Clement of Rome, and the Apocryphal New Testament, copies of *Osservatore Ro-*

mano and a tract from the Society for the Prevention of Premature Burial. *De Contemptu mundi, Historia di tutte l'Heresie, Christ and the Powers of Darkness, De Locis Infestis, Libellus de Terrificationibus Nocturnisque Tumultibus. Malay Magic, Religions des Peuples Noncivilisés, Le Culte de Dionysos en Attique, Philosophumena, Lexicon der Mythologie.* On a volume of Sir James Frazer (open to the heading, Sacrifice of the King's Son) lay opened *The Glories of Mary,* and there underlined,—There is no mysticism without Mary. Behind the yew trees, whose thickly conspired branches and poison berries guarded the windows, night after night passed over him, over the acts of Pilate, Coptic narratives, the *Pistis Sophia,* Thomas's account of the child Jesus turning his playmates into goats; but the book most often taken from its place was *Obras Completas de S Juan de la Cruz,* a volume large enough to hold a bottle of schnapps in the cavity cut ruthlessly out of the *Dark Night of the Soul.* (23)

In addition to indicating Gwyon's interests and reading habits, the passage also serves to anchor in a character, "to motivate" as the Russian formalists would say, the extreme erudition that pervades the novel. Here, as in the welter of voices that rises from almost every page, we see the same medley of the profound and the trivial, the serious and the humorous, the authoritarian and the suspect—in short, a whole range of erudition from the most real to the most fake and fantastic. It is precisely through this kind of mixture that the novel will enact a "carnivalization" of knowledge.[3]

As a result of the "Spanish affair"—as Reverend Gwyon and the New England townspeople refer to Camilla's death—the Reverend seems to have turned back not only toward Catholicism and the mystery of the Virgin birth in all its earlier cultic variety and strangeness but even further, beyond Catholicism and the early practices of the Christian church to primitive sun worship, Mithraism, and worship of the Golden Bull, to the solar mysteries and sacred rituals of seasonal change. Reverend Gwyon's attitude toward Christianity's triumph over Mithraism is revealing here:

> —It didn't fail because it was bad. Mithraism almost triumphed over Christianity. It failed because it was so near good. He mumbled something, and then added,—That's the trouble today. No mystery. Everything secularized. No mystery, no weight to anything at all. . . . (57)

In stressing that Protestantism has demystified ritual and turned it into routine—exemplified in *The Recognitions* by the ridiculous and ineffectual activities of the church ladies' Use-Me Society—Gwyon clarifies his own spiritual and intellectual reversion back to an entirely different conception of religion, one involving ritual magic and esoteric knowledge communicated to initiates in sacred mysteries. He soon begins to disturb his congregation with strange gleanings:

> They had never been treated this way from the pulpit. True, many stirred with indignant discomfort after listening to the familiar story of virgin birth on December twenty-fifth, mutilation and resurrection, to find they had been attending, not Christ, but Bacchus, Osiris, Krishna, Buddha, Adonis, Marduk, Balder, Attis, Amphion, or Quetzalcoatl. They recalled the sad day the sun was darkened; but they did not remember the occasion as being the death of Julius Caesar. And many hurried home to closet themselves with their Bibles after the sermon on the Trinity, which proved to be Brahma, Vishnu, and Siva; as they did after the recital of the Immaculate Conception, where the seed entered in spiritual form, bringing forth, in virginal modesty, Romulus and Remus. (56)

The problem is not merely that the Reverend's sermons become increasingly larded with the arcane lore of Sir James Frazer and the comparative religionists, although that is certainly true. Rather, it is as if all temporal perspective, not to mention the hierarchy imposed by God's truth, has been skewed; not just that his text becomes a revelation of the layered nature of Western religion, so that behind Christianity, itself a tangled strand of many beliefs, stands the pagan belief in gods and goddesses and behind that the fertility cults and tree worship and so on backwards toward the origins of human consciousness; but that all of this in its variegated detail is simultaneously present in his text, inscribed in an immense and echoing chatter in which sacred and profane history is mixed together. Not surprisingly, the local townspeople can hardly tolerate or sustain such a state of mind, and eventually (some hundreds of pages later in the novel) the Reverend Gwyon's attempts to translate his obsessions into practice—he sacrifices a neighbor's bull and begins to redecorate the interior of the church more in accordance with the practice of Mithraism—bring his evident "madness" to public light and lead to his breakdown.

Much of Gwyon's erudition and something of the attitude it embodies is communicated to his son Wyatt, who at age three, with the death of his mother, is left to be raised by Gwyon and Aunt May. Aunt May is Gwyon's aunt, a spinster whose rigid Calvinist beliefs have a disabling effect on the development of the young boy's psyche. She fills him with stories of suffering and martyrdom, her favorite being that of John Huss, and has him read John Foxe's *Book of Martyrs*. In general, she would like to instill in him a *contemptus mundi* and strong sense of his own sin and guilt in a world bereft of pleasure and interest. From the moment his mother appears to him in a white sheet at the time of her death, a vision Aunt May attempts to discredit as sinful, Wyatt begins to find the "Christian system suspect." Yet he is not strong enough to resist her overbearing and forceful personality. When he develops a precocious talent for drawing, she identifies his work with the sin of Lucifer:

> —He tried to become original, she pronounced malignantly, shaping that word round the whole structure of damnation, repeating it, crumpling the drawing of the robin in her hand,—original, to steal our Lord's authority, to command his own destiny, to bear his own light! (34)

But Wyatt continues to draw in secret, convinced all the more that he is damned. Aunt May does permit him to copy certain religious works, however, and one of his first successes is an exact reproduction of Hieronymus Bosch's *Seven Deadly Sins*. As mentioned earlier, his father had obtained it by sneaking it through customs disguised as a "copy." Wyatt will later steal the supposed original, having replaced it with the near perfect copy he has made, and use it to finance his expenses at art school in Europe. (Actually, Wyatt only reveals these details later, and then as a story he claims to have heard about someone else.)

When Wyatt is twelve, Aunt May dies suddenly (and somewhat mysteriously, just after Heracles, the ape Gwyon brought back from Europe, destroys her prized hawthorn tree), leaving Wyatt free to pursue his interest in painting. Three years later, he himself is visited by a mysterious burning fever, which the doctors, though they submit his body to every probe and test imaginable, can neither diagnose nor cure. All their efforts, organized by the fiendishly persistent intern Doctor Fell (who, like many minor characters, will turn up hundreds of pages later, this time to experiment on another character), the Reverend Gwyon denounces to his congregation as so much modern quackery and malignant superstition, a modern example of human sacrifice to the god of science. Gwyon soon resorts to his own methods: following a primitive ritual cited by Frazer, he literally sacrifices Heracles after bringing it into the presence of his delirious son. Whether as a consequence of the ritual or not, Wyatt's fever finally passes. But it never altogether leaves his eyes, and their burning green intensity becomes a sign by which we later "recognize" him. As he continues to paint, Wyatt also develops intense powers of concentration which consume his whole consciousness and leave him subject to delirium, his speech halting and broken. This tendency becomes another identifiable trait, especially marked in a book filled with characters who are facilely articulate.

Another important influence on the young Wyatt is that of Camilla's father, the Town Carpenter and the antithesis of Aunt May in every respect. Said to have Indian blood, the Town Carpenter (he is given no other appellation) is a harmless village eccentric who spends most of his time at the Depot Tavern. Both a loquacious talker and a voracious reader, he contributes greatly to the store of "nonsense" that Wyatt absorbs and against which Aunt May battles so valiantly:

> Between the two men, she could never be quite sure where Wyatt picked up his prattle about griffins' eggs, alchemy, and that shocking, disgusting story about the woman and the bull; but when his curiosity turned upon great voyages, and figures like Kublai Khan, Tamerlane, and Prester John, she knew she had the Town Carpenter to thank. (36)

As one might expect of a barroom storyteller, the Town Carpenter is prone to embellishment, as when he recounts Odysseus's adventures to Wyatt. Feeling the voyage had grown too short, he introduces Odysseus to Prester John at Ogygia, thus comically mixing, in a way typical of the book, stories from the classical and Christian heritage. In Part I, we last catch sight of him escaping from the house with both volumes of Tissandier's *Histoire des ballons,* the perfect book to inflame one of his curious obsessions.

Gwyon takes only an intermittent interest in his son's artistic preoccupations. Every now and then, his attention is caught by an unfinished portrait of Camilla, which he completes each time in a different way in his mind's eye. He even insists, unsuccessfully, that Wyatt complete the portrait; otherwise, he warns, it will always be with him. But Wyatt can only finish works that are copies: "The original works left off at that moment where the pattern is conceived but not executed, the forms known to the author but their place daunted, still unfound in the dignity of the design" (60). In a word, Wyatt espouses the Platonic theory of Praxiteles, according to which the artist merely brings into realization or material embodiment a perfection that preexists the work. As Wyatt himself says, in regard to the unfinished portrait of his mother,

> —There's something about a . . . an unfinished piece of work, a . . . a thing like this where . . . do you see? Where perfection is still possible? Because it's there, it's there all the time, all the time you work trying to uncover it. (65)

But uncertainty and ambiguities crowd around his attitude, ambiguities concerning the theory's relevance to the making of art in the modern world, his relationship with Aunt May and his Puritan heritage, as well as to his mother. The question as to why he can't complete an original painting will be posed again, and his response will form part of the central religio-aesthetic dialogue that threads through the novel.

At this point in his life, moreover, a painting is not the only thing he cannot complete. After one year at divinity school, which was to prepare him for the role borne by all his male ancestors since the family first settled in America, he returns home, having decided to study art in Munich.

Chapter I thus establishes the familial and cultural matrix that will frame Wyatt's activities and shape his consciousness. Clearly, his inheritance forms a rich and contradictory mixture, but also a heavy burden. His father's line carries a legacy of necessity and guilt, an endless repetition of the same: "Each generation was a rehearsal of the one before"; each life is "conceived in guilt and perpetuated in refusal" (18). Only one Gwyon has been able to break free, significantly, by drowning himself. Striving to continue the family tradition and to prepare Wyatt to carry it on, Aunt May communicates most strongly the Puritan heritage of Election, and the pain and torment of the individual conscious open to God's scrutiny. On Wyatt's maternal side, his inheritance is more complexly suggestive. His grandfather, the Town Carpenter, with his Indian ancestry and spirit of pagan adventure, stands in obvious counterpoint to Aunt May. Years ago, he had fallen into a well, where, from the depths below, he could discern through broad daylight the pattern of stars in the sky above. The incident has a special importance for Wyatt, who, like the medieval astronomers, thinks of the sky as a celestial sea. Camilla, too, offers a rich set of associations. Since she dies on the voyage by accident, she evokes chance and incompletion, and the flux of the sea. In opposition to Gwyon's Apollonian worship of light and the sun, she bequeaths an aura of darkness, death, and absence. Yet these associations are soon reversed: Gwyon reverts to the more "irrational" cult of Mithras, and Camilla appears to Wyatt as a bright, visionary image. Camilla, moreover, wanted to name Wyatt "Stephen" after the first Christian martyr, but Aunt May had prevailed. As one critic has pointed out, since *stephanos* means crown or ring, the name stands in clear antipathy to the regressive linearity of "Wyatt Gwyon," and explains why Camilla's large, hooped Byzantine earrings later become one of Wyatt's few treasured possessions from his past.[+]

Chapter II opens on a scene at the Café Dome in Paris, where a young American tourist sits reading a copy of *transition*. The shift in tone is immediately evident. Nearby, a group of drunken Englishmen are singing "The Teddy Bear's Picnic"; Moroccan children in the street are harking their wares ("peanuts from the top of the basket, hashish from the bottom"), and amidst a chorus of unidentified voices uttering inanities and cultural clichés ("You'll like Venice. It's so like Fort Lauderdale"), a satiric portrait of the city famous for its art begins to take shape. A chapter epigraph strikes the dominant theme: "Très curieux, vos maîtres anciens. Seulement les plus beaux, ce sont les faux" (63). Aswarm with the fake, the copied, the stolen, and the second-rate, Paris is a phantasmagoria of the counterfeit; from the Napoleonic era onwards "this faked Imperial Rome lay in pastiche on the banks of its Tiber," in effect a copy of a copy. The spirit of collecting art in a city where everything is for sale has had predictable results. The Church of the Sacred Heart, we learn in a digressive capsule history, was granted official papal "recognition" (the word begins to recur in varying contexts) only after Pope Pius IX received a petition with twelve million signatures, although three-fourths were demonstrably counterfeit. Though the city's prestige remains formidable, knowing tourists take Paris at her own valuation only when she presents another figure: the sick prostitute, hiding her cancerous breast, painted and daubed for the night.

Wyatt, we learn, has been there a year, having spent the previous year studying early Flemish painting in Munich. Intensive study of Memling, the van Eycks, Bouts, and van der Weyden, however, has hardly prepared him for the venalities of the contemporary art scene. In what is a foreshadowing or "first version" of a later temptation, a corrupt art critic named Crèmer makes Wyatt a proposition: he will write a laudatory review of Wyatt's first exhibition for a percentage of the commission on whatever is sold. Wyatt declines, and his paintings fail to stir any interest. In the chapter's last paragraph, as Wyatt turns away from a café where he has been reading an article in a German art magazine about the recent discovery of a new Memling (the painting is obviously his own earlier student imitation), his "shadow falls back seven centuries to embrace the dissolute youth of Raymond Lully." Thus is accomplished, in a manner indebted to Joyce, Wyatt's passing identification with that celebrated figure—"a scholar, a poet, a missionary, a mystic, and one of the foremost figures in the history of alchemy" (77).

Chapter III opens in New York several years later. Wyatt has been married for a year to Esther, an aspiring young novelist, and works as a draughtsman copying plans for bridges while continuing to paint at night, although most of his time is actually spent restoring old paintings. The chapter is mainly concerned with the disintegration of their marriage. Exasperated with Wyatt's withdrawn and abstracted behavior, as well as with his "lack of ambition" (his own paintings still remain unfinished), Esther first betrays their privacy by discussing him with friends and then is drawn into an affair with Otto, another aspiring young writer.

The episode constitutes a psychological drama, but not one presented with special psychological emphasis or subtlety: we simply see Esther becoming more frustrated by Wyatt's inwardness and less willing to tolerate his strange and elusive behavior. Although they share intellectual interests—they discuss Baroque music in detail and Picasso's *Night Fishing in Antibes*—she cannot seem to move beyond conventional assumptions about life and art and only voices the social clichés of Greenwich Village in the late 1940s. She becomes upset, for instance, when she discovers that her favorite poet is a homosexual (like most of the literati in the novel, she is more interested in a writer's life than in his work), and later, she accuses the unresponsive Wyatt of being one. As a modern intellectual woman, she seeks to possess through an assertive rationality and demands a psychological intimacy that seems oppressive. She has no sympathetic grasp of the cultural heritage Wyatt incarnates, nor of the mysteries that draw him away.

Wyatt, on the other hand, is racked with seemingly unconscious, unresolved tensions and tormented by strange dreams, which Esther takes to be signs of guilt. In one recurrent dream, his hair is on fire; in another, he desperately tries to account for missing steps. He is also obsessed with the idea that maybe "we are fished for," and often ponders a story he heard as a child—his father tells him it is Clement of Rome's monogram—about a man coming down out of the celestial sea to free an anchor caught on a tombstone, and then drowning. These signs, perhaps, are to be taken as evidence of a religious sensitivity or even a saint's calling. Wyatt, moreover, always dresses in a plain black suit without a tie, and physically resembles John Huss. What others find most striking about him at this juncture, however, is the way his work and attitudes separate him from other people. As Esther puts it: "this restraint, this pose, this control you've cultivated, Wyatt, it becomes inhuman..." (97). His silent inwardness, his insistency on the "privacy of suffering" and the arrogance of his solitude cause Esther much anguish and unhappiness. She even admits that she feels comfortable with him only in the dark, an aspect of their relationship later encapsulated allegorically: "Persephone then, Proserpina now, the same queen in another country, she stared at the doorway to his kingdom and faltered forward" (396).

In the meantime, Wyatt develops a curious friendship with Otto, who instantly recognizes Wyatt's special intensity and complex inwardness. Early in the relationship, Otto begins to jot down Wyatt's statements in a notebook, in order that he may incorporate them later into the play he is writing. Wyatt's aesthetic, for example, is ironically compressed into a shorthand jotting: "Orignlty not inventn bt snse of recall, recognition, pattrns alrdy thr, q." (123). Not surprisingly, the play's central character "Gordon" becomes a rather stiff, unintended parody of Wyatt. The irony is furthered by the fact that Otto himself is a diluted version of Wyatt. As Esther perceives, and it forms the basis of Otto's appeal, Otto has several of Wyatt's qualities without the latter's disturbing intensity. We also discover that all this time Wyatt has actually been designing the bridges he was supposedly only copying, or perhaps has "derived" them (the distinction remains ambiguous) from the designs of the Swiss engineer Robert Maillart, and all out of friendship for a young architect named Benny. Such reversals and retrospective shifts in our perception of characters and their relationships begin to increase noticeably, in fact, as we penetrate further into the novel.

In the most important scene in the chapter, Wyatt is reading and listening to music in his apartment after Otto and Esther have gone out to a party. Distracted by a black poodle that he has rescued temporarily from the street, Wyatt half-seriously begins to practice the cabalistic art of letter combinations in the manner of Raymond Lully's *Ars combinatoria*.⁵ The music stops, he hears the dog scratching on the floor, but is unable to see it.

> —Dog, he whispered in a hoarse tone.—Dog! Dog! Dog! No sound contested his challenge, no recognition of men imprisoned in the past for spelling the Name of God backwards, no response to God, if not the Name, reversed three times in his whisper. (139)

Suddenly, he jumps to his feet, spilling ink all over his papers and cursing the dog repeatedly. At this point, there is an insistent knocking at the door, and in walks Recktall Brown, as if conjured out of thin air. Or perhaps his sudden appearance is merely coincidental. In any case, Brown is a "businessman" who seems to know a lot about Wyatt and quickly proceeds to tempt him into an agreement to forge "undiscovered" paintings by the Flemish masters.

Again, the dramatic emphasis of the scene is not psychological, nor is the underlying pattern of Faust's temptation insisted upon. Comprising neither an ironic commentary nor a parodic parallel, the scene simply echoes, somewhat modestly, this famous literary moment. Wyatt himself accepts Brown's proposal without much hesitation. By way of motivation, he forthrightly states that the time is not propitious for original work, since its "inner necessity" would not be recognized: "And if everyone else's life, everyone else's work around you can be interchanged, and nobody can stop and say, This is mine, this is what I must do, this is my work . . . then how can they see it in mine, this sense of inevitableness, that this is the way it must be" (144). This sense of "inevitableness" has nothing to do with originality, as Wyatt had explained earlier in response to Esther's begging plea that he fulfill his talent by finishing something "original." By quoting his old teacher Herr Koppel, he pronounces his own aesthetic:

> "That romantic disease, originality, all around we see originality of incompetent idiots, they could draw nothing, paint nothing, just so the mess they make is original . . . Even two hundred years ago who wanted to be original, to be original was to admit that you could not do a thing the right way, so you could only do it your own way. When you paint you do not try to be original, only you think about your work, how to make it better, so you copy masters, only masters, for with each copy of a copy the form degenerates . . . you do not invent shapes, you know them, auswendig wissen Sie, by heart . . .". (89)

While the novel as a whole explores more fully the implications of "copying the masters," at the level of the plot Wyatt's aesthetic attitude appears rather ambivalently motivated. When he was a little boy, Aunt May had not only influenced him to associate originality with rebellion and damnation, but had also inspired him with the idea that he would be a hero, someone "who serves something higher than himself with undying devotion" (32), just as the Town Carpenter had inspired him to be a voyager. Having rejected the family tradition of Calvinist ministry, Wyatt, like Joyce's Stephen Dedalus, who is also fascinated by temptation and specifically by Lucifer's rebellion, turns to art as a spiritually infused, higher principle. As in Joyce, the overlapping of the religious and the aesthetic insures that Wyatt will conceive art in epiphantic terms. The question, then, is why Wyatt agrees to make the pact with Brown.

The answer comes later, when more details in the pattern of analogies emerge. Brown, we discover, is more than a Mephistophelean figure (his devilish nature is parodically accentuated by his physical appearance: strange, fleshy ears, eyes like black pin-points, and a general toad-like demeanor). As the raunchy pun in his name suggests, he embodies a cluster of anal associations, most obviously with the lowest degree of unredeemed matter. Furthermore, as an art collector (suggestions of an anal-retentive character), a publisher, the head of an art forgery ring, an enterprising businessman, and con man with a hand in any number of shady deals, Brown also evokes the native American figure of the "confidence man."⁶ Yet, as an allegorical and somewhat comic father figure, Brown is crass but never really wicked, exploitative but also sympathetic. Finally, as Basil Valentine, a corrupt art critic in league with Brown points out to Wyatt, in a materialist and commercial culture, "Recktall Brown is reality" (244).

In making a pact with Brown, then, Wyatt is essentially "making a pact" or formalizing a relationship with modern secular reality, which he hopes to redeem and transform through his art. Brown himself asserts that buying art even redeems money, but in fact, Wyatt's pact constitutes an attempt to deny secular history and to transcend time in a sacred repetition. As he explains his quixotic but religious dedication:

—And . . . any knock at the door may be the gold inspectors, come to see if I'm using bad materials down there, I . . . I'm a master painter in the Guild, in Flanders, do you see? And if they come in and find that I'm not using the . . . gold, they destroy the bad materials I'm using and fine me, and I . . . they demand that . . . and this exquisite color of ultramarine, Venice ultramarine I have to take to them for approval, and the red pigment, this brick-red Flanders pigment . . . because I've taken the Guild oath, not for the critics, the experts, the . . . you, you have no more to do with me than if you are my descendents, nothing to do with me, and you . . . the Guild oath, to use pure materials, to work in the sight of God. . . . (250)

Having identified completely with the master painters of the Flemish guilds, Wyatt uses the same pure materials and emulates their working conditions; he also seeks to experience their holy reverence, which finds expression in the painting's execution: "Because they found God every-where. There was nothing God did not watch over, nothing, and so this . . . and so in the painting every detail reflects . . . God's concern" (251). What makes Wyatt's forgeries so convincing, therefore, are not only the surface details and execution, but the seeming authenticity of the patterns themselves, which evoke "recognitions that go much deeper, much fur-ther back," as he explains. So, in an act of artistic creation that recalls because it is based upon Plato's doctrine of anamnesis—of remembering rather than inventing eternal forms—Wyatt fabricates a work of art from an earlier historical period.

The esoteric knowledge passed down through the guilds, its hermetic assumptions and occult significations, have not been lost upon Wyatt either. Earlier in the novel, he tells Esther that alchemy was not just about making gold but about the redemption of matter itself (129). In a lengthy digression, the narrator traces the loss of this mystical meaning attached to gold and elaborated by such alchemists as Albertus Magnus, Paracelsus, and Michael Majer, "who had seen in gold the image of the sun, spun in the earth by its countless revolutions, then, when the sun might yet have been taken for the image of God" (131), to what gold now means to the likes of such as Otto: "cuff links, cigarette cases, and other mass-produced artifacts of the world he lived in, mementos of this world, in which the things worth being were so easily exchanged for the things worth having." A whole network of associations in the novel delineates this debased economy of exchange, which depends nonetheless on a certain kind of "recognition."[7] Thus, when a prostitute in a bar tells Otto that her gold cigarette lighter is "supposed to be gold but I have to go and have it redipped every two or three months" (510), a network of references to gold flashes with ironic significance. The lighter was a gift from her husband; now that they're divorced, it has become a "sacred memory." Furthermore, since she turned Catholic when she got married, now she doesn't know "what she is."

Wyatt's faith in the alchemical and occult significance of art, and its power even to redeem money, keeps him at a distance from this "fallen" realm.[8] As far as he is concerned, it intrudes irrepressibly only through the agency of mechanical reproduction, which provokes him to ire on several occasions. Yet obviously, there is a contradiction: while on one level Wyatt's occult interests serve to motivate several textual digres-sions—a catalogue of the mystical analogies to the "seven lilies" in his painting of the Annunciation, for example (285)—on another, the problem posed by mechanical reproduction brings his aesthetic theory into direct confrontation with social reality, since mechanical reproduction renders problematic the very idea of a tradition.

In an essay entitled "The Work of Art in the Age of Mechanical Reproduction," first published in 1936, the German critic Walter Benjamin attempted to address this problem directly. Benjamin argues that a work of art's uniqueness is "inseparable from its being embedded in a fabric of tradition," which establishes not only the conditions of the work's creation and transmission but defines the very nature of its "originality." In Benjamin's analysis, the unique value of the "authentic" work of art has its basis in ritual—"the location of its original use value." Enshrined in a tradition, a work of art has an "aura" or visible sign of this location and of the distance from which it "returns our gaze." By entirely bypassing the traditional context in which the work of art was originally executed and seen, mechanical reproduction destroys the "aura" and the distance which paradoxically insured the work's meaning and replaces it with a factitious air of familiarity. With the advent of photography, Benjamin argues further, the criterion of authenticity ceases to be applicable to artistic production, and "the total function of art is reversed. Instead of being based on ritual, it begins to be based on another practice—politics."[9]

Benjamin's analysis would suggest that Wyatt's absolute dedication, indeed obsession, with the material and spiritual conditions of guild painting in the Northern Renaissance is what enables him to simulate the "aura" of these paintings. It also indicates why the contradiction noted above cannot be "resolved" at the level of representation. For although Wyatt exhibits no understanding of how his own practice is intimately related to mechanical reproduction, in order for him to forge or "simulate" these paintings successfully, he must utilize an exacting knowledge of the art of detection, particularly of scientific techniques such as X-ray and chemical analysis, paint-stroke identification, and stylistic projection. "There isn't one test they [the experts] don't know, and not one that can't be beaten" (248), he proudly proclaims. Significantly, when he is charged with calumniating these artists with his forgeries, Wyatt defends himself with an appeal to a "return to origins," which of course only displaces the contradiction:

> ... Do you think I do these the way all other forging has been done? Pulling the fragments of ten paintings together and making one, or taking a ... a Dürer and reversing the composition so that the man looks to the right instead

of left, putting a beard on him from another portrait, and a hat, a different hat from another, so that they look at it and recognize Dürer there? No, it's ...the recognitions go much deeper, much further back, and I...this...the X-ray tests, and ultra-violet and infra-red, the experts with their photomicrography and...macrophotography, do you think that's all there is to it? Some of them aren't fools, they don't just look for a hat or a beard, or a style they can recognize, they look with memories that...go beyond themselves, that go back to...where mine goes. (250)

In an important sense, therefore, Wyatt's "forged" paintings have a curious double and contradictory status. On the one hand, by reproducing exactly the spiritual and material conditions under which, for example, Hugo van der Goes painted and through a profound act of emulation, Wyatt paints an *Annunciation to the Virgin* as if van der Goes himself had painted it. Like the Memling "imitation" discussed earlier, the result is neither an "original" nor a "fake" copy, but a more genuine work of art than the "true" originals of Wyatt's contemporaries. On the other hand, the painting is a forgery and is passed through Brown's ring into the world as an "original," heretofore "undiscovered" painting by Hugo van der Goes solely in order to make money. It is as if, in a totally commodified culture, the high exchange value of painting threatens to reduce its use value to mere ornamental status, and a "genuine" new work must pass itself off as a fake old masterpiece in order to enter the culture at all.[10]

Of this second contradiction Wyatt is fully aware, but in theological rather than social or historical terms. As Basil Valentine quickly points out in response to Wyatt's defense of his forgeries, "corruption enters" when Wyatt attaches another's signature. Wyatt's dialogues with Valentine, which thread through the novel and form its central intellectual debate, are the chief means by which these contradictions are brought out. As one of the most intelligent characters in the novel, Valentine provides a cynical counterpoint to Wyatt's naive and deluded faith. And, in his own way, Valentine is as mysterious as Wyatt. Raised as a Catholic, he admits to being a failed priest turned aesthete. As a secret partner in Brown's counterfeiting ring, he uses his knowledge and influence as an art critic and connoisseur to cast doubts of authenticity on the newly "discovered" paintings, and then, after further examination and new evidence, reverses or retracts his first pronouncement, thus making the claims for authenticity seem all the stronger.

A complex, composite figure with many facets to his identity, Valentine also works at mysterious purposes of his own as part of an international monarchist conspiracy that will have Father Martin assassinated in Rome much later in the novel. In a flagrant exhibition of the novel's "textual logic," Wyatt "recognizes" this aspect of Valentine's identity via a treatise on alchemy:

> —*The Triumphal Car of Antimony.* Now I remember your name, Basil Valentine, the alchemist who watched pigs grow fat on food containing stibium, wasn't it . . . you tried it on some fasting emaciated monks and they all died. . . . (384)

The name Basilus Valentinus, the fifteenth century alchemist Wyatt refers to, actually derives from the combination of Basilides and Valentinus, the two leaders who organized the largest Gnostic sects in opposition to Christianity in the second century A.D., and thus suggests another dimension of Valentine's identity. But although associated with gnosticism and heresy, Valentine reveals himself to be a rational skeptic whose strongest feeling is a revulsion for the vulgar masses and their "dirty hands." His distaste for physical contact is so strong in fact that he always wears gloves and washes his hands obsessively. As a type, Valentine is a vaguely homosexual aesthete whose sophistication becomes an end in itself. When asked by a fellow conspirator if he enjoys posing as an art critic, he replies:

> —There is always an immense congregation of people unable to create anything themselves, who look for comfort to the critics to disparage, belittle, and explain away those who do. And I might say, he added with slight asperity,— it's not entirely a pose. (651)

The gist of his response could well be applied to his identity as a whole: one pose does not exclude another, and they are not mere poses anyway. Put another way, there is no way to dissociate the original person from his mask, his simulacrum, or his double. Yet one thing is clear amidst this shifting and mercurial complex of poses and associations: as their ensuing dialogues reveal, Valentine functions as Wyatt's shadow self and demonic interlocutor (an aspect of their relationship taken up again in Chapter Three).

To return to the action: his "pact" with Brown concluded, Wyatt immerses completely in the counterfeiting of paintings by Bouts and van der Goes. Esther in the meantime has begun an affair with Otto. When soon thereafter Wyatt moves downtown to an obscure area near Horatio Street, he drops out of view, appearing only intermittently between the desultory comings and goings of a large number of minor characters. Wyatt's recession into the background is accentuated by the fact that he is no longer referred to by name, although other characters sometimes allude to him.

Esther, abandoned in turn by Wyatt and then by Otto, takes up with Ellery, who works in advertising. This change in lovers is accomplished within the ellipses of a conversation, with the confusion in pronoun antecedents (a device used throughout *The Recognitions*) underscoring the interchangeable nature of the characters and their acts:

—Otto?
—What.
—You . . . Oh nothing but, I liked you better a boy, she said from the closet where she stood putting on her slip:
　The women who admonish us for our weaknesses are usually those most surprised when we show our strength and leave them.
—I . . .
—We . . .
—You . . .
—Esther?
—Ellery? . . . Oh, Otto? Otto went away, says Esther from the closet where she stands, taking off her slip.—He went to Central America, to work on a banana plantation. (151–152)

Doomed to repetition, with each new lover failing to fill the absence created by Wyatt's failure to "recognize" her, Esther soon becomes pregnant, and her search for a doctor to perform an abortion is counterpointed by the desperate attempt of another couple, Arnie and Maud, to adopt a baby. Such ironies, both sad and comic, begin to proliferate. Ellery works for Necrostyle, a large corporation that manufactures a large assortment of consumer items, from sleeping pills to prophylactics. The company name boldly declares the deadly nature of its products. Later, one of the characters summarizes its thematic significance:

—But it isn't that simple. Don't you wonder why . . . why everything is negative? Stanley craned round to look up at both of them.—Why just exactly the things that used to be the aspirations of life, those are just the things that have become the tolls? I mean like . . . well like girls having babies? They used to be the fruit of love, the thing people prayed for above everything, and now, now they're the price of...Everything's sort of contraceptive, everything wherever you look is against conceiving, until finally you can't conceive any-more. Then the time comes when you want something to work for you, the thing you've been denying all your life, and then it won't work.... (459)

From this world, Chapter IV shifts abruptly to a banana plantation in Central America, where Otto, having finished his play *The Vanity of Time,* is about to return to New York." The play sounds like a stiff, drawing room rehash of Oscar Wilde, but without the brilliant aphor-isms, as we gather from Otto's reading a part of it to a fellow worker on the plantation, the tattooed Jesse Franks. The latter's suggested "im-provement" is an unconscious parody of the "tough guy" or hard-boiled fiction of the Hemingway line, and the collision between the two ob-viously derivative styles and the characters who represent them generates a great deal of humor.

In Chapter V, Otto returns to New York tanned and cultivating a "new look." His obsession with his image—he is always regarding himself in a mirror—is now firmly established as his special "tic." As a ploy to make himself more interesting, he fakes a wound by putting his arm in a sling—"There was a revolution. Why, they're a regular occupational hazard..." (174) he awkwardly explains—but it fails to arouse any no-tice. Although the previous chapter's epigraph, culled from Rimbaud ("Les femmes soignent ces féroces infirmes retour de pays chauds"), heaps ridicule on a portrait already heavily satirized, Otto is not the only one singled out. As he carries his play around the bars and cafés of Greenwich Village, he encounters artists, critics, reviewers, models, agents of all sorts, advertisers, and drug addicts—in short, a motley gallery of char-acters who while talking, drinking, and screwing try to con each other in every imaginable way. The satire, commensurately, intensifies.

Many of these characters congregate at a large party in the Village to celebrate the unveiling of the painter Max Schling's latest artwork, a blotchy abstraction called *The Worker's Soul* because it consists of a work-man's shirt stretched on a frame and painted over. Max's party is the first in an important series of parties that organize large sections of the novel and in fact constitute a series of "mock-cena" : by providing the occasion for much of the novel's saturnalian ribaldry, the parties contribute sub-stantially to its pervasive air of decadent festiveness. They also bring various characters into collision, provoking through "syncrisis" and "an-

acrisis" the extended and polyphonic dialogues so important to its texture.[12] *The Recognitions* is not just the *Satyricon* writ large, however.
Evelyn Waugh, Ronald Firbank, and Aldous Huxley have also contributed measureably to its manner of presentation, as evidenced by the
characters' zany and often absurd antics and their intellectually sophisticated discussions. But these exchanges make up only part of a larger
polyphony of voices into which Gaddis weaves gossip, crude jokes, and
innuendo, most of which is obliquely significant and always thematically
relevant.

Of the characters present at Max's party a number have important
minor roles in the novel. Agnes Deigh, a beautiful and sophisticated
literary agent, is present with her gay entourage (the phrase "queerer
than queer" begins to recur with some frequency in this section), among
whom Big Anna the Swede, a flamboyant "queen," and Herschel, a ghost-
writer who fakes "copy" for a senator in hilarious ways, stand out in
particular. On this occasion, Herschel laces the cocktail party chatter with
witty quips that counterpoint the exaggerated and heavily stylized drawl
of the other homosexuals. Also attending the party is a critic in a green
wool shirt who will later review a book which sounds like *The Recognitions,* after having read only the jacket blurbs; Mr. Feddle, a befuddled
old man who writes poetry (which he pays to have published) but who
spends most of his time autographing whatever book happens to be lying
around; Hannah, a dumpy bohemian artist who sometimes lives in the
subway; Don Bildow, the editor of a small, intellectual review; and many
other assorted Village types. Other characters, such as Sonny Byron,
Charles Dickens, Buster Brown, and Adeline Thing, have no fixed or
identifiable traits but fill out the social space with activity and chatter.
Otto's former Harvard chum Ed Feasley, who has no established oc-
cupation or identity but who is usually recognized by his "Chrahst"
followed by some exclamation of bewilderment, is also introduced. A
running dialogue over a theological matter between Stanley and Anselm,
two characters who assume a greater importance as the novel progresses,
contributes a more serious note to the party chatter. Stanley, one of the
genuine artists in the novel, composes music, and his persistent attempt
to link art with his devout Catholicism exasperates Anselm, who is obsessed with finding a base or material motive behind every spiritual act.

Otto's attention is quickly drawn to Esme, a wispy and vacant-looking
but beautiful blonde. During the course of the party, she is variously

referred to as a drug addict, "schiz," model, whore, and mother, a signal that she will be viewed from multiple vantage points. All of these rumors turn out to be true, although she is a "mother" now only in that she serves as a model for a painting of the Virgin Mary. She also writes poetry, and later, her discussions with Otto comically puncture an academic assumption of the 1950s—parodically incorporated into the text—that "poetry should not mean but be." At the party, unbeknownst to Otto, Esme is high on drugs, so that his seduction of her recalls that of Eliot's house agent's clerk ("Exploring hands encounter no defense; /His vanity requires no response, / And makes a welcome of indifference"). As the two leave together, the party collapses into chaos, with Anselm taunting Esme with the accusation that she is a succubus and an actual fist fight breaking out between Hannah and Herschel.

Chapter VI opens with Otto awakening the morning afterward in Esme's apartment to the sound of Verdi's *Aïda* (references to opera begin to proliferate noticeably beginning in Chapter III). At breakfast later in the morning, he discovers that Esme doesn't even remember going to bed with him and that he has a rival in the person of Chaby Sinisterra, a dissolute young drug addict. Esme takes pity on him, however, and they return to her apartment and make love, after which, curiously, they both dream of Wyatt. Otto, who has lost touch with him, does not know that Esme is his current model and would-be lover. Ironically, Esme's drug habit explains the particularly successful look of repose in the Virgin of one of Wyatt's forged van der Goes. But only in part: as Wyatt explains to her, he studies her face "not to find what was there, but to find what he could put there, and take away" (270). Yet her face has a strange affective power and becomes a source of fascination for many of the characters.

The dreams are worth recounting. In Otto's dream he pretends to be blind and is walking in a park with a stick with a retracting point. The stick splits down the middle and he is alone, abandoned by the woman who was walking beside him. Then he sees that "pale, thin man [obviously Wyatt] standing in the park vividly silent, watching him without recognition as he approached, blind, with the stick and its retracting point" (220). Esme dreams that Wyatt is caught in a system of mirrors (his painting technique, significantly, relies on the manipulation of mirrors) which have "terrible memories . . . they know, and they tell him these terrible things and then they trap him" (221). The dreams are deciphered easily enough: Otto, self-blinded, requires a crutch, which is usually a woman who will abandon him, and has lost the "recognition" he sought in Wyatt. In Esme's dream, Wyatt is trapped, not liberated, by the "recognitions that go way back," and doomed to replication. To some extent, the dreams merely recapitulate what we have already discovered, but they also anticipate later turns in the narrative. For example, Chapter VIII in Part II concludes with a strange last encounter between Wyatt and Otto that appears to actualize or at least echo Otto's dream.

Chapter VII, the conclusion to Part I, is chiefly devoted to a meeting between Wyatt, Recktall Brown, and Valentine at Brown's sumptuous, art-filled apartment. The purpose of the meeting is to discuss the possibility of a more daring forgery than any accomplished heretofore: a painting by Jan van Eyck's brother, Hubert van Eyck, a painter whose very existence is questioned by many. In this setting, the theologico-aesthetic dialogue between Wyatt and Valentine begins to unfold. We also witness the vying claims on Wyatt's attention. Brown is cautious and protective, almost paternalistic, and sees danger in Valentine's inquisitive regard for Wyatt. Valentine, on the other hand, recognizes Wyatt's talents and sees in him an intellectual equal with whom he must engage, even if it endangers their project. Valentine even goes as far as to draw out a comparison between the madness of van der Goes, who believed himself eternally damned, and Wyatt's own distracted state.

Their intellectual exchange provides sharp contrasts: Valentine speaks in clever aphorisms, whereas Wyatt's speech is halting, his sentences never completed. Valentine is by turns provocative and knowledgeable, cynical and sophistic ("If the public believes that a picture is by Raphael, and will pay the price of a Raphael, then it is a Raphael") (239). But he is also lucid and forthright, whereas Wyatt appears naive and deluded, even crazy, as an inspired artist moved by forces beyond his control: "I don't live, I'm . . . I am lived," he stammers (262). Together they discuss techniques of forgery and detection and the history of private art collecting from its halcyon beginnings in the early days of Republican Rome, through its displacement by the collecting of holy relics with the advent of Christianity, to its return in the Renaissance. But the most important thread of the dialogue turns on the notion of "inherent vice," a phrase that refers to the policy whereby insurance companies refuse to accept responsibility for a painting's decomposition, often caused by improper or inadequate mixing of its materials. Valentine plays on the term's obvious theological implications. He argues that Wyatt's simulations may be genuine works of arts, but "corruption enters" the painting as soon as Wyatt affixes a signature. This leads to a discussion of the "fatal dissension" as well as "fatal attraction" between the priest, "the guardian of mysteries," and the artist, who is driven to expose them. There is some irony here, of course, since these terms don't exactly correspond to either of their positions.

Another game that Valentine plays is that he is the only one of them who exists, the other two being projections of his unconscious. Valentine claims to be writing a novel about Recktall Brown, so much of their talk reflects, both seriously and parodically, on the novel we are reading. For example, Valentine remarks on the function of the hero in the novel, and the interplay between accident and design in life and art, two motifs that begin to assume more importance in *The Recognitions*. And, in a further flaunting of the novel's artifice, he jokingly predicts Wyatt's fate: "I suppose you ... well, let's say you eat your father, canonize your mother, and ... what happens to people in novels? I don't read them. You drown, I suppose" (262). In a telephone discussion with a friend, Valentine also refers to a certain "Willie" who is writing a novel which sounds very much like *The Recognitions*.[13] Yet on a casual reading, these self-reflexive references hardly obtrude but blend almost invisibly with the seemingly more naturalistic dialogue.

Wyatt agrees to dine with Valentine but then abruptly abandons him in a cab they share downtown. Burdened with country-fresh eggs for his tempera medium and an armful of lilies (whose mystical associations are important for the new van Eyck *Annunciation*), Wyatt unexpectedly encounters his old friend John from divinity school walking in the street. The two retire into the nearest bar, where John brings Wyatt up to date on Reverend Gwyon's most recent activities. The first in a series of bar scenes, it is interesting primarily for the way in which several conversations are reported simultaneously, those of unidentified drinkers and "regulars" providing ironic counterpoint to the exchanges between the characters we know. Because the bars usually consist of dark, mirrored interiors, the shadow play of images and voices gives the entire scene a phantasmal quality. As for the encounter between John and Wyatt, it will occur again, many pages later, under similar circumstances. These encounters—between Wyatt and John, Wyatt and Otto, and especially Wyatt and Valentine—all have the same eerie and hallucinatory strangeness. They suggest both an encounter with a shadow self and a stark, Dantesque epiphany in which the characters' spiritual plight is suddenly illuminated. Not surprisingly, references to the *Inferno, Faust, The Harrowing of Hell,* and other literary texts involving Hell begin to recur. This network of allusions makes the city a netherworld or infernal landscape, a compositional strategy that, as Bakhtin points out, is basic to Menippean satire.[14]

In the following scene, Wyatt has returned to his studio, where Esme has come to model for him. The painting is finished, and they fall into desultory conversation after she reads a passage from *Grimm's Fairy Tales.* Suddenly, seeing something in her face, he takes out another painting (apparently the unfinished portrait of his mother), and begins to work. As Esme moves to look at the painting, a feeling of intimacy develops between them, but Wyatt abruptly turns away and sends her off. Upon returning to her apartment after this moment of unconsummated intensity, she tries to write poetry. Recalling the fear and terror of a recent, possibly heroin-induced trance, she begins to write from memory the opening lines of Rilke's first *Duino Elegy.*

Mock-Cenae in New York: *The Recognitions,* Part II

Except for two chapters set in Wyatt's New England hometown, Part II takes place entirely in New York. At the level of the plot, two series of events predominate: Wyatt's futile attempt to expose his forgeries and the consequent break-up of the counterfeiting ring, and assorted encounters between many minor characters which illustrate every possible kind of misrecognition. The action in this part is comprised almost entirely of extended dialogues at parties, bars, and restaurants, and in streets and apartments scattered around the city. The impression created is that life is a mad carnival, that identity—both social and sexual—is a masquerade, and that most human activity has become aimless and decadent. This impression is set and sustained primarily by means of three large parties: a "drag" dance party in Harlem, a Christmas cocktail party at Esther's, and then another at Recktall Brown's. Rather than give a chapter-by-chapter account, I shall simply examine these events in some detail.

In several meetings with Valentine and Brown, Wyatt declares his intention to make public the fact of his forgeries. In response, both insist

that no one will believe him. Now that the forgeries have been ac-
credited—both critically and financially—they have been invested with
a value that will not be easily controverted, even though Wyatt has kept
certain "fragments" or trimmings from the edges of the canvases that
will furnish material evidence of his claims. It also emerges in these
confrontations that Wyatt is distracted almost to the point of incoherence.
In an exchange with Valentine, Wyatt discovers that the tabletop painting
by Hieronymus Bosch in Brown's collection that he thought was the
original is only a copy (see quotation cited earlier, page 10). This discovery precipitates Wyatt into a delirium, and his speech dissolves into
a fragmentary mixture of allusions to his obsession with theological problems. Valentine quickly counters Wyatt's incoherence by remarking that
Wyatt reminds him of his own seminarian friend Martin (a double of
Wyatt's friend John), one of those who "wake up late. You suddenly
realize what is happening around you, the desperate attempts on all sides
to reconcile the ideal with reality, you call it corruption and think it new"
(383). He continues: "We live in Rome, Caligula's Rome, with a new
circus of vulgar bestialized suffering in the newspapers every morning."
But Wyatt is special, Valentine admits, "one who could do more," "this
other self" who will not be recognized by the vulgar public. Valentine
then tries to convince Wyatt to join him in a "conspiracy" against the
masses to protect the beautiful things of the world. Wyatt rejects the
overture, and after stealing a golden bull from Valentine's apartment,
flees into the street.

Earlier in the day, Wyatt had taken his latest painting, a van der Goes's
Death of the Virgin he had "damaged" in order to make it appear more
authentic, to Brown's apartment. Brown, now "so damned familiar," has
become a "luxury" (in the sense of vice) Wyatt can no longer afford. As
Brown tries to persuade him to continue making the forgeries, Wyatt
simply gets drunk. The important exchange seems to have occurred earlier
with Brown's black manservant Fuller, while Wyatt was awaiting Brown's
arrival. Fuller has made several attempts—always foiled—to escape from
Brown and now believes that Brown employs magic powers to hold him,
even using his black poodle to spy on his activities. Fuller's simple but
probing theological questions make a strong impression on Wyatt, as
does his story of a recent encounter with one Reverend Gilbert Sullivan
(who is later arrested for hawking counterfeit wares). Approaching Fuller
in the streets, the Reverend had suddenly asked, "Am I the man for

whom Christ died?" (348). Although it only becomes evident retrospectively, this conversation with Fuller leads Wyatt to return home in an effort to resume his "original calling" immediately after the confrontation with Valentine described above.

Chapter III traces this return. Actually, it begins at the conclusion of Chapter II, when Wyatt again encounters his seminarian friend John on his way to catch a train. Their brief exchange is almost unintelligible, however, because Wyatt's journey back is described mythologically as the movement of the sun (the pun providing the motivation) through subterranean passages to the east where it will make a triumphal appearance at dawn as Baal, the sun god. In the opening pages of Chapter III, as Wyatt approaches his home, his state of mind is rendered in a stream-of-consciousness manner through the suppression of external references and syntactic connections. As an expression of Wyatt's dazed and delirious consciousness, this polyglot collection of fragments blends the erudite, the trivial, and the fantastic into a nearby unintelligible mishmash, although phrases echo earlier passages (see especially pages 390–394).

The reunion with his father brings about a partial recovery. Wyatt then attempts to account for himself:

> —Yes, now here we are, and . . . because down there, things got confused down there, dreadfully confused. I couldn't begin to tell you everything that happened, everything . . . I hardly know myself, except . . . I hardly believe it now, I hardly believe they actually did happen. And so I . . . well there, so I just left it all there, it was getting to be so unreal anyhow that it . . . and I . . . well here, here to go on from where reality left off, to recover myself, and . . . the ministry, a career with the times, in keeping with the times. He took a hand from the edge of the table to rub it over his face.—And all that . . . fabrication, there's no reason to believe it ever existed, and she . . . that city? If I fell among thieves? Why, there are places more real, there are places in books, there are people in plays more real than . . . all that. It was turning into a . . . a regular carnival. (427)

In the security of his home, where he feels that he is always being watched—"How safe I am from accident here," he says—Wyatt thinks he has escaped from this carnival world. But his security soon dissolves when he discovers that his father's conception of the ministry is not at all what he had assumed; it is Mithra's priesthood that his father wants to prepare him for, and for that he must "die at the hands of Pater Patratus, like all initiates." Gwyon explains:

—No one can teach Resurrection without first suffering death himself. No one can be reborn without dying. No one can be Mithras' priest without being reborn . . . to teach them to observe Sunday, and keep sacred the twenty-fifth of December as the birthday of the sun. Natalis invicti, the Unconquered Sun, Gwyon finished, turning his face to the window.

—But I . . . you . . . to worship the sun?

Gwyon let go his wrist abruptly, and he drew it back.

—Nonsense, said Gwyon, brisk now.—We let them think so, he confided,—those outside the mysteries. But our own votaries know Mithras as the deity superior to it, in fact the power behind the sun. (432)

In several ways, this reversal has already been anticipated. It is noted earlier, for example, that Gwyon is reading the chapter on the sacrifice of the King's son in Frazer. More directly, Wyatt himself brings home the stolen golden bull as a present for Gwyon, perhaps unwittingly leading his father to suspect that he knew all along what he was engaged in. In any case, immediately after the discovery of Gwyon's atavistic practice, their encounter is interrupted by the arrival of the church Use-Me Ladies' group. When Wyatt realizes that they don't recognize him as Gwyon's son, he manages his escape as the "Reverend Gilbert Sullivan."

This interplay between mis-recognition and disguise operates on several levels, but primarily through the confusion of the literal and the symbolic. At some level of his consciousness, Wyatt strongly identifies with John Huss, and his mental state is certainly aggravated by the fact that no one "recognizes" him as the minister's son. Furthermore, Janet, the household serving girl, takes him for Christ in the Second Coming. When she decides he is the Antichrist instead, she lapses into a strange brooding state and then, on a stormy night, tumultuously offers herself to a bull in the carriage barn. I have already discussed how this section functions textually; dramatically, it presents the final, heightened confrontation between father and son. As the scene of Janet's mad act stands revealed before them in a crash of lightning and thunder, Wyatt turns to his father and repeats the question Fuller was asked by the Reverend Gilbert Sullivan: "Father . . . Am I the man for whom Christ died?" (440).

Although he doesn't realize it at the time, Wyatt's meeting with his maternal grandfather, the Town Carpenter, offers a more hopeful counterpoint. Though he may be joking (one can never be sure), the Town Carpenter takes him initially for Prester John, newly arrived "from Ethiopia and the three Indies" (408). In a long speech which ironically echoes one of Valentine's, his grandfather reflects on the fact that none of the townspeople has any idea of what a hero is, nor of the meaning of their own activities. Lucky for them, they can stay out of important matters by making money. "Fortunately," he continues, "men like you and myself appear every century or so, to keep the way open" (409). However, he concedes, people are now intruding more and more into the important things in life, such as art and voyaging, thus making it more difficult for those capable of real experience. It's the difference between going somewhere in a balloon or in an airplane, he explains. His last words, which Wyatt will echo in his own last reported words, suggest a radical solution: "Later on we shall simplify things. Why, all the others are drowning in details. That's what happens to them, you know. That's where we'll outwit them. We must simplify . . ." (411).

Wyatt, however, is not yet ready for this advice. The Town Carpenter's friendly avowal of recognition—"Of course I'd have known you anywhere"—is not enough to offset the loss of his bearings occasioned by his discovery of his father's plight and the fact that none of the townspeople recognize him. So, in what is clearly a major turn in the plot, Wyatt returns to New York.

Except for an occasional glimpse, Wyatt now disappears from the reader's view. In Chapter IV, Esme visits him one night at his Horatio Street studio. When he doesn't respond to her words (apparently he is unconscious), she takes his mother's Byzantine earrings and leaves him a letter that concludes: "Paintings are metaphors for reality, but instead of being an aid to realization obscure the reality which is far more profound. The only way to circumvent painting is by absolute death" (473). Apparently ready to act on this belief, Esme goes home and attempts suicide.

We soon hear that Wyatt's studio has burned down and all of his things destroyed, just as earlier the warehouse storing his first paintings had also burned down. At his next appearance, a brief meeting with Valentine at the city zoo, Wyatt complains that there is little money in his bank account, although there should have been thousands of dollars as his share of the profits on the forged paintings. Valentine later admits to Brown that he has robbed Wyatt in a futile effort to control his behavior.

On the night of Brown's party, where critics, buyers, and art connoisseurs have gathered, Wyatt makes a last desperate attempt to expose his forgeries. Earlier, Valentine had warned him that it wouldn't be easy—

"This putting off the old man"—an allusion to the change in identity brought about through Christian faith (the old man, of course, being the Adam of the sinful self). Wyatt compounds his difficulties by appearing at Brown's party wearing two suits—one on top of the other—in a travesty of the Christian belief. A pompous member of the Royal Academy of Art (referred to as the R.A.) takes him for a lunatic and dismisses his claims as drunken ravings. (To complicate matters, this entire scene is reported indirectly, in later conversations between Fuller, Valentine, and Brown.) Leaving the party, Wyatt goes to Esther's apartment in search of his material proof, the fragments cut from the edges of his forgeries.

Apparently unhappy at the imminent dissolution of his pact with Wyatt, Brown begins to drink heavily and then, in another travesty, decides to put on the suit of Italian Renaissance armor in his collection, his favorite work of art. Significantly, the footgear is of a German make and markedly incongruous with the Italian design. As Brown is clanking around inside the suit on the balcony above, the pompous R.A. is reminiscing about a scholarly paper he once wrote:

> —Yes, yes, here it is. The devil, wearing false calves, do you recall? Mephistopheles, don't you know, in mffft that ponderous thing by Goethe. Good heavens yes, wearing false calves, don't you know, to cover his cloven feet and his mphhht calves, yes. Well my thesis, don't you see, was that these things weren't simply a disguise, to fool people and all that sort of things, but that some sort of mfft... aesthetic need you might say, some sort of nostalgia for beauty, don't you see, he being a fallen angel and all that sort of thing, rather ...unpleasantly different in his mphhht appearance from mphhht....(676)

Before we can fully grasp the ironies generated by this juxtaposition of travesty and intellectual theory, Wyatt arrives upon the scene—"Here's your lunatic come back again," the R.A. says—and Brown, in the full panoply of armor, falls from the stairway to the landing below, causing his instant death.

In the ensuing confusion, the party breaks up, leaving only Wyatt and Valentine for a final confrontation. Valentine wants to carry on, just the two of them together. When Wyatt shows no interest, Valentine lashes out,

> —Vulgarity, cupidity, and power. Is that what frightens you? Is that all you see around you, and you think it was different then? Flanders in the fifteenth century, do you think it was all like the Adoration of the Mystic Lamb? What

about the paintings we've never seen? the trash that's disappeared? Just because we have a few masterpieces left, do you think they were all masterpieces? What about the pictures we've never seen, and never will see? that were as bad as anything that's ever been done. And your precious van Eyck, do you think he didn't live up to his neck in a loud vulgar court? In a world where everything was done for the same reasons everything's done now? for vanity and avarice and lust? and the boundless egoism of these Chancellor Rolins? Do you think they knew the difference between what was bizarre and what was beautiful? that their vulgar ostentation didn't stifle beauty everywhere, everywhere? the way it's doing today? Yes, damn it, listen to me now, and swear by all that's ugly! Do you think any painter did anything but hire himself out? These fine altarpieces, do you think they glorified anyone but the vulgar men who commissioned them? Do you think a van Eyck didn't curse having to whore away his genius, to waste his talents on all sorts of vulgar celebrations, at the mercy of people he hated? (689–690)

Picking up a thread from an earlier dialogue, Valentine continues:

—Yes, I remember your little talk, your insane upside-down apology for these pictures, every figure and every object with its own presence, its own consciousness because it was being looked at by God! Do you know what it was? What it really was? that everything was so afraid, so uncertain God saw it, that it insisted its vanity on His eyes? Fear, fear, pessimism and fear and depression everywhere, the way it is today, that's why your pictures are so cluttered with detail, this terror of emptiness, this absolute terror of space. Because maybe God isn't watching. Maybe he doesn't see. Oh, this pious cult of the Middle Ages! Being looked at by God! Is there a moment of faith in any of their work, in one centimeter of canvas? or is it vanity and fear, the same decadence that surrounds us now. A profound mistrust in God, and they need every idea out where they can see it, where they can get their hands on it. Your . . . detail, he commenced to falter a little,—Your Bouts, was there ever a worst bourgeois than your Dierick Bouts? and his damned details? Talk to me of separate consciousness, being looked at by God, and then swear by all that's ugly! Talk to me about your precious van Eycks, and be proud to be as wrong as they were, as wrong as everyone around them was, as wrong as he was . . . .—Separation, he said in a voice near a whisper,—all of it cluttered with separation, everything in its own vain shell, everything separate, withdrawn from everything else. Being looked at by God! Is there separation in God? Valentine finished, and held out his hand again, but more slowly, less steady, to withdraw it immediately the two retreating before him came up, breaking the surface as the voice broke the silence he left. (690)

The outburst, like many others in the novel, illustrates how ideas voiced by characters take on a dramatic intensity in confrontations that are more or less tangential to the plot. (In this we see an affinity with Dostoevsky's fiction.) Valentine's assertion here that things haven't changed histori-cally, that the present is really not different from the past, and that we should have the courage to face this fact brings the religio-aesthetic dialogue with Wyatt to a culminating point.

Wyatt's "response" will not come until much later. In this scene, as Valentine reiterates his plea that they renew their complicity ("You and I" he repeats insistently), Wyatt goes berserk and stabs him repeatedly with Brown's penknife. The scene concludes with Wyatt and Fuller going their separate ways, Fuller feeling "free as the day I was born" after years of enslavement to Brown, and Wyatt, coherent again, in search of Esme. (Actually, Valentine doesn't die as Wyatt thinks and the reader assumes. He will reappear later in the novel, but without ever being identified again by *name*.)

Since this scene brings the main plot to a head, we can now turn to the series of mis-recognitions that form the basis of the subplots devel-oped in Part II. Chief among these is Otto's comically bungled attempt to meet with his father, which clearly parallels Wyatt's attempt at reunion with Gwyon. Mr. Pivner's portrait is presented in the opening pages of Part II. More than any other character in *The Recognitions,* he represents modern "mass man." When not working at the office, his time is occupied with reading the newspaper and listening to the radio, his experience pitifully reduced to the repetition in his consciousness of mass-media clichés and stereotyped thoughts. For him, the newspaper externalizes in "the agony of others the terrors and temptations inadmissible to him-self" (288); the radio offers a series of substitute gratifications—a sermon, then a deodorant advertisement—all while constantly reminding him that he "is under absolutely no obligation." Fretting alone in his apartment, itself a testament to utter anonymity, Mr. Pivner amiably accepts every imprecation from the mass media; he even waits courteously for the announcer to finish speaking before turning the radio off. Pathetically, these communications are his only contact with anything outside himself. Yet, in spite of the fact that he leads such an abstract life—existing only in "aggregate" (303), as the narrator more precisely puts it—Mr. Pivner somehow elicits our compassion.

This is perhaps explained by the fact that he illustrates so sadly a kind of relationship with others that Jean-Paul Sartre calls *seriality.* As Sartre describes it, a serial relationship is one predicated on neither individual face-to-face encounters nor on the sharing activities of group action, but rather on the essentially anonymous repetition of what others are doing or would do in the same or in a similar situation.[15] Thus, reading a newspaper or listening to the radio, walking home from work or taking a bus (the activities we observe Pivner doing) are all characterized by their identity with the acts of others in similar situations, and so, whatever the uniqueness of the particular experience, it is undermined by an anonymity and statistical quality. For Sartre, developing this Heideggerian theme, such an experience is a quintessential form of the inauthentic: since I am no longer at the center of my action, but doing just what everybody else is doing, the center of my act is elsewhere, outside me, in other people. But, since everybody else feels the same way, there is really no center, no external model that everyone is imitating. The feeling of togetherness derived from being with the collectivity, or the "aggregate," like the phenomena of "public opinion" or the science of statistics, is revealed to be founded on a kind of optical illusion.

Formulated in these terms, Pivner's plight obviously parallels Wyatt's different kind of serial repetition, and the latter's "failure" to appear as a hero (an important theme I shall return to in Chapter Three). In a digression "inspired" by Pivner, the narrator animadverts upon the results of "Reason":

> Here in the foremost shambles of time Mr. Pivner stood, heir to that colossus of self-justification, Reason, one of whose first accomplishments was to effectively sever itself from the absurd, irrational, contaminating chaos of the past. Obtruding over centuries of gestation appeared this triumphal abortion: Reason supplied means, and eliminated ends.
>
> What followed was entirely reasonable: the means, so abruptly brought within reach, became ends in themselves. And to substitute the growth of one's bank account for the growth of one's self worked out very well. It had worked out almost until it reached Mr. Pivner, for so long as the means had remained possible of endless expansion, those ends of other ages (which had never shown themselves very stable) were shelved as abstractions to justify the means, and the confidently rational notion that peace, harmony, virtue, and other tattered constituents of the Golden Rule would come along of themselves was taken, quite reasonably, for granted. (290–291)

In reality, this "Reason" produces a fretting anxiety and feeling of inadequacy which Pivner is constantly exhorted by the mass media "to overcome." Hence, he becomes an avid reader of Dale Carnegie's "masterwork," *How to Win Friends and Influence People,* as well as such books as *How to Speak Effectively, Conquer Fear, Increase Your Income, Develop*

Self-Confidence, "Sell" Yourself and Your Ideas, Improve Your Memory, Increase Your Ability to Handle People, Win More Friends, Improve Your Personality, and *Prepare For Leadership.* Of course, it is a vicious circle, for the means of escape from this condition simply involve Pivner more deeply in another seriality.

There is a sad irony then in referring to Mr. Pivner's son Otto as "part of a series of which the original doesn't exist": as the father or "origin" of Otto, Mr. Pivner is almost a nonentity, so it seems hardly surprising that Otto lacks an identity of his own and is obsessed with his self-image. In Chapter V, seeking relief from the insubstantial encounters with Village types and similar people in the advertising and publishing world, Otto arranges to meet his father, whom he has never seen, in a midtown hotel bar. Unfortunately, Mr. Pivner, worried that he will be late, neglects to give himself his diabetes injection. As a result, he has a hyperglycemic reaction outside the hotel and is mistakenly arrested as a heroin addict. Meanwhile, Otto sits at the bar inside, idly thinking about picking up a blond prostitute named Jean sitting beside him. When the counterfeiter Mr. Sinisterra enters, he immediately takes Otto for the "pusher" of his newly minted fake twenty-dollar bills. Because Sinisterra is wearing a green scarf, a previously established sign of "recognition," Otto mistakes him for his father. The two take a table and sit through a rather awkward dinner together in a very funny but credible scene. The timid and faltering Otto does not realize there has been a mix-up, and assumes the bag full of money Sinisterra hands him is an unusually generous Christmas present. Only later, after Stanley is arrested for possession of a counterfeit bill Otto has loaned him, does the latter realize that the money is "queer." Eventually, Otto will have to flee to Central America to escape the police, but in the meantime, he tells all his friends that he has sold his play for a large sum.

Sinisterra, realizing his mistake, will pursue Otto from place to place, but his attempts to grab him are always foiled by an accident or the intervention of some other party. Sinisterra is indeed unlucky, and his name has to be taken in the sense of unfortunate rather than ominous and threatening. It is Sinisterra's son Chaby who is sinister in the latter sense. Chaby's activities, in fact, remain shrouded in mystery. All we really know about him is that he is a heroin addict and that he thwarts Otto's attempts to become Esme's lover.

Like Otto and Mr. Pivner, as father and son the Sinisterras provide numerous comic analogies and displacements. The father in particular, who is portrayed as an "authentic" counterfeiter and "genuine" Catholic, provides the foundation for a series of parallels, analogies, and contrasts with Wyatt's activities. When he first appears in Part II, Sinisterra has just been released from prison, where he made the plates for the twenty-dollar bills. (He has also repented for his responsibility in causing Camilla's death.) Bemoaning the lamentable state of his craft, he especially feels the loss of the old masters: "I miss him [Johnny the Gent] when a great artist dies like that. He was no bum. It's no place for bums to get into, but they're ruining it every day. There hardly is a single old master left. A real craftsman, like Johnny, or Jim the Penman" (519).[16] A fervid reader of the periodical *The National Counterfeit Detector,* where reviews of his own work have not appeared for years, Sinisterra provides the motivation for long historical forays into the "art." He is justifiably proud of his achievements and his "identity" as a counterfeiter:

> And do you think nobody knows who I am? The minute they spot a piece of this stuff, they've got it under a microscope. They've got work of mine they picked up thirty years ago, and they can compare it. They're not dumb, with a microscope in their hand, the Secret Service, they can find the smallest resemblance, even after thirty years they can see my own hand in there, a little of myself, it's always there, a little always sticks no matter what I do. (491)

Sinisterra's claims parallel some of Wyatt's statements on the detection of forgeries in art, and there are similarities in attitude, such as Sinisterra's reverence for his work, which he approaches as a master in a secret, artisanal guild. Both forgers use certain materials in common—particularly lavender—and come to be associated with its scent. (This motif is parodied in turn by the emergence of a new perfume on the market called *Fuissi deam,* a title that derives from and vulgarizes a topos in classical poetry.) The parallels between Wyatt and Sinisterra are further heightened in Part III when they actually cross paths in Spain. Here I shall merely note that, in bringing together Sinisterra and Wyatt late in the novel, Gaddis offers a parodic commentary upon the meeting of Stephen Dedalus and Leopold Bloom in Joyce's *Ulysses.*

To insure that this parody of the father/son theme will not be missed, it is echoed by other mis-recognitions. In Chapter IX, the last chapter of Part II, we return to Wyatt's home town to witness the institutionalization of the Reverend Gwyon in a mental hospital after he sacrifices his neighbor's bull and during one Sunday sermon begins to offer "sacrifice unto Mithra." He is replaced by a bland young minister named "Dick," who sets about immediately to make the parsonage and church "cheery" and "cozy." "Dick" decides to cultivate one "sin" in public— smoking cigars—since he feels that "an entirely virtuous man . . . occupies an untenable position in society" (715), it being wise therefore to give one's neighbors "some small vice upon which to latch their rancor at the absence of larger ones." "Dick" is thus a perfect representative of the church in a period of historical decline. In hommage to his predecessor, Dick imitates Gwyon's style in one of his sermons, yet the congregation doesn't recognize this gesture of respect, just as Dick himself doesn't recognize its profoundly pre-Christian implications. In a funnier misrecognition, Dick goes to the sanatorium Happymount in order to visit the Reverend, and is constantly mistaken there for the son Wyatt.

Dick's worst mistake occurs after the Reverend dies. Having placed the latter's remains in an airtight oatmeal tin, he sends it to the monastery in San Zwingli, as directed in the will. But then, he misplaces the address to which he must also send an explanatory letter. As a consequence, at San Zwingli the Reverend's remains are assumed to be the flour he usually sends and so are baked into rather crumbly loaves of bread. What's more, Wyatt, who at that point is staying at the monastery, eats the bread, and father and son become consubstantial in a black parody of Holy Communion.

The father/son relationship is also the source of other examples of grotesque humor. Mr. Pivner never hears from Otto again after receiving a dressing gown as a Christmas present (he never knows of the mix-up that occurred inside the hotel) and soon befriends Eddie Zefnic, an office boy he will later adopt as his own son. In another mix-up, Eddie unwittingly incriminates Pivner, who is arrested again, this time for counterfeiting when the police apparently confuse father and son. Persistently maintaining his innocence, Pivner is finally forced to submit to a lobotomy intended to "cure" him of his tendency to lie. Filial through it all, Eddie writes to Pivner from school (financed by his new father) to explain how an experiment in science class throws some light on Pivner's gruesome fate:

> I have been in the laboratory here where they took a sheep's brain apart so I could see what it must be like having those nerve tissues between the frontal lobes of the brain severed off of the midbrain which is where you have the emotions, so I can see where the prison psychiatric doctor said how it might

be a good thing because things like counterfeiting and forging aren't crimes
of violence but more something emotional maybe that gets mixed up so if
you sever it off then it can't get mixed up anymore and you don't want to do
things like forging and counterfeiting any more. Which even though they
aren't crimes of violence they sort of mean something's wrong somewhere.
(933)

As a caustic satire on the "scientific" attempt to explain human behavior,
the passage is thus linked to a whole series of harangues and diatribes
against Reason and rationality.

Another source of humor in *The Recognitions* is generated by the masquerading and mis-recognition of sexual identity. This theme corresponds
to a comic playing out of the serious theological question occupying
Wyatt and which was a matter of debate in the formation of early Christian doctrine: were God and Jesus homo*ou*sian or homo*oi*sian (of *one* or
like substance?). Since a homosexual was commonly regarded as a sexual
counterfeit in the conservative 1950s (as in Edmund Bergler's *Neurotic
Counterfeit Sex,* 1951), much of the novel's play with sexual identity
involves a suspicion of homosexuality, a suspicion that is extended to
money as well. For example, the counterfeit money fabricated by Sinisterra is repeatedly referred to as the "queer."

The sexual counterfeit theme is worked with many variations. One
character, Charles Dickens, is discharged from the army because he is
caught wearing women's clothing, although apparently he is not a trans-
vestite. However, a number of characters do attempt to disguise their
sexual identity or preference: Big Anna, a blatant queen, pretends to
faint in order to receive artificial respiration from a group of Boy Scouts;
another queen joins the Catholic Church so that he can adopt a young
Italian boy.

These scattered incidents are given a more concentrated thematic focus
in Part II when many of the characters attend a "drag" party in Harlem.
The first of three parties that punctuate Part II, it most strongly conveys
the sexual confusion and mayhem of life in New York as a carnival
masquerade: Agnes Deigh is punched in the face and Adeline Thing
rebuffed by her dancing partner when it is discovered that the two women
really are women and not transvestites; Ed Feasley pursues "a gorgeous
creature in organdy" only to unexpectedly meet up with "her" at the
men's urinal; and Esme sleeps with a woman she mistook for a man the
night before. While these various mishaps and mis-recognitions do not

amount to a serious questioning of the basis of sexual identity, they do suggest that something as seemingly fundamental as sexual identity is a matter of role or position adopted rather than underlying essence.

That same evening, the ancient Greek practice of carrying ithyphalli through the street is travestied as Ed Feasley and Otto carry an amputated leg around the city, looking for a suitable victim on which to play a prank. They intend to offer the leg to Stanley, claiming it to be the Pope's and therefore a Holy "relic." Unbeknownst to them, the leg is probably the same one amputated from Stanley's mother earlier that day. Unable to find Stanley, they finally leave it to decay on a subway seat.

Such saturnalian escapades continue throughout the many bars and cafés in the Village, where the characters often meet. A favorite spot is the Viareggio, where a large unshaven man who resembles Hemingway is always to be found using the resemblance to welsh drinks from the writer's young admirers. As a gathering place for pseudo-intellectuals, writers, and artists, it provokes the narrator to satiric ire:

> Neighborhood folk still came, in small vanquished numbers and mostly in the afternoon, before the two small dining rooms and the bar were taken over by the educated classes, an ill-dressed, underfed, overdrunken group of squatters with minds so highly developed that they were excused from good manners, tastes so refined in one direction that they were excused for having none in any other, emotions so cultivated that the only aberration was normality, all afloat here on sodden pools of depravity calculated only to manifest the price-lessness of what they were throwing away, the three sexes in two colors, a group of people all mentally and physically the wrong size.
>
> Smoke and the human voice made one texture, knitting together these people for whom Dante had rejuvenated Hell six centuries before. The conversation was of an intellectual intensity forgotten since Laberius recommended to a character in one of his plays to get a foretaste of philosophy in the public latrine. There were poets there who painted; painters who criticized music; composers who reviewed novels; unpublished novelists who wrote poetry; but a poet entering might recall Petrarch finding the papal court at Avignon a "sewer of every vice, where virtue is regarded as proof of stupidity, and prostitution leads to fame." Petrarch, though, had reason to be irritated, his sister seduced by a pope: none here made such a claim, though many would have dared had they thought of it, even, and the more happily, those with younger brothers. (305–306)

Yet the satire is "self-directed" as well, since the author's surrogate and parodic stand-in "Willie" is often seen there, reading such books as *The Destruction of the Philosophers* and *The Destruction of the Destruction* (two actual books, the first by al-Ghazzālī and its refutation by Averroës). At the Viareggio, the characters sit around gossiping and drinking, while discussing their "work." Otto's play sounds "familiar," yet no one can quite place where it comes from. Max's newly published poem, actually a plagiarized English translation of Rilke's first *Duino Elegy* (which he has copied from Esme, thinking she is the author), arouses interest. Topics such as who is sleeping with whom, artificial insemination, the "queer conspiracy," or the latest reproduction in *Collector's Quarterly* never fail to stir up lively controversy.

The most interesting exchanges are the recurrent confrontations between Stanley and Anselm. Critics of *The Recognitions* all seem to agree that Stanley, a would-be artist and sincere Catholic, is one of the few completely "positive" characters in the book. Like several of the other characters (Ed Feasley in particular), he is obsessed with the entropy and expendability, indeed programmed ephemerality, of material things in contemporary culture. His horror of "entombment" prevents him from taking the subway; he stares for anxious hours at a lengthening crack in his ceiling, and always carries concealed in his pocket a small hammer and chisel—his "escape tools." Articulate about the gaps and fissures that characterize modern existence, he is always arguing that we live amidst "fragments" and "palimpsests," as in the following summary of his "aesthetic":

> —This self-sufficiency of fragments, that's where the curse is, fragments that don't belong to anything. Separately they don't mean anything, but it's almost impossible to pull them together into a whole. And now it's impossible to accomplish a body of work without a continuous sense of time, so instead you try to get all the parts together into one work that will stand by itself and serve the same thing a lifetime of separate works does, something higher than itself, and I . . . this work of mine, three hundred years ago would have been a Mass, because the Church . . . . (616)

As a serious artist (he is composing an organ concerto), Stanley echoes many of Wyatt's concerns. His obsession with fragmentation, for example, parallels Wyatt's notion that "separateness"—"everything withholding itself from everything else"—is the source of what is wrong with modern life. And many of Stanley's pronouncements, like Wyatt's, seem to apply self-reflexively to *The Recognitions*.

But though he adumbrates a serious theory, Stanley also appears to be a victim of "separation." Afraid of expending himself, he refrains from all sexual contact and keeps baths and haircuts to a minimum. (His ascesis has comic as well as serious repercussions, as both Agnes Deigh and Hannah pursue him sexually.) At one point he thinks that "every created work is the tomb of its creator," thus acknowledging metaphorically but also anticipating literally his own death for art. His life's ambition is to play his perfected composition on the organ of a medieval cathedral in Fenestrula, Italy. In the closing pages of the novel, he finally accomplishes this end, but the powerful organ, installed by an American industrialist, is too much for the fragile building, and Stanley's performance of the piece brings the entire edifice crashing down on his head.

Anselm, Stanley's persistent interlocutor, provides a strong contrast to Stanley's yearning spirituality. As one critic observes, Anselm is the novel's Diogenes, the one who confronts others with their base animal nature.[17] Unlike his namesake Saint Anselm, whose doctrine of *credo ut intelligam* allowed him to harmonize faith and intelligence, Anselm (who is also called "Arthur") has no means to control or harmonize his conflicting impulses and falls prey to an obsessive desire to disrupt Stanley's spiritual balance and to distract himself from an absolute spiritual trauma. Stanley remains his friend nevertheless because he recognizes that Anselm, like Dostoevsky's Kirilov in *The Possessed,* can neither believe nor live without belief. Without the constraints of faith, Anselm's intellect, which is formidably developed (he is one of the most learned of the characters), has no constructive outlet and becomes only a source of torment. At the same time, his intellect shows up the intellectual shallowness of the other characters. Since Anselm can move with ease from the writings of Saint Jerome to Vaihinger's *Die Philosophie des Als Ob,* he is quickly drawn into intellectual discussions. His intellectual jokes, however, usually pass unrecognized by the others, as when Otto begins to discuss Praxiteles' theory of art and Anselm jokes on the name "Phyrne" (Praxiteles' statue). Though capable of wit—after hearing that Stanley has spent the night with Hannah, he asks him if he's been making the beast with two backs with a palindrome—Anselm is more frequently given to crude, adolescent humor. When Stanley asks him the name of a tune he is humming, he replies: "Yes, it's called I can give you anything but love . . . Bach wrote it when he was three . . . for Mother's Day" (523).

Anselm does more than show up the falsity and shallowness of his friends' learning: he denounces the green wool shirted critic (never identified by name)— "a three time psychoanaloser" (453) he calls him—

for his fake conversion to the church. He also perceives that Otto's arm is not really injured, and he is the only one to recognize that Max's poem is a plagiary. Angered by Stanley's humility, which he says is a form of defiance, he also argues against simplicity ("simplicity today is sophisticated . . . simplicity is the ultimate sophistication today") (457), an argument that will echo and hence qualify Wyatt's last reported words, which also urge "simplicity." Yet Anselm is a faker too. In a comic reversal, he carries a copy of Tolstoi's *Kingdom of God* concealed within the folds of a girlie magazine. As an ex-medical student, he uses his knowledge of medicine to pass himself off as a doctor in various hospitals in order to take advantage of young female patients. Not surprisingly, many characters think he is completely mad. Both Stanley and Esme continue to defend his behavior, however, even though he calls her a succubus (we later discover that he has made love to her), and he never ceases to abuse Stanley.

In several ways, Anselm serves to connect the heavily satirized activities of the Viareggio crowd with the more spiritual yearnings of the serious characters. This is underscored in an interesting way. One day while out with Don Bildow's daughter, whom he baby-sits, Anselm runs into Max, Stanley, and Otto in the street and tells them that the green wool shirted critic used to take a tiny little girl who associated with the Viareggio crowd home with him where he would dress her in children's clothes and then rape her. "Too much Dostoevsky" is Max's response. Later, another character claims that it was Anselm himself who had done this. Hence, the entire episode echoes in *structure* Wyatt's forgery of the Bosch original, which he tells as a story he heard about someone else, and *in content* the rape of the girl canonized in San Zwingli. (The incident also links Anselm again with Dostoevsky's fiction.) So, while Anselm, like most of the Viareggio characters, is a "flat character" defined mostly by tics and obsessions, he is also a center or node of multiple textual connections and allusions.

The cocktail party, I observed earlier, is a basic compositional unit in *The Recognitions*. There are three in Part II alone: the "drag" party in Harlem, Esther's cocktail party on Christmas Eve, and Recktall Brown's on the same night. I have already discussed the first and the last, but Esther's cocktail party, as the fullest "mock-cena" of the series, illustrates most directly how Gaddis appropriates a basic Menippean form. It is also the setting where the confrontations between Stanley and Anselm come to a head, just as the theologico-aesthetic colloquy between Valentine and Wyatt comes to a head at Recktall Brown's party.

Esther's party occupies almost all of Chapter VII, which concludes with several brief scenes from its aftermath. The chapter epigraph, drawn from Darwin's *The Origin of the Species,* suggests that the central concern will be the struggle for existence. This "struggle" is presented as a series of confrontations and seductions that emerge out of the background of fragmented cocktail-party chatter continually running at cross-purposes. The Darwinian theme is further enhanced by fleeting references to the apartment as a jungle floor where strange flora and fauna interact: an orchid worn upside down is dropped, a lady's fur pelt is appropriated by one reveller and then sullied, children and babies crawl about, a cat is crushed when sat upon and ends up in Agnes Deigh's purse. As the narrator notes, even the environment against which change would be reckoned is changing:

> And they [an older man being seduced by a younger] passed under the eyes of the Paleosoic poet, glittering open from features whose prehistoric simplicity was faintly shadowed with apprehension at the sight of the opportune mutations going on around him, denying, by their very existence, the finality of his old-world wisdom, and suggesting, as they took to the air manipulating the baubles so helplessly evolved with a pretense of having designed them themselves, that perhaps, for all his belligerent cooperation with environment, that environment itself was changing, and not only he, but the entire species upon which he depended while living, and rescue from anonymity, perpetuation afterward, was to become part of the sodden floor, and the mat, and finally only traces of the crust itself. (627)

Another perspective is provided by the anxious expectation and then finally anticlimactic arrival of the poet mentioned above, who is the honored guest of the evening. Since it is a Christmas Eve party, his "coming" is obviously a travesty of Christ's coming. The effect is underscored by the unexpected arrival of Wyatt, who is initially mistaken for the famous but never named poet and then later, after Wyatt has gone, by the unexpected arrival of Otto. For Esther, all three are substitutes for one another, as the repetition of the pronoun "he," which here has an interchangeable reference, neatly indicates. Wyatt, not knowing about the party, has come only to get a change of clothes for Brown's party but then is immediately drawn into an extended confrontation with Esther. When he admits that today there doesn't seem to be "much that's worth doing," she lashes out that everything in his life—especially his "guilt complexes"—have only gotten worse: "I watched you turn into no one right here in front of me, and just a . . . pose became a life, until you were trying to make negative things do the work of positive ones" (629). Wyatt, thinking of his intention to expose his forgeries, can only respond rather abstractly: quoting Fichte, the German Idealist philosopher, he asserts that the boundaries between good and evil must be defined again, that "the only way we can know ourselves to be real, is this moral action, you understand don't you, the only way to know others are real . . . that the only way to reality is this moral sense . . . " (631). But Esther senses that he has something specific in mind, which he vaguely alludes to as "crucial," and correctly predicts that it won't work.

Esther's confrontation with Otto repeats with variations her confrontation with Wyatt. Whereas Wyatt is distracted to the point of a schizoid absence of self, Otto is so narcissistically self-entranced he cannot acknowledge or even see Esther as a real person with her own needs and desires. Yet, in an exchange that echoes her earlier one with Wyatt, Esther succeeds in bringing Otto to certain "recognitions." As he admits:

> —If I didn't trust you then, I mean mistrust you, then I wouldn't have learned to mistrust myself and everything else now. And this, this mess, ransacking this mess looking for your own feelings and trying to rescue them but it's too late, you can't even recognize them when they come to the surface because they've been spent everywhere and, vulgarized and exploited and wasted and spent wherever we could, they keep demanding and you keep paying and you can't . . . and then all of a sudden somebody asks you to pay in gold and you can't. Yes, you can't, you haven't got it, and you can't. (621–622)

The passage is significant in that a character comes very close to stating that "recognition" is no longer possible in a totally counterfeit world, while also echoing Bernard's statement in *The Counterfeiters* cited earlier. Otto's admission of his "true" feelings, which he analogizes to paying with gold, is also funny in that he now literally possesses only counterfeit money. As his confusing choice of words seems to suggest, there's no way back to feelings (i.e., values) that have been "spent everywhere and, vulgarized and exploited and wasted." Similarly, Wyatt's attempt to repossess "reality" through a completely quixotic gesture of confession and atonement—though perhaps to be taken more seriously—appears equally futile. Yet while Esther somehow understands all this, she is nevertheless condemned to frustation. Her famous guest arrives and then slips away unnoticed, and—in a savage touch of final humor—after the party she ends up going to bed with the green wool shirted critic, who only wants her to watch him masturbate.

During the party this same critic, who is looking for a job writing television scripts anonymously, had been drawn into a confrontation with Benny, who is now Ellery's friend and works in television advertising. We learned earlier that Benny's idea for a publicity gimmick—a man in trouble financially will commit suicide by leaping from a church steeple, at the very moment television cameras happen to be on the location—has met with enthusiastic acceptance at Necrostyle. When the critic insinuates that Benny has "sold out," the latter responds with a long harangue:

> —I offered you work, and you were too good for it. We buy stuff from guys like you all the time, writing under pen names to protect names that are never going to be published anywhere else, but they keep thinking they'll make it, what they want to do, but never quite manage, and they keep on doing what they're too good for. It's a joke. It's a joke, Benny repeated, and it was now that his voice began to rise.—I know you, I know you. You're the only serious person in the room, aren't you, the only one who *understands,* and you can prove it by the fact that you've never finished a single thing in your life. You're the only well-educated person, because you never went to college, and you resent education, you resent social ease, you resent good manners, you resent success, you resent any kind of success, you resent God, you resent Christ, you resent thousand-dollar bills, you resent Christmas, by God, you resent happiness itself, because none of that's *real.* What is real, then? Nothing's real to you that isn't part of your own past, real life, a swamp of failures, of social, sexual, financial, personal, . . . spiritual failure. *Real life.* You poor bastard. You don't know what real is, you've never been near it. All you have is a thousand intellectualized ideas about life. But life? Have you ever measured yourself against anything but your own lousy past? Life! You poor bastard. (602–603)

Benny perceives that the critic's intellectual stance is sustained by resentment, yet he also admits that his own life is a hollow sham. But what's important here is not a dramatization of moral self-awareness but rather the opportunity for extended verbal assault. In a conventional novel, Benny's harangue would probably be "out of character," but here it serves to "relativize" (in Bakhtin's sense) the self-privileging viewpoint of someone dedicated to the "purity" of a literary vocation.

The culminating confrontation between Stanley and Anselm involves more of the other party goers and so has a disintegrating effect on the party as a whole. Stanley arrives early and is immediately pulled into a tête-à-tête with Agnes Deigh, who at their last meeting tried to draw him into bed after declaring her love for him. Stanley had flown from the physical contact, though he hasn't given up in his attempts to convince this lapsed Catholic to return to the Church (her name of course is a pun on "lamb of God"). At the party, Stanley resumes his explanations of the fragmentary nature of modern life and argues that without the Church we are doomed to live among palimpsests. Even art, standing in self-sufficiency, becomes a force separating people. Anselm soon arrives, but remains aloof, merely staring at them from the distance. Then suddenly, he breaks into their conversation with such intensity that Stanley must abandon Agnes. At the mention of the Church, Anselm begins to quote Christ's "separation" speech ("For I am come to set man at variance against his father, and the daughter against her mother in law ... and a man's foes shall be they of his own household"), a speech suggesting the more subversive side of Christianity. When Stanley tries to calm him, Anselm lashes out in a speech that echoes Valentine's response to Wyatt's naive faith in an earlier time. In the ensuing verbal to-and-fro, Anselm charges that Stanley's faith and humility is a selfish refuge, that it amounts to a refusal of love: "You're the one who refuses love, you're the one all the time who can't face it, who can't face loving, and being loved right here, right in this lousy world, this God-damned world where you are right now, right ... right now" (678). Anselm appears to be right—at least his charge qualifies the value of Stanley's assertions. As they continue, the exchange becomes a debate about the nature of love, with Stanley arguing for its spiritual, transcendent powers ("love has to be something greater than ourselves ... "), while Anselm, in carnivalesque fashion, wants to bring love back through scatological comparisons and a quotation from Suckling's poem ("love is the fart of every heart ... "), to the dimensions of the human body, with its physical needs and desires. Of course, the argument is never resolved. Instead, as Anselm becomes wilder and more hysterical, others are brought into the mêlée, with the result that Anselm is finally knocked down and then disappears from the party.

These confrontations do not occur as sequentially as the summary here implies, but fade in and out of the intermittent chatter of the other party-goers as we move around the apartment. Amidst a polyphony of dialogue and conversations often running at cross-purposes, a number of seductions are in progress: Arny is seduced by a young black homosexual named Sonny Byron while his wife Maude becomes preoccupied with a baby she finds crawling on the floor; Ellery is faithless with a blond secretary while Esther is busily engaged with Wyatt and then Otto. And there is much of the zany and unexpected. Ed Feasely, whose father is an arms manufacturer, manages to sell a battleship to an Argentinian who's at the wrong party. The eccentric Mr. Feddle is busy autographing all of Esther's books. The author of the best-selling book *Trees of Home* is in the corner "shooting" whiskey with a hypodermic syringe in order to "prevent hangover." Amidst echoing references to a "Swiss conspiracy" and to the classical music playing in the background, we discover that Esther's pregnancy is a "false" or hysterical one, that Max's poem for Don Bildow's magazine is a plagiary of a Rilke poem, and that Esme, whose absence from the party is conspicuous, has attempted suicide.

In spite of the fact that the party is a convivial social gathering, there is little communication among the characters. As one commentator has observed: "Symposiums usually end in communion or resolution; here, clashing emotions and ideas increase the tension between the emotions and ideas without reaching a synthesis."[18] This effect is created and sustained by a device employed throughout *The Recognitions*: the juxtaposition of snippets of conversation that are satirically self-deflationary, as in the following passage:

> Behind him, a girl said, to someone else,—So I started this personalidy course where they have you stand in front of a mirror and repeat your name over to yourself in a nice gentle tone . . . and now I'm Mister Wipe's personal secretary . . .
> —So I said to her, you just go ahead and *be* pathological . . . .
> —So I said to them when we got back to Florence, of course there's no place I'd rather live than Siena if I had my analyst there with me . . .
> —So he said to me, Oh, Sappho, he was queer too wasn't he. . . . (610)

Anti-Semitism, homophobia, pretentious knowledge of art, and cultural snobbery are especially noticeable in the cocktail-party chatter. Interwoven with these satirized exchanges are the more serious confrontations between Stanley and Anselm, Esther and Wyatt, and Esther and Otto. But at neither level is any important issue resolved, and the party finally disintegrates.

In the construction of these polyphonies, Gaddis employs hyperbole, juxtaposition, parody, and camp humor—all to suggest the inauthenticity and exchangeability of the characters' ideas and emotions. Yet this "inauthentic" language does not serve to hide and thereby suggest some deeper, more authentic feeling stirring below the degraded crust of every-day speech, as in Natalie Sarraute's notion of the "sub-conversation."[19] However hollow and debased, it is the only medium of exchange through which the characters encounter each other at all. So, in order to prevent the reader from wearying from the inundation of clichés and sterotypes, Gaddis often inflects the speech (as in "personalidy course" above) toward a certain recognizable idiolect. Or sometimes he constructs jokes around a character's ignorant use of a cultural fact or allusion:

> At her elbow, someone said,—Well Ruskin dated his life from the first time he saw them.—Well, of course *Rus*kin, said the other.—He was in town just last week, wasn't he? said the tall woman.—I heard my husband talking about him. They had lunch together, I think . . . he's doing a book about stones . . . ? (571)

But more interesting is the way this fragmentary speech echoes, even in a completely trivial context, references to people, places, and books mentioned or important in other parts of *The Recognitions*. This kind of repetition creates a haunting sense or familiarity or a constant déjà vu, but without suggesting which repetitions are significant or why.

After Esther's party breaks up, the chapter concludes with several brief scenes. In one, Anselm crawls on all fours into a subway station where he encounters his mother, whom he refuses to recognize. Quickly evading her, he crawls into a men's room and castrates himself with Reverend Gwyon's razor, which he has taken from Esther's bathroom. In another, Agnes Deigh is mugged while waiting for Stanley to call a cab; little does she know that her purse contains only Esther's asphyxiated cat. Stanley coaxes her into accompanying him to church, but she bolts suddenly and enters a bar. When Stanley tries to pay with the counterfeit bill he borrowed earlier from Otto, he is arrested. The chapter concludes with several drunks cursing Jews and joking about Christmas.

Voyaging: *The Recognitions,* Part III

Just as the party is the main compositional unit in Part II, so the voyage plays a similar structural role in Part III. The importance of the voyage as a motif is established at the very beginning of *The Recognitions* with the Reverend Gwyon's trip to Spain and Italy. Yet so is the futility of the voyage as a quest for spiritual fulfillment or renewal, insofar as Gwyon only becomes more convinced during his travels of the failings of Christianity. In Part III, nearly all the main characters and many minor ones take some kind of trip or voyage, and following the pattern established by Gwyon's experience, nearly all turn out to be parodies of true religious quests or pilgrimages or end in the character's death. Instead of leading to fulfillment or spiritual rejuvenation, the voyage becomes a mechanism of dispersion.

The first chapter opens on the Central American port of Tibieza de Dios, which in appearance has "the transient air of a ragged carnival never dismantled" (771). Tibieza is Otto's destination, though he doesn't know it when he boards an airplane in New Orleans in a desperate effort to avoid arrest for passing counterfeit money. The episode modulates from slapstick comedy to black humor. Unknown to the passengers or pilot, another man seeking escape is clinging to the airplane's tail assembly (Otto notices, as he climbs aboard, that it looks curiously bent). As the plane flies high over the Caribbean, we catch a glimpse below of the *Island Trader,* on which Fuller, having successfully escaped after Brown's death, is working as a cook. When the airplane lands on the beach in Tibieza, the half-frozen extra passenger is discovered. Before he can be questioned, however, the airplane is overwhelmed by a truckload of island revolutionaries who mistakenly believe it to be carrying an arms shipment. The pilot immediately takes off, leaving the passengers stranded helplessly. Soon afterward, the revolution breaks out in full fury, and Otto is accidentally knocked out and his arm broken. Upon regaining consciousness he discovers he is under the "care" of Doctor Fell (under whose ministrations Wyatt had almost died earlier in the novel). Fell hopes that Otto has contracted "something entirely original," and consoles him with the possibility that a new disease may be named after him. Traveling without identity papers, Otto now assumes the name of Gordon, his own fictitious creation. As a prisoner of Doctor Fell, his plight recalls Tony's in Evelyn Waugh's *A Handful of Dust,* who must read Dickens to his captor; yet there is an irony special to *The Recognitions,* since Otto's fate is a grotesque realization of a fantasy he had fabricated in order to embellish his personal identity.

Chapter II returns us to New York, where the false saint theme is immediately picked up. Necrostyle is sponsoring a new television series based on *The Lives of the Saints.* In the studio, some brisk dialogue between Ellery and his associates informs us of a new state of affairs in American life: advertising is the "new Wall Street," and this new industry is being "taken over" by the Ivy League, which supplies its executives. Predictably, their conversation is heavily satirized, as when we hear one complain: "What's a basilica? What was she, Eyetalian? They didn't teach Eyetalian at Yale" (733). One of these new executives explains how things are too simple for "unamerican intellectuals" to understand:

> They still think their cigarettes would cost them half as much without advertising. The whole goddam high standard of American life depends on the American economy. The whole goddam American economy depends on mass production. To sustain mass production you got to have a mass market. To sustain a goddam mass market you got to have advertising. That's all there is to it. A product would drop out of sight overnight without advertising. I don't care what it is, a book or a brand of soap, it would drop out of sight. We've had the goddam Ages of Faith, we've had the goddam Age of Reason. This is the Age of Publicity. (736)

One may well wonder if these exchanges qualify as what Bakhtin calls the "language of the marketplace." It is certain, in any case, that the television production of *The Lives of the Saints*—to single out only one example—demands that repetition in *The Recognitions* also be situated in relation to the commodification of older cultural forms and themes through mass-media representation.[20] At one level *The Recognitions* attempts to neutralize the effects of such contamination through unremitting satire; but at another level, as we'll later see, its strategies are much less conventional.

The spirit among the executives at Necrostyle is not all buoyant optimism. We soon discover that Benny, having set up his advertising gimmick involving the suicide of a young man in financial trouble, has decided to substitute himself for the young man. His suicide has only a momentarily disturbing effect on his friend Ellery, who presents a satirized portrait of the "businessman" as ruthless predator in a completely commercialized culture (in this sense Ellery is clearly Pivner's opposite number). Minutes after witnessing the suicide in the Necrostyle studio, he is back to "business as usual" and lunch at "Twenty-one."

Benny's is only one of the many suicides scattered throughout *The Recognitions*. In concert with the omnipresence of disease, they create the impression of a sick and desperate society, and thus establish the novel as another prose version of Eliot's *The Waste Land*.[21] Shortly after Benny's successful suicide, we hear about Agnes Deigh's failed attempt. When Stanley decides to visit her in Bellevue where she is recuperating, he unexpectantly encounters Esme, who earlier had also attempted suicide after discovering Wyatt in a catatonic state. Esme is now clearly schizoid and refers to herself only in the third person. Struck by her air of genuineness and the delicate feelings she reveals, Stanley decides to rescue her and take her with him to Italy. But first, he must tend to an infected tooth. In one of the novel's many comic coincidences, he happens to choose Dr. Weisgall, the same sadistic character whom Agnes had seen from her apartment window tormenting a young child. Agnes had immediately called the police, but it turned out that the young girl was Weisgall's daughter, so Agnes is threatened with legal reprisals. The episode precipitates so much guilt in her that she seeks consolation from Stanley—one day, she even briefly enters a church—and begins to overwhelm Weisgall with letters of apology. This attempt to expurgate her guilt culminates in one long letter (produced in full on pages 808–814), rambling and effusively abstract, a perfect example of the mock-profound. The letter also recalls Esme's long letter to Wyatt, which she leaves before attempting suicide. Both letters, the one serious, the other a comic mockery, show up the poverty and ineffectiveness of "personal confession" as a mode of discourse: Esme's is so inward and subjective as to be only intermittently intelligible, while Agnes's is a collection of the most blatantly clichéd "spiritual truths."

The last four chapters alternate between Stanley's voyage to Italy, where he seeks to play his completed concerto on the organ at Fenestrula, and Wyatt's encounter with Sinisterra and activities in the monastery at San Zwingli. In satiric counterpoint to these events, the activities of mostly unnamed tourists and snatches of their conversation weave in and out of the exposition.

The end of Chapter II and the whole of Chapter IV are set aboard a ship bound for Rome carrying Stanley and Esme, a group of pilgrims led by Father Martin who are all to attend the canonization ceremonies for the new eleven-year-old "saint," Don Bildow, who is seeking sexual adventure in Europe, and several journalists and American senators. The pilgrims, whom we see counting off their prayers on recording rosaries and reading luridly sensational "convent confessions," present a comic mockery of the early Christian pilgrims. Even Father Martin, we later discover, is actually using his habit to disguise his mysterious conspiratorial activities.

During the voyage the focus centers on Stanley's developing relationship with Esme. Although he soon falls in love with her, his main efforts are directed toward bringing her to accept the Church and its teachings as the true fulfillment of her spiritual longing. In this, he has no more apparent success than he had with Agnes. At one point, their ship takes on survivors from the wreck of the *Purdue Victory* (the same ship Gwyon and Camilla had taken to Europe some twenty years earlier) which has broken up in a storm. One of those taken aboard, nearly drowned, is revived long enough to receive the last rites from Father Martin. When Esme sees the man being plucked from the water and raised to the deck, she thinks he is Wyatt. Stanley, who has never known Wyatt, tries desperately to keep her away from what he thinks is only an ordinary Spanish sailor; besides, he is fearful, so precarious is her state, that Esme will attempt another suicide. In any case, the appearance of the dead man, ministered over by Father Martin, whom Esme refers to as "the black androgyne," precipitates a spiritual crisis which goes rapidly out of Stanley's control. When Stanley tries to get her to pray, she begins to laugh hysterically. To make matters more strange, from the very beginning of the voyage no one has taken any notice of Esme or acknowledged her existence in any way, except for a mysterious figure on the upper deck whom she refers to as the Cold Man and who gives some indication of being Valentine.

At the height of the confrontation between Stanley and Esme, which collapses into a physical struggle, a sinister and grotesque fat lady, one of the pilgrims, intervenes. She ignores Esme, whom she does not appear to see, and ushers in Father Martin, so that Stanley might be "exorcised" by the priest. The possibility that Esme may be only a demon inhabitant of Stanley's fevered imagination or a succubus, as Anselm had charged earlier, finds some support here in the fact that Stanley often feels assaulted by her "simulacra." Whatever the case—and the chapter remains interesting for the way a number of possibilities regarding both Esme and Wyatt are left suspended—this fantastic episode is enough to send Stanley spinning into a delirium. Much of what transpires, in fact, is recalled retrospectively from within the confines of the ship's hospital, where he is held captive by a tyrannical nurse until the ship reaches Rome.

Between these two chapters set aboard the ship bound for Italy, Chapter III jumps to Spain where Wyatt's encounter with Frank Sinisterra becomes a brief "partnership." The chapter is subtitled "The Last Turn of the Screw," and brings Wyatt full circle to the side of his mother's grave, just as the first chapter, "The First Turn of the Screw," chronicled his father's voyage to Europe and his mother's death.[22]

Sinisterra, disguised as a Rumanian named Mr. Yák, has come to Spain fleeing counterfeiting charges in the U.S. He, too, is something of a voyager: earlier he had "allowed himself a moment to dream, saw himself voyaging (for the Eternal City, in a Holy Year, lay before him) like those early pilgrims to the Holy Land, Lententide in Rome, Holy Week at Compostella" (496). Reading that an Egyptologist named Señor Kuvetli is searching for the lost mummy of a young princess, Yák (Sinisterra) contrives to counterfeit a mummy out of the bodily remains of a young girl buried at the San Zwingli graveyard. The plan seems doomed from the start, for the reader knows that Kuvetli's search is only a disguise for a complicated political intrigue. At the San Zwingli graveyard, Yák encounters Wyatt, who is looking for the grave of his mother in what is referred to as a gesture of atonement (810). Neither knows that Camilla's body, mistaken for that of the little girl who is about to be canonized after a number of "miracles" are traced back to her influence (references to the canonization recur throughout the last part of the novel), has already been exhumed. Sinisterra immediately suspects that Wyatt, who behaves rather mysteriously and refuses to give his name, is a criminal like himself. Since Sinisterra needs help in order to counterfeit the mummy, he tries to enlist Wyatt's aid in return for a Swiss passport bearing the name "Stephan Asche." Wyatt hardly seems interested, but when Sinisterra reveals that he is an artist and a craftsman, Wyatt lets himself be taken in hand. Only intermittently coherent, Wyatt begins to drink heavily, with Sinisterra pursuing him from bar to bar. After intimidating the sacristan and parroco at the graveyard with simple chemical changes which he displays as "magic" (an obvious parody of Clementine's portrait of Simon Magus in Egypt), Sinisterra finally gets hold of the little girl's body. Then, in a hilarious episode, he and Wyatt disguise the decaying corpse as an old woman covered with a full-length shawl and take it on the train to Madrid. While Sinisterra goes off to find a cab at the Madrid train station, the police announce they are looking for a North American counterfeiter, and Wyatt (Stephen) disappears. Though Sinisterra succeeds in getting the body back to his hotel room, where he immediately goes to work on the mummification (Wyatt has explained the basic principles), he nevertheless becomes "engulfed in the sense of something lost" (821). He soon thereafter dies under mysterious circumstances, probably assassinated by agents who think he is the real Mr. Yák.

The grotesque comedy of the episode involves several thematic complications. First of all, Gaddis's bringing together of Wyatt and Sinisterra parodies Stephen and Bloom's crossing in *Ulysses,* and further mocks the resolution of the father/son theme. However, it is through this parodic father figure that Wyatt's originally intended name is restored to him, though ironically it comes from a phony passport. Throughout the episode, Sinisterra continues to insist on calling Wyatt "Stephen," and by the end of the episode, so does the narrator. Thus, through a counterfeit, Wyatt (re)gains what was to have been his original name. Secondly, in this espisode the religious theme is also refracted into several parodic registers. When Sinisterra offers the Swiss passport to Wyatt, he alludes to the biblical injunction that assuming a new identity will be like putting off the "old man" and putting on the new. Furthermore, in their discussions of sin, guilt, and atonement, we witness a complicated play of perspectives. A firm and orthodox believer, Sinisterra always takes the traditional Christian view. When he berates Wyatt/Stephen for sinful living—meaning, his heavy drinking and dallying with the prostitutes Marga and Pastora—Wyatt's Faustian reply is that it is "always the prospect of sin that draws . . . us on" (814). While Wyatt/Stephen affirms that he is a Pelagian, he agrees with the unorthodox but nevertheless Christian view that "they let the path [to Heaven] stay dirty . . . to fool the reasonable people" (803).

In one of his few coherent statements of any length, Wyatt tries to describe Spain's special significance:

> —Why in this country you could . . . just sail on like that, without ever leaving its boundaries, it's not a land you travel in, it's a land you flee across, from one place to another, from one port to another, like a sailor's life where one destination becomes the same as another, and every voyage the same as the one before it, because every destination is only another place to start from. In this country, without ever leaving Spain, a whole Odyssey within its boundaries, a whole Odyssey without Ulysses. (816)

The passage both provides a veiled description of *The Recognitions* (it is indeed a "whole Odyssey without a Ulysses") and indicates the paradoxical nature of the voyage, in which sameness and difference, emptiness and plentitude, are somehow reconciled in movement. Mr. Yák's (i.e., Sinisterra's) response is a simple "anyways you couldn't drown on the land," to which Wyatt in turn replies: "You couldn't! Well it's . . . like that. It's like drowning, this despair, this . . . being engulfed in emptiness" (816). The drowning motif thus links together a number of passages, beginning with Clement of Rome's motto (*gettato a mare con un ancora*) which has so fascinated Wyatt because of his family history. Secondly, speaking as a mock-surrogate author, Valentine had predicted Wyatt's "drowning" earlier. Wyatt's reply to Sinisterra emphasizes the metaphorical sense of his drowning, an effect complicated by both the displacement onto the drowned Spanish sailor whom Esme mistakes for Wyatt and his linkage of drowning with suicide (815). This kind of displacement and condensation around a thematic node is typical in *The Recognitions,* and illustrates how it often unfolds according to a dynamic of textual determination sometimes at odds with mimetic representation.

In this section Wyatt also adds to the aesthetic dialogue running through the novel, though now his interlocutor is Sinisterra rather than Valentine. When Sinisterra discovers that Wyatt has been spending the better part of his days at the Prado, he draws him out on the difference between El Greco and the painters of the Northern Renaissance. Wyatt argues that it is difficult to see the El Grecos—with so many hanging side by side—because El Greco is a visceral painter. There is so much plasticity and movement that when the paintings are hung together the "forms stifle each other." But this is not the case with the Northern painters such as Bosch, Breughel, Patinir, and even Dürer, whose compositions do not disturb each other. As Wyatt explains, in the latter "every composition is made up of separations" (807).

Wyatt's insistent valorization of a composition based on " separations" is of course thematically significant. I noted earlier how the psychological consequences of this aesthetic bias have been emphasized within the novel, and they are again demonstrated when Wyatt rejects or abandons Sinisterra. A brief exchange prefigures this "separation." When Sinisterra offhandedly begins to address him, "Then you and me can . . . ," Wyatt responds almost violently:

> Damn it just . . . stop saying that. That you and me. Will you? Damn it. What do they want me for? What do you want me for? Damn it, what do they all want me for? (790)

Recall that it was Valentine's similar gesture, which also started with a "you and me . . . ," that provoked Wyatt to stab him with Brown's penknife. The shift or oscillation between "you" and "they" is also significant, for Wyatt's tendency is to deflect an appeal voiced from the "you" position by returning it transformed into a demand voiced as a "they." On the verbal level, at least, this is the way he rigorously maintains his separation from others. Yet Wyatt is the character whose consciousness is most permeated by the voices of others, both in the sense that his speech is traversed by cultural quotations and allusions, and in that he is constantly giving voice to the wants and desires of the other characters. At the same time, his speech pattern, marked by its fragmentary and halting rhythms, is the most distinctive of all the characters in the novel. In his reported speech, then, we find a contradiction implicit in the novel as a whole: on the one hand, he urges "separation" and all the values it sustains, but in his actual words (that is, at the level of the signifier), there is very little separation and the contours or boundaries of his speech are often blurred.[23]

In Chapter V, we discover that Wyatt/Stephen has apparently taken Sinisterra's advice that he should retire to a monastery for awhile, though it is difficult to ascertain whether Sinisterra feels that Stephen is spiritually troubled or just insane. Stephen's mental state will also be a mystery to Ludy, the "distinguished" (for which, read "popular") novelist from whose point of view Chapter V is rendered. Ludy has come to the monastery at San Zwingli in search of a religious experience, preferably one that he will be able to transmit in a "delicately elevated" prose (but which turns out to be, as samples indicate, unctuous and cliché-ridden). Given this point of view, not surprisingly the entire chapter satirizes the decay of Christianity, perhaps most bitingly when a group of tourists visiting the monastery for lunch reveal a complete ignorance of the fundamental tenets of Catholicism.

The chapter's central incident involves Ludy's two encounters with Stephen, who is staying at the monastery as a penitent. In the first, Ludy happens upon Stephen at work "restoring" several of the paintings that belong to the monastery. It is not clear in what sense Stephen is "restoring" the paintings, since he is actually erasing parts of the composition, as Ludy discovers. Wyatt's speech is even more broken and fragmentary than usual, although in the accumulated context of the book as a whole, much of what he says is recognizable.[24] Ludy's smug attempt to interpose himself is futile, but like many of the characters, he is held rapt by Stephen's strange intensity, even when the latter begins to mutter and talk to various people who are not present. Stephen claims to have passed all the scientific tests, and like the master whose painting he is working on, to have studied with Titian. After explaining that it was "Separateness, that's what went wrong" (874) he passes into a long verbal delirium in which he describes all the scientific tests to which a painting could be submitted: X-ray and microscopic examinations, pigment analysis, defraction tests, and so on. The speech is a harangue against scientific attempts to explain art but presented as a mosaic of jumbled references to various aspects of his identity as a character, most of which are rather abstruse. At one point, he casually asks if Ludy remembers the passage in the *Paradoxa* where Cicero describes the sculptor Praxiteles creating a figure by merely removing the excess marble "until he reaches the real form which was there all the time" (875). Ludy, of course, doesn't remember; in fact, he hasn't read any of the books Stephen mentions. But then, Ludy suddenly sees an old man standing there, the porter, who appears "as though he had emerged from the stone" (875). It is difficult to tell whether the joke is Stephen's or the narrator's; in any case, as Stephen explains, the old man is a fellow penitent (and the rapist of the little girl to be canonized, we soon realize). All the while, Stephen has been munching on some slightly discolored and crumbly bread, which, we discover in a few pages, was unwittingly baked from the ashes of Reverend Gwyon. And so, Stephen becomes "consubstantial" with his father.

In thus weaving together several plot strands and thematic connections in this preposterous manner, Gaddis surely intends an elaborate joke, but one that doesn't deny more serious possibilities, particularly in relation to black humor and the grotesque.[25] Another exchange has a similar effect. In response to Ludy's query about the murder that Stephen supposedly committed, Stephen gives a totally unexpected account of an episode in Algeria in which he shoots and kills a legionnaire. It's a compact and exotic tale about an old friend named Han from his student days (Herr Koppel is also mentioned). When Han, who feels that Stephen has betrayed him ("There was something missing," he says), attacks Stephen, the latter is forced to shoot him. Despite its Hollywood flavor, the tale sounds convincing. Yet at the conclusion of the telling, Stephen reveals inexplicably that when they took down the legionnaire's pants, they discovered that he had a face tattooed on his "fundament." That the tale concludes with this quintessentially carnivalesque image neither helps to establish nor contravert its authenticity. What it does, rather, is to put the reader suddenly in the same uncomfortable and disturbing position held by Ludy, whom the reader can easily feel superior to.

The second encounter between Ludy and Stephen takes place on a hill above the monastery on the morning after Ludy has seen from his window the old man bar Stephen's entry into the church. Ludy is frightened at the prospect of another confrontation with someone he regards as a lunatic and, as a defensive gesture, begins to ask him questions in a faltering voice. Though Stephen answers in the same discontinuous and highly allusive manner, only intermittently intelligible, the most casual-seeming references to various sights and incidents begin to dovetail into a lyrical affirmation of his life as a voyage. The old man, he explains, has sent him on, so that he might find redemption by "living it through." "Hear the bells!" Stephen exclaims, "the old man, ringing me on." While these details suggest that Stephen is moving toward a Faustian redemption ("Whoe'er aspires unweariedly / Is not beyond redemption," Goethe's *Faust* concludes), there are other patterns as well. Stephen alludes to having a daughter, and to returning home as an Odysseus-like figure:

> Oh Christ! not slaying the suitors, no never, but to supersede where they failed, lie down where they left. Where they lost their best moments, and went on, to confess them in repetition somewhere else without living them through where they happened, trying to reshape the future without daring to reshape the past. Oh the lives! that are lost in confession. (900)

And though he seems committed, "Now at last, to live deliberately," his last words and departing gesture are hauntingly ambiguous:

> —You and I . . .
> —No, there's no more you and I, Stephen said withdrawing uphill slowly, empty-handed. (900)

Early in the scene, Ludy had tripped and fallen in fright, cutting his hand. At the same time, he had startled a bird, which had fluttered up and been caught by Stephen. For most of the exchange, Stephen holds the bird clutched tight in his fist. Ludy's continued expression of worry about the bird and complaints about his own bleeding hand only draw peals of mirthful laughter from Stephen. At the last moment, as Stephen hears the bells again and says goodbye, he releases the bird into the air, and it flies free. When Ludy returns to his room, the bird is sitting on one of the framed pictures hanging on the wall. It may even be the same bird that has fluttered outside his window since his arrival. As Ludy now tries to shoo it back out the open window, it hops back and forth from portrait to portrait, with him pursuing frantically from one side of the room to the other. As he chases it, the narrator tells us, he passes himself in the mirror in both directions, "where he might have glimpsed the face of a man having, or about to have, or at the very least valiantly fighting off, a religious experience" (960).

Ludy's sentimental and wholly conventional expectations about what constitutes a "religious experience" are reflected in his hackneyed and formulaic prose account of his spiritual pilgrimage to the monastery and sojourn there. The falseness of his writing is all the more marked in contrast with the narrator's spare but suggestive registration of the sights, sounds, and conversations in and around the monastery. The quoted examples of Ludy's writing convey only attitudes established beforehand toward what he assumes will make up his "religious experience" and read like a Hallmark card from a Spanish monastery. There is nothing to suggest that what happens there will not be amenable to an objective and rational account. Hence, Ludy is totally unprepared and profoundly shaken by his encounter with Stephen and the bird.

The incident with the bird is not without significance in relation to Stephen, either. As a child, Wyatt/Stephen had accidentally killed a wren with a rock; he buried the bird—significantly, in the same place he had also buried his drawings—but never managed to suppress his guilt. Years later, during his mysterious raging fever, he confesses the stoning to his father, who dismisses the incident by reminding him that the early Christian missionaries used to have it hunted down and killed: "the wren was looked on as a king, and that . . . they couldn't have that" (47). Thus, in Part II, when Wyatt returns home for the last time, he tells his father that he will go out like the Christian missionaries and hunt down and kill the wren (430). More obliquely, the incident also recalls the end of Chapter I (Part I) when Gwyon, having received a letter from Wyatt explaining why he can't return to divinity school (because of guilt feelings), ponders telling Wyatt the "truth," but is quickly caught up in pagan reveries: "his memory vaulted through centuries. The letter he had torn in pieces lay on the moving air for an instant, was caught, spread up over the ground and blew away from him like a handful of white birds startled into the sky" (62).

One interpreter of *The Recognitions,* Bernard Benstock, having noted these recurrences, reads their significance in light of Joyce's development of the wren motif in *Finnegans Wake:* "Both Stephens then are recognizable as the wren, the scapegoat, the sacrificial lamb, the uncrowned king, the creative Demiurgos that rivals the God of the Creation, the first martyr of the true religion and the surviving martyr of the true art and the false which both Joyce and Gaddis offer in lieu of religion."[26] Continuing this Joycean reading, Benstock goes on to associate the bird with Wyatt's guilt at his mother's death, though there is no textual evidence for such guilt, and to assert that "it is certainly her emanation that flies into his hand at the monastery."

The entire incident, particularly in regard to its strategic location (Stephen's last appearance in the novel), clearly calls out for interpretation. Benstock's reading, based on the assumptions of the symbolist aesthetic, appears reasonable, but much more needs to be said. Earlier I mentioned that throughout the confrontation with Ludy, many references to Wyatt/Stephen's multitudinous experience dovetail into a lyrical affirmation of his resolve to overcome his admitted despair and to continue on. Most readers have in fact read this part as a qualified but positive resolution of Wyatt's life problems.[27] A closer reading, however, would suggest that this matters less than something else which is at work: the way a series of multiplying and resonant references and identifications produce contradictory and unresolvable effects. Surely there is something strange about the assertion that Wyatt/Stephen is continuing indefinitely on his Faustian quest, with the old man ringing him on with the bells, that he is also a homebound Ulysses, with wife and child awaiting his return, and that he is also comparable to a martyred saint, having found release from his guilt and suffering. There is something forced and contradictory about this reading, just as Benstock's list of associations seems a little remote from the surface tenor of Gaddis's text. I would suggest instead that Wyatt/Stephen is moving beyond these patterns and roles, which are dissolving into incoherence (they no longer cohere around him), and that, if he has achieved any degree of freedom, it is from the cultural past and the roles these allusions imply.

This alternative reading finds some support in Tony Tanner's provocative remarks regarding Stephen's erasure of paintings in the monastery: they are signs that "he is pushing on to a more comprehensive idea of restoration—namely the restoring of reality to itself, symbolized by his erasing of the interpositions of art, and all the filterings and fixities which a work of art involves."[28] Tanner would like us to view Stephen in terms of "decreation" (in the sense that Simone Weil and Wallace Stevens use the word), a reading that takes on added weight when we recall that the artist Robert Rauschenberg did his famous "erasure" of a Willem de Kooning drawing about this time.[29] However, since it is not at all clear what the "restoring of reality to itself" means, I prefer to say that at this point the novel is attempting to represent its own "decoding," with decoding understood to mean the unraveling of the literary and cultural codes that allowed the text to be articulated in the first place.[30] In Stephen's last words to Ludy, Tanner also hears the suggestion that Stephen "is going to try to move on to a state beyond separate identities, as well as beyond the separations of art." Yet instead of pursuing this idea beyond the level of representation, Tanner concedes that perhaps "Stephen is living in a mental world all his own now—alcoholism, inanition and a series of extraordinary adventures having taken their toll."[31]

Much more could be said at this point, but since I return to this important issue in Chapter Three, here I shall simply stress the state of uncertainties towards which the narrative leads: Has Wyatt/Stephen moved beyond the claims of the past and, hence, given way to a desire to get beyond art and artifacts altogether, as Tanner would argue? Is he now to "simplify" and live "deliberately," as he says, possibly with a Spanish wife and child? Or rather, is he insane and no longer in possession of a coherent identity? Is his laughter at the end, repeated and insisted upon in the text, the laughter of spiritual victory and freedom, or is it the laughter of a madman, as Ludy believes? Perhaps there is no way to choose among these possibilities. One thing however is certain: insofar as these possibilities no longer provide stable oppositions and elide into one another, we are witness to the *state of reversibility* toward which the text is tending. In relation to the novel's carnivalization, this effect exemplifies what Bakhtin insists is the literary celebration of the "unfinalizable" and "unobjectifiable" in man, a reading that Wyatt's laughter would certainly support. Yet in a last twist, we must also acknowledge that Wyatt's rich cultural inheritance has come to nought: no frame could contain the energies collected there, and so his final dispersal and disappearance comes with a certain tragic inevitability.

Exeunt Omnes: *The Recognitions,* Epilogue

An unnumbered epilogue, prefaced by a notice posted in brothels along the rue d'Aqueduct in Oran (Algeria), brings the novel to a conclusion.

The notice ("Aux Clients Reconnus Malades L'ARGENT ne sera pas Remboursé") emphasizes both the wasteland motif and its harsh economy of exchange. Most of the action in the epilogue takes place in Rome and centers on the activities of Stanley, who has joined the pilgrims touring the Vatican while awaiting the imminent celebration of the eleven-year-old saint's canonization. About midway through the epilogue, Gaddis intercalates a series of brief scenes depicting the fates of minor characters in a narrative montage that parodies the ending of the long conventional novel.

Stanley seeks to accomplish two things: to find Esme and to play his completed organ concerto at the church at Fenestrula. He goes about the first by simply wandering through the streets and cafés of Rome. Encounters with a group of homosexuals there to celebrate the "marriage" of Rudy and Frank, and later, with a public relations man (who may be Ellery) seeking Esme for the star role in an upcoming movie about the Virgin Mary, eventually bring him the news that she has planned to enter a convent and has been to the church of Portiuncula in Assisi seeking indulgences for Wyatt, whom she thinks is in purgatory. To accomplish his second aim, Stanley goes to see Mrs. Deigh, Agnes's mother, a wealthy expatriate and religious eccentric and one of the novel's most comic characters. In her sumptuous, art-filled apartment on the via Flaminia, where she keeps a (fake) Dominican friar named Dom Sucio and a dog named Hadrian with a skin disease and a hearing aid, Mrs. Deigh receives Stanley graciously and easily arranges for him to play the organ at Fenestrula, since she knows a cardinal with a particular fondness for musical young boys. (In a comic mix-up, Stanley receives not the letter the cardinal writes on his behalf but his grocery list.) Mrs. Deigh also arranges for Stanley to be transported to Fenestrula in her chauffeured automobile, the back seat of which contains a prie-dieu and stained-glass windows. Stranger still, Mrs. Deigh bears an uncanny resemblance to the fat lady aboard the ship that brought the pilgrims.

Stanley soon encounters Don Bildow in the streets of Rome. While on the ship, Bildow had been frantic to get his hands on some testoserone pills and now he is looking for prophylactics. (Thus, through Mrs. Deigh and Bildow, the "American abroad" theme is satirized at both extremes: worshipping at the shrine of culture and sexual adventure.) Stanley is short with Bildow until he learns that the latter has a copy of Anselm's just published confessions, supposedly written in a monastery. Stanley borrows the book and retires to a café to read it but there spots the Cold Man (Valentine) conversing intimately with a man we know to be the assassin Mr. Inononu. The latter, presumably, has murdered Sinisterra (thinking he was Mr. Yák) and now receives instructions to murder Father Martin, whom Valentine will betray by pointing out in the street. (The details of this "international murder intrigue" are meager and shadowy, and can only be pieced together after several readings.) After these arrangements which Stanley overhears but does not understand are concluded, Inononu leaves, and his seat is immediately taken by Esme, who now has a noticeable sore on her lip (she will soon die from an infection contracted after kissing Saint Peter's statue). The "absolved quiet" on her face holds Stanley where he is, and unseen, he listens to their conversation. Unexpectedly, Esme proposes marriage to Valentine, who refuses and insists that she carry through with her plan to enter a convent. At that moment, Bildow rushes upon Stanley with news that his six-year-old daughter is pregnant. In a hysteric fit, he begins to tear pages out of Anselm's confessions.

In the next scene, Stanley has returned to Mrs. Deigh's apartment, where, in a dazed state, he tells her that Esme proposed to *him*. It is not clear whether he met with her afterward or if this is his hallucinated version of the café scene. In any case, Mrs. Deigh seeks to console him and suggests that they pray together. Moments later, she returns carrying lighted candles but completely nude. Shocked, Stanley runs from the apartment, as he had earlier run from the naked embrace of the daughter (in Chapter I, Part II); when he reaches the street below, he is almost run over by a Fiat.

The name of the car—Latin for "so be it"—is humorously significant. Throughout the novel Gaddis plays on names and phrases that formerly referred to something of religious or spiritual significance but that now only designate some secular or commercial item. In addition to operating within this general textual strategy, "Fiat" also brings to conclusion a series of parodic echoes of the language of excommunication. The implication is that Stanley, though overtly the only sincere Catholic believer in the novel, has been excommunicated, since his "spirituality" is founded on too insistent a denial of the flesh's claims. We can also note in this section that, in spite of the general atmosphere of sterility and decadence, there are many ironic signs of fecundity: Bildow's daughter is pregnant, Esme is apparently pregnant, even "Huki-lau," the dog of a tourist couple who wander through the novel complaining about missing the Narcissus Festival in Hawaii, turns up pregnant, though it was forced to wear a chastity belt. Furthermore, much of this satiric humor is offered in the vein of Ronald Firbank's *Concerning the Eccentricities of Cardinal Pirreli*, to which the epilogue also pays hommage. In a Firbankian touch, for example, Mrs. Deigh's "religious path" was set on the day when, floating naked on her back off the blue waters of Portugal, a group of peasant children mistook her for an apparition of the Virgin. Similar mis-recognitions thread through the epilogue, which begins with the Roman police mistaking the pilgrims for a notorious political group.

After the scene at Mrs Deigh's apartment, the narrative fragments into a number of vignettes depicting minor characters in some final charac-teristic act. Otto, his counterfeit money stolen, is now doing menial work for Doctor Fell in Tibieza, and has named the native field workers after his New York friends (Ed, Max, Anselm, and Chaby). Ed Feasley is now managing the sanatorium near his father's estate in Hudson Valley, New York, and has also named the patients, or "feebs" as he calls them, after his New York friends. In a letter to Mr. Piver (quoted earlier), Eddie Zefnic explains in a gruesome parody of scientific thinking why the frontal lobotomy Pivner has been given for counterfeiting is appropriate. Mrs. Sinisterra, after receiving a newspaper clipping reporting the supposed suicide of her husband in Spain from Memento Associates, which offers to "permanize" it, discovers the drugs from her medicine cabinet have been stolen by her son. In New York, Mr. Feddle is trying to palm off reviews of Anselm's book as reviews of his own. Following an encounter in the street with a critic (who is reviewing a novel that sounds like *The Recognitions* after having read only the jacket cover), Mr. Feddle with-draws to a café to read his own book. But only the book jacket is his; underneath the cover is Dostoevsky's *The Idiot*. As he reads, the scene is literally subsumed into an exchange between Prince Myshkin and Ip-polite. The next scene is a condensed repetition of the entire Paris chapter (Chapter II, Part I). Crèmer, the critic who had attempted to corrupt Wyatt years before, now makes the same offer to Max, who immediately accepts: "any good publicity agent charges ten per cent" (940) he says. Hannah now dances nude in a "cave" in Paris. Rudy and Frank are unable to live comfortably in their Paris apartment because of a recent suicide from the window. When Arny Munk opens the window in his Paris hotel room, the building's facade collapses, causing his death. In the next fragment numerous *faits divers* from all over the globe are reported in a language blending distorted versions of the "Stars and Stripes Forever" and the "Pledge of Allegiance to the Flag" as recited by a student at the Essex County Boys Vocational and Technical High School in Newark, New Jersey. In the next scene, Valentine is dying in a Budapest hospital from chronic insomnia.

Returning to Rome, we find Stanley now reconciled with Mrs. Deigh. Soon after he "confesses" to Father Martin, who also arranges for the trip to Fenestrula, the latter is shot dead in the street. Stanley then decides he will go to Fenestrula and play his organ concerto on the day of the canonization. On the train, he again encounters Don Bildow, now on his way to Paris. In the last of a series of literal travesties, we see Bildow take off his old suit and flush it down the toilet before donning his new, tailor-made Italian suit, all in order to avoid paying the customs duty. Much to his chagrin and our amusement, he discovers that the box supposedly containing his suit contains only a little boy's sailor suit, with Dante Alighieri embroidered on the cap.

In Fenestrula, after attending an early mass, Stanley discovers he is more mindful of three souls ("equally dear, and equally beautiful") (955) than of his music. We can only guess at the identities of the three: Esme, Father Martin, and Anselm (but Agnes or even Wyatt, though Stanley didn't know him, are possibilities). In any case, thinking of the three, he looks at his composition,

> which was all that was left. He looked at it with sudden malignity, as though in that moment it had come through at the expense of everything, and everyone else, and most terribly, of each of those three souls: but there was this about him, standing, running a hand through his short hair, pulling up his belt, and staring at that work, which since it was done, he could no longer call his own: even now, it was the expense of those three he thought of, and not of his own. (955)

The church is old, and Stanley is warned not to play the organ with the lower tone stops pulled out. He either doesn't understand the grave danger (the warning is in Italian) or throws caution to the winds and begins to play through the composition without restraint. Soon, the walls begin to quiver, and then the church collapses upon him. The narration concludes:

> Everything moved, and even falling, soared in atonement. He was the only person caught in the collapse, and afterward, most of his work was recovered

too, and it is still spoken of, when it is noted, with high regard, though seldom played. (956)

Thus, Stanley's life ends, as does the novel, in ambiguous terms. Is his death an accident or suicide? Is his music an enhancement or betrayal of life? Does this concluding statement also apply to the novel we have just read? Like Wyatt's disappearance, Stanley's art and the death it leads to raise questions which the novel refuses to answer unequivocally.

Most critics have wanted to see Stanley's end as a victory, just as they have wanted to see Wyatt's epiphany on the hill as a sign of redemption ("it's only living through sin that redeems it"), with these two "positive" moments thus qualifying an otherwise rather nihilistic conclusion. However, one cannot read them in simple opposition or contrast without taking into account both the texture and pattern of the larger "system" of which they are a part. In relation to the latter, these characters must be examined both as representations and textual figurations, which is what I intend to do in the next chapter.

Chapter 3

Subject and System

> The assumption of one single subject is perhaps unnecessary; perhaps it is just as permissible to assume a multiplicity of subjects, whose interaction and struggle is the basis of our thought and our consciousness in general.
>
> My hypothesis: the subject as multiplicity.
>
> —Friedrich Nietzsche, *The Will to Power*

Modern theories of literature, elaborated in the wake of modernist writing, have come to question the assumption that a subject can preexist its articulation in language, thus denying the commonsense assumption that there can be an author (a subject) with a story to tell (about certain subjects) which he or she then "expresses" in language. This illusion of idealism and positivism alike—that language is a transparent medium that simply represents a prelinguistic subject (in both senses)—may once have served as a basic assumption of the novel, but it no longer sustains postmodern writing.

In structuralist theory, especially that of Louis Althusser and Jacques Lacan, subjectivity is seen as the result of the subject's "construction" through his or her insertion into a discourse, and of the "contradictions" which result from that insertion.[1] The displacement of subjectivity across a range of discourses thus implies a range of positions from which the subject may grasp himself or herself and, hence, his or her relations with the real. Within its varied discourses, *The Recognitions* offers a number of possible subject positions, but those that might initially seem the most privileged (and least vulnerable to satire) turn out to be the most unstable. Consequently, there is little possibility for the reader to establish a non-contradictory identification with a unified subject of the *enunciation* (an author) or with a subject of an *énoncé* (a character); nor is there any clear hierarchy of discourses that would insure a stable, transcendent position from which the reader could recognize unequivocally the text's "truth." As a dialogic structure, the novel sustains a number of contradictory relationships among its various elements but no coherent and unified subject, in the sense that a single subject does not emerge and cohere at any level.[2] To explore these points in specific detail, I shall focus simply on one category of the subject, the represented characters.

Fragmented Selves and Spatial Form

A rapid survey of *The Recognitions* yields the following simple typology of characterizations. At one extreme, there is the seemingly authentic self on the "schizophrenic" voyage, not so much of self-discovery as self-dispersal, a self that passes through a series of intense states which include fevers, dreams, delirium, hallucinations, and schizophrenia.[3] This self is presented as fundamentally discontinuous, at least in the sense that the character's behavior is not "explained" psychologically, although it is given partial or momentary definition through allusion to mythic patterns or cultural figures. The central protagonist Wyatt Gwyon, his father Reverend Gwyon, Esme, Stanley, and perhaps Anselm belong to this type. At the other extreme are the characters who are merely referred to by name or who exist only as voices, often anonymous, that float in and out of the many social scenes depicted in the novel. Though devoid of individualizing qualities, these characters do perform individual acts. The important thing about them, however, is that they exist only as part of one of the various groups in the novel: the Viareggio crowd, the publishing world, the homosexuals who cluster around Agnes Deigh, the pilgrims, the tourists, or the Use-Me Society ladies. These characters appear therefore to be partial crystallizations out of a social multiplicity, rather than individuals in their own right, and their actions and speeches make sense generally in relation to a specific group. Between these two extreme types of character is a third type distinguished by some kind of inauthenticity. For this type, identity is always a mask or persona, a counterfeit or patchwork fabrication with no underlying substance, and the self is only "part of a series of an original that never existed." In this category belong all manner of the novel's fakes and phonies, each one individualized, but only in relation to its own special kind of inauthenticity. Otto, Max, Benny, Ellery, Mr. Pivner, Sinisterra, Esther, Valentine, Brown, and many others clearly belong to this type. Finally, while obviously the boundaries between the three types are not absolute, even the few migrations back and forth and borderline cases like Anselm and Valentine do not jeopardize the cogency or usefulness of the typology.

For the most part, the characters of the second and third types are presented as "flat," although not exactly in E. M. Forster's sense, inasmuch as they are not to be contrasted with "round" characters. What we see of them in any given scene is all there is, for they cast no shadows of an interior psychological complexity; indeed, they seem to possess little interiority at all, or seem only intermittently self-aware. But in this regard, they do not form an opposition to the first type, whose members would be distinguished by their psychological complexity. For if psychological complexity is taken to mean either some perceptible development in self-awareness and moral perception or some obscurity of motivation, then it is fair to say that none of the characters in *The Recognitions* consistently exhibit such an attribute.

Instead, they are defined along other axes altogether. What we find are characters who are delineated in terms of multiple identities, who occupy one or more places—even if only briefly—in a symbolic system (i.e., they are identified with mythic, historical, or literary figures) or in terms of single and overriding obsessions, which are revealed in their passing encounters with other characters or in their professional and social ambitions. Some, like Brown, Valentine, and Anselm, are defined in both ways. The primary overall effect of this manner of definition is that the characters often appear to be figures in a psychodrama or splinter selves reflecting a single trait or aspect of human personality with abnormal intensity. Their "tics" or personal attributes are usually only surface effects and seldom point to or suggest the depths of a subjective interiority. Like Dickens, most of whose characters are also flat, Gaddis relies on recognizable types and caricatures; the green wool shirted critic, Ellery, the "Rammer-Jammer" man, and the tourists are obvious examples. But whereas Dickens's characters vibrate with a vitality that seems to emanate from the author,[+] Gaddis's exhibit an intensity that results from thematic and textual mechanisms intrinsic to the system of which they are part. This is most evident in the case of characters who are "objectified" only as voices or mouthpieces for opinions and satiric quips, tidbits of information and gossip that hardly express or reveal a subject (as understood in either sense) but only articulate a position or "point" in the novel's polyphonic discourse. For all its variety of characters, then, the novel does not represent a single autonomous and fully developed self—nor could it do so, given its manner of representation.

The typology thus suggests the extent to which the individual subject as it is represented by the characters has disintegrated into various component parts and affects that have been rearticulated as "figures" and partial selves having only a momentary and precarious stability. Such an impression is confirmed by what the characters themselves occasionally say about one another. For example, late in the novel, Ed Feasley, who is obsessed with the way things are constantly wearing out and falling apart, begins to talk about how he has scattered little parts of himself everywhere—"these pieces of me and pieces of other people all screwed up and spread all over the place" (749)—and how he could never collect them all if he wanted to. The Viareggio crowd in particular remind him of "parts of me that never grew up."

This kind of disintegration extends even to the individual body. In the course of the novel, various body parts—limbs, particularly arms, teeth, and in one case an entire corpse—circulate or recur just enough to intimate a loosening and potential dissolution of the body's boundaries and its integrity as an organic unity. Besides producing effects of the grotesque, this morcellation has an obvious thematic importance in the context indicated above and perhaps augurs some schizophrenic breakdown and the imminent collapse of social reality. However, it may also echo an older, entirely different image of the body, one more befitting the novel's carnivalesque roots: the body as open to the world and interpenetrating with it through a circulation of partial objects. In his study of Rabelais, Bakhtin shows that this image of the body signifies a point of imminent reversal from death to new life and productivity:

> The unfinished and open body (dying, bringing forth and being born) is not separated from the world by clearly defined boundaries; it is blended with the world, with animals, with objects. It is cosmic, it represents the entire material bodily world in all its elements. It is an incarnation of this world at the absolute lower stratum, as the swallowing up and generating principle, as the bodily grave and bosom, as a field which has been sown and in which new shoots are preparing to sprout.[5]

Obviously, I cannot insist on this half-buried image of the body, barely perceptible within this forgotten framework, as a substratum image rising to the surface through the agency of the carnivalesque: it is far too "integrative" for Gaddis's text. Here it will suffice simply to note this underlying ambivalence of the novel's body imagery, while also remarking that its most obvious significance derives from psychoanalysis, according to which an image of the morcellated body signifies an incoherent collection of desires, and hence a fragmented subject.

However, I must insist on one important point: this evidence of character-splitting and disintegration—the fragmentation of individual identity, in short—is not to be interpreted as a necessary prerequisite to its reintegration at another, more symbolic level, so that, for example, several characters would "add up" to a more coherent and rounded character, as in the classic examples of late Victorian and early modern fiction—Stevenson's *Dr. Jekyll and Mr. Hyde,* Wilde's *Dorian Gray,* and Conrad's *The Secret Sharer*—where a second character or double is used to dramatize a secret, buried, or repressed side of the self. Earlier, of course, Dickens had made full thematic use of split-personality types, and often decomposed individuals into two or more parallel or contrasting "flat" characters: Carker in *Dombey and Son* epitomizes what Dombey might have become; Pip and Orlick in *Great Expectations* are a symbolic representation of a personality divided in the Freudian sense of rational and libidinal components.[6] Similar examples abound throughout Dickens's novels, but the purpose usually remains the same: to dramatize a psychic reality and demonic world that coexists with the seemingly natural one by revealing hidden correspondences and secret affinities between apparently remote characters and areas of life. Such a use of doubling and symbolic projection has always been fairly common in literature. But the effect concerning us here was first fully adumbrated by Dostoevsky, who was, of course, a great admirer of Dickens. Dostoevsky used such strategies more methodically, and pushed them to the point where they began to mutate into something altogether different, a whole new kind of structure, in fact, which is what we shall find in *The Recognitions*.

Significantly, it was the appearance of doubles in Dostoevsky's fiction that led Bakhtin to formulate the essentials of what he perceived to be a new strategy of fictional representation:

> This stubborn urge to see everything as coexisting, to perceive and show all things side by side and simultaneous, as if they existed in space and not in time, leads Dostoevsky to dramatize, in space, even internal contradictions and internal stages in the development of a single person—forcing a character to converse with his own double, with the devil, with his alter ego, with his own caricature (Ivan and the Devil, Ivan and Smerdyakov, Raskolnikov and Svidrigailov, and so forth). This characteristic explains the frequent appearance of paired characters in Dostoevsky's work. One could say, in fact, that out of every contradiction within a person Dostoevsky tries to create two persons, in order to dramatize the contradiction and develop it extensively.[7]

In *The Recognitions*, we can perceive a similar strategy at work. For example, Wyatt has several doubles: a serious one (Stanley) and a caricature (Otto). He also converses with a shadow self, the Jesuit turned aesthete, Basil Valentine, and with a devil figure, in the person of Recktall Brown. In Frank Sinisterra, he sees a reflection of his own dual identity as medieval artist craftsman and counterfeiter, as well as an older father figure. But despite these similarities, *The Recognitions* does not seek to dramatize the contradictions that may be found within a single person. In this respect, Dostoevsky remains closer to Dickens. What links *The Recognitions* to Dostoevsky's fiction, rather, is this tendency to "dramatize in space," which is where we must pursue the similarity.

As Bakhtin reads it, the primary categories of aesthetic projection in Dostoevsky's fiction are coexistence and interaction in isolated moments of time rather than evolution over a longer period. Dostoevsky's tendency to dramatize conflict "in space" is thus diametrically opposite to that of most nineteenth-century thinkers, such as Goethe and Hegel, who perceive all existing contradictions as various stages of some unified development. Goethe or Hegel might see in every manifestation of the present traces of the past, the epitome of contemporaneity or a future tendency, but these relationships would always be conceived temporally, as unfolding in a chronological progression. Dostoevsky, in contrast, perceives these stages in their simultaneity, juxtaposed and counterposed in a complex configuration whose relationships are neither causal nor sequential. It is a style of vision, Bakhtin says, that resulted from Dostoevsky's tendency to apprehend the profound ambiguity of everything:

> In every voice he could hear two contending voices, in every expression a crack, and the readiness to go over immediately to another contradictory expression; in every gesture he detected confidence and lack of confidence simultaneously; he perceived the profound ambiguity, even multiple ambiguity of every phenomena. But none of these contradictions and bifurcations ever became dialectical, they were never set in motion along a temporal path or in an evolving sequence: they were, rather, spread out in one plane, as standing alongside or opposite one another, as consonant but not merging or hopelessly contradictory, as an eternal harmony of unmerged voices or as their unceasing and irreconcilable quarrel. Dostoevsky's visualizing power was locked in place at the moment diversity revealed itself—and remained there, organizing and shaping this diversity in the cross-section of a given moment.[8]

Again, we can observe a similar strategy of presentation at work in *The Recognitions,* which is also poised precariously between a harmony of unmerged voices (as evidenced in the novel's polyphony as a whole as well as within Wyatt's or Gwyon's consciousness) and ceaseless, hopeless agrument (between Wyatt and Valentine, Stanley and Anselm, and Benny and the critic). But whereas Dostoevksy felt impelled to dramatize in space out of a need to capture and present the ambiguities latent in all human action and expression, in Gaddis's novel this tendency is closely connected to the reversal from original and imitation (or model and copy) to the simulacrum and phantasm that I described earlier as the novel's central event. In order to explore this relationship in detail, we must first consider how this tendency to dramatize in space is linked to other aspects of the novel's characterization.

Dostoevsky's inclination to organize and formulate "diversity within the cross section of a given moment" bears certain affinities with the tendency Joseph Frank calls the spatialization of narrative or "spatial form," by which he means the attempt to organize a poem or novel "in space," independently of narrative, sequential, or syntactic connections.[9] But while it is true that *The Recognitions* is "composed of a vast number of references and cross-references that relate to each other independently of the time sequence of the narrative," as Frank says of *Ulysses,* the concept of spatial form has only limited application to Gaddis's novel, as we shall see in a moment. In his discussion of the concept, however, Frank does raise two relevant problems.

First, Frank suggests that the "loss of self" which characterizes much of modern and postmodern literature is to be seen as a symptom of what he calls "the transmutation of the time-world of history into the timeless world of myth." As he explains, "the self no longer feels itself to be an active, individual force operating in the real world of history and time; it exists, if at all, only through its assimilation into a mythical world of eternal prototypes." In other words, Frank is suggesting that Joyce's (or Eliot's) mythical method is really a sign of the breakdown of the individual subject, rather than a revelation of an unsuspected and underlying continuity with his archaic past, as it is usually interpreted to be. Frank's reading could thus be taken to mean that the very appearance of the mythic method both hides and reveals a shake-up and possible mutation in the symbolic order of Western culture.

A comparison between how Joyce and Gaddis employ the mythical method to structure their novels will both clarify this point and indicate what is at stake. Joyce's manipulation of a "continuous parallel between contemporaneity and antiquity," as Eliot puts it, with the mythic parallels assuming primarily an organizational or purely aesthetic function and serving, like the literary tradition itself, as a grid against which the welter of details depicting everyday life are to be seen, clearly demanded a "classical frame" or ground—a well-known narrative with bold outlines and of universal significance.[10] In contrast, Gaddis's use of the Faust myth amounts to a "romantic frame," and the patterns it provides are more esoteric, even occult. (In this respect, as in many others, *The Recognitions* may be profitably compared with Malcolm Lowry's *Under the Volcano,* which has a similar relationship to *Ulysses.*) Moreover, if for Joyce an elaborate system of correspondence serves as an organizational rather than an interpretive scheme—by providing a check on the potentially limitless proliferation of surface details made possible by the dissolution of traditional narrative unities—for Gaddis these correspondences have a more uncertain role. For one, they no longer occupy a background position but have been foregrounded by being named explicitly in the text: the *Clementine Recognitions,* the Faust legend, and the lives of John Huss and Raymond Lully, as well as other narratives apparently relevant to the novel's structure and implicit meaning, are not only referred to but sometimes discussed—albeit fragmentarily—by the characters. Yet the precise nature of these references remains an open question. In contrast, while Joyce refers directly to Homer's epic only in his title, it remains implicit throughout the book, and serves as the central armature in the elaboration of an ironic structure. But whereas in *Ulysses* the terms of the structure are always clear—Bloom is to Dublin as Odysseus is to the world of the Greek epic—the parallels and analogies in *The Recognitions* remain shadowy and ambiguous, intermittent and truncated. Wyatt Gwyon, the young artist turned forger of Renaissance paintings, is identified with Clement of Rome, Faust, John Huss, and others, but the narrative of his own life presents no clear, consistent parallel or contrast with the lives of the latter. They establish not so much a background scaffolding, which would have, as in *Ulysses,* a stable meaning "in itself," as a series of partial frames and implied perspectives whose privilege and authority remain in question.

This point can be further illustrated by considering for a moment how the network of schemes and systems of correspondence function in a reading of *Ulysses.* Umberto Eco provides a succint summary of this process for the modern reader:

> We only have to identify and accept Joyce's schemes in order to penetrate effortlessly into the universe of Ulysses. We henceforth have at our disposal

an Ariadne's thread, ten compasses, a dozen different plans. We can enter this polyhedric city that is Dublin as into a house of mysteries or a palace of mirrors, and move around there without difficulty. That Molly has a role derived from the Trinity, that in an anthropological perspective she is Cybel or Gea Tellus, or even that, following the abscissa of Greek myth she is identified with Penelope—all that doesn't prevent the reader from having access to her individuality, nor from recognizing her as a universal type. On the contrary, it is then that it becomes possible to crystalize the perceptual flux of the character, to discover centers of intention and signification, and to give diverse interpretations to her gestures. It is when one is surrounded with rigid schemes, as in a wax museum, schemes so intellectual and scholarly that they would kill the characters of any other poet, it is precisely then that one sees Molly's humanity appear, her distress and dissatisfaction, the glory and misery of her fleshly state, the enveloping immensity of her telluric femininity. If in a medieval poem symbols and allegories only exist as instruments of an Order to be celebrated, in *Ulysses* it is the Order that serves as an instrument for the establishment of symbolic relationships. If one should refuse to take into consideration this order, and believe that it reveals a penchant for intellectualist interpretations, the book comes unhinged, disintegrates, and loses all power of communication."

At first, given the many cultural echoes, correspondances, and mythic allusions in *The Recognitions,* the reader may suspect that Gaddis has worked out a similar scheme. But while the schemes in *Ulysses* provide a way of grasping the characters in all their "individuality" and "humanity," insofar as we see them in and through (and against, one might add) these schemes, those implied in *The Recognitions* only render the characters' individuality and the discreteness of their identities more uncertain. The main character, Wyatt Gwyon, both the most "original" of the characters and a bundle of repetitions from the cultural past, can only be problematically related to such schemes, while most of the other characters appear to be fragmented personalities or partial selves who echo earlier cultural figures only parodically. Their acts, in relation to an invoked mythic past, appear psychotic rather than "universal," as when Janet gives herself to a bull, or Anselm castrates himself in an apparent religious conversion. If myth retains its integrity in *Ulysses* and suggests a fixed and immutable order, such is not the case in *The Recognitions,* where the myth of Faustian man, the myth of the artist as heroic artificer, and a myth of religious martyrdom are all dismantled and dispersed. So, while in *Ulysses* a palpable tension between a surface naturalism and a mythic background or depth perspective is maintained throughout, in

The Recognitions these two poles are no longer held apart; the myths no longer exist as unities in some separate and ideal cultural "background" realm but are present in the text as fragments and echoes. It is as if what was the framing principle in *Ulysses* has in *The Recognitions* collapsed into the novel's texture or has been projected "inside" the frame, where it exists only in fragmentary allusions.[12]

Although *The Recognitions* hardly conforms to Eliot's demands for a form that would subsume temporality and "the immense panorama of futility and anarchy which is contemporary history" under the timeless recurrence of myth, the Faust myth nevertheless resonates through the novel's "past" and "future": the narrative re-enacts what scholars have interpreted to be the "original" version, while also registering the comic and potentially infinite repetition of the myth as a movie ("We're shooting Faust now, a sort of bop version, we've changed him to this refugee artist, and now Mephistopheles is..." [661]). Yet at neither end of the spectrum of echoes does this version bear a strong resemblance to Goethe's. The obvious point is that the myth clearly doesn't function as an "origin" or source that would ground the novel's meaning or provide a stable basis for interpretation. Its repetition has been "problematized" —in both parodic and serious registers—and must itself be explained.

This difference between Joyce's and Gaddis's manipulation of the mythic method has important consequences. Despite the dispersive effects of Joyce's pyrotechnic verbal display and stylistic variety in *Ulysses,* his reliance on myth as a stable symbolic order allows for a strategic recontainment of the unity and individuality of his characters. This is especially evident in the phantasmagoric Nighttown or Circe chapter, where Stephen's and Bloom's hallucinations have a cathartic effect. As Fredric Jameson has observed, rather than seeing their psyches dissolve into external determinations under the pressure of delirium, we are given a depth-psychological perspective on the wellsprings of their fantasies; thus the unity of the psyche is not only maintained but finally reconfirmed.[13] This is possible because the symbolic order provides Joyce with an authoritative reference system outside and apart from the flux of registered sensations of Dublin life. Thus, while Bloom may be perceived by Joyce's text as Elijah, Bloom never confuses himself with the Hebrew prophet.

But the order by which Joyce constructs a complex array of symbolic relationships—hence, his valorization of myth and symbol—exists only fragmentarily in *The Recognitions*. Just as Gaddis's schemes often dissolve or blur into one another and no longer offer fixed and secure points of reference, so confusions of symbolic and imaginary identification frequently occur, undermining the characters' stability and leaving them subject to fragmentation and dispersal. This important structural difference between *Ulysses* and *The Recognitions* may be taken as evidence of the emergence of a different process of structuration, one perhaps best described by Jameson (in reference to Wyndham Lewis's novels) as a postmodernist or schizophrenic aesthetic, since it stresses "discontinuity, allegory, the mechanical, the gap between signifier and signified, the lapse in meaning, the syncope in the experience of the subject."[4] Such a description highlights precisely the kind of structure that concerns us here. What must be emphasized is that this difference between Joyce and Gaddis (or the modernist and postmodernist aesthetic) hinges on the stability of a symbolic order. In the terms of contemporary (Lacanian) psychoanalysis, we can say that in Gaddis's text the symbolic order, which guarantees the stability of linguistic and hence all articulated oppositions, has come partly unhinged, causing a collapse of certain oppositions on the imaginary plane.[5] We have already seen evidence of such destabilization in the threatening dissolution of the copy/counterfeit opposition. But this disruption of the symbolic order is also manifest in the occasional freeing of signifiers from their signifieds and their recombination in various unexpected ways, as when words from Esme's poem later "return" in the novel as the names of characters. Compared with the "schizophrenic" textual logic at work in *The Recognitions,* Joyce's play with language seems motivated and expressive—in short, modernist.[6]

Gaddis's novel thus draws our attention to a shake-up or mutation in the symbolic order implicit in Joyce's method but not fully visible there, since it is obscured by the new autonomy granted to aesthetic orderings. But whether or not the difference between *Ulysses* and *The Recognitions* corresponds to a mutation in the symbolic order of Western culture, it undeniably correlates with an important conceptual shift—from cultural symbols to the symbolic function—evident within the social and human sciences.[7] More important here, this difference in the stability of the symbolic order points to the kind of novel Gaddis actually writes. While Gaddis was clearly drawn to an epic frame and structure such as *Ulysses* incarnates, his own novel ultimately took another formal direction, one predicated on a dialogic structure and exfoliating as a carnivalesque, rather than an epic fiction. As Bahktin shows, Menippean satire (which was the first historical form of carni-valesque fiction) arose in opposition to the epic ethos and constitutes a formal deconstruction of its assumptions. Perhaps this inversion also corresponded to a profound shake-up in the symbolic order of Greco-Roman culture. Whatever the case, there can be little doubt of the intrinsic relation between carnivalesque fiction and the kind of instability of the symbolic order found in *The Recognitions*.

This digression brings us back to the second problem to which Frank draws our attention: the spatialization of character relationships in *The Recognitions*. In contrast to the modern psychological novel, *The Recognitions* assumes that human identity is not a substance revealed through self-awareness and the coherence of its intentional acts but rather a matter of roles assumed and positions occupied, with these always defined in relation to one another. In the narrative, the characters' individual psychological motivations count for less than the various patterns and connections that are established, to the extent that the "meaning" of the relationship is more a function of the characters' positions vis-à-vis one another in a network of correspondences than their conscious attitudes. Since these relations are, in part, apprehended synchronically in a kind of spatial configuration, the term "spatial form" has some pertinence. Valentine and Brown, Stanley and Anselm, Reverend Gwyon and Aunt May, and Ellery and Mr. Pivner, to cite several examples, form oppositional pairs; Esther, Esme, Marga, and Pastora form a contrapuntal array in their relationships with Wyatt; Agnes Deigh, Hannah, and Esme form another in their relationships with Stanley. Not surprisingly, the relationships of the couples echo one another: Wyatt and Esther's relationship is echoed by Esther and Otto's, by Stanley and Agnes's, and more parodically, by Arnie and Maud's.

But more significant than this kind of relationship is the obvious fact that the characters do not grow or develop in the course of the novel. Instead, their relationships undergo displacements and changes of position relative to one another. In Esther's life, Otto replaces Wyatt and is in turn replaced by Ellery. "Dick" replaces Reverend Gwyon as minister of Wyatt's New England hometown, where he is mistaken for Wyatt the son when he visits the Reverend in the sanatorium; in fact, he has assumed the position Wyatt has abandoned. Father/son substitutions in particular are especially important: Brown replaces Gwyon as Wyatt's father figure, only to be replaced in turn by Sinisterra, and Eddie Zefnic replaces Otto as Pivner's son. Only one son, Ed Feasley, "falls into line" and assumes his filial obligations, but that, satirically enough, turns out to be managing the family-owned lunatic asylum, whose inmates he nicknames after his former New York friends.

At first blush, these various substitutions underscore the novel's carnivalesque quality, especially insofar as "carnival celebrates change itself, the very process of replaceability, rather than that which is replaced," as Bakhtin states.[18] In the characters' relationships with one another, this sense of replaceability is so strong that most of the novel's multiple plots appear simply to actualize substitutions and displacements along two axes: the "vertical" or father/son filiation, and the "horizontal" or friend/lover affiliation.

Such a pattern also provides direct evidence of the "molestation of paternal authority" and problem of generation and filiality that Edward W. Said has analyzed as underlying much modern writing.[19] In *The Recognitions,* the problem is further complicated by the absence of the mother. Recall that the narrative begins with the death of the protagonist's mother, Camilla, and that his youth is dominated, indeed psychologically molested, by her substitute Aunt May. Later, Wyatt's wife, Esther, will complain that his mother is her rival, as if his unfinished portrait of Camilla literally hangs over their relationship as an malign spirit. And later still, it is when Esme models for Wyatt that he is almost able to complete the portrait and, at the same time, to consummate his relationship with her. That Wyatt's story will end near his mother's gravesite does not so much resolve the problem as round out the pattern.

As if to mock interpretation, one character flippantly remarks that Wyatt's problems stem from "a father complex or a mother complex or something vulgar" (173). What is certain is that the pattern anchors at the literal level of the story a whole freight of symbolism centered on the Great Mother and motivating a complex of nocturnal, lunar, and marine imagery.[20] If a novel like *Ulysses* maintains a delicate balance or tension between literal and symbolic relationships, both paternal and maternal, in *The Recognitions* the scale has tipped dramatically toward the symbolic. Moreover, in the light of Frank's remarks, it seems reasonable to see this shift as compensating for the overwhelming lack of stability in the characters and their relationships and, as I have suggested, a weakening of the symbolic order. I shall return to this important problem, but for the moment, let us note that this instability is emphasized at the level of representation in many ways, by the high number of suicides (more than ten), for example. Another obvious emphasis is the satire directed against what appears to be the novel's only "normal" married couple, Arnie and Maud. After a series of failed attempts to adopt a baby (evidently, the couple is unable to have one of their own), Arnie is seduced away by a group of homosexuals. Meanwhile, Maud takes home to raise as her own the baby she finds crawling on the floor at Esther's apartment. Other scenes echo and magnify the satire: Big Anna tries to adopt an Italian boy, presumably for sexual purposes, and near the end of the novel the recently "married" homosexual couple, Rudy and Frank (whose relationship is described by one critic as the only happy one in the book), celebrate their honeymoon in Paris. The celebration is marred, however, by a suicide attempt from their balcony apartment. Thus, even a travesty of the conventional happy ending is not proof against molestation at the level of plot.

As a novel, *The Recognitions* seems less interested in explaining such a state of affairs than in presenting as fully as possible conditions under which we could not expect anything else. Most of the interactions and encounters between the characters constitute one form or another of mis-recognition, sometimes because a character's identity is a fabrication or mask but more often because their identities are too inchoate to sustain more than glancing contact. In psychological terms, the characters appear too self-absorbed or absent from self, too distracted or obsessed to notice or fully acknowledge the reality of others. At least since Hegel, "recognition by the other" has been considered constitutive of identity, so that these failures of recognition are linked on a thematic level with the general troubling or instability of identity observable throughout. Moreover, the mirrors and mirror reflections, identifications, and phantasmal images that pervade *The Recognitions* constantly remind the reader that identification and image projection are the two modes by which the characters achieve definintion, both for themselves and others, while also reinforcing the novel's self-reflexivity.

These features—the general instability and collapse of the characters as integral selves, the importance of mis-recognition and "position" in a symbolic network in regard to identity, the high incidence of mirroring and image identification, as well as certain peculiarities of the narrative, which sometimes operates according to a textual logic or "logic of the signifier"—all suggest that character is represented in *The Recognitions* in a manner that exhibits clear affinities with Jacques Lacan's psychoanalytic theory of the subject. Perhaps this should come as no surprise, given the "protostructuralist" tendencies in the dialogical approach to characterization. There may be historical reasons for the similarities as well. Lacan's theory, developed for the most part in the 1950s, was directed—rather trenchantly, in fact—precisely against American ego psychology and the notion of the conscious, rational ego as the subject's center.[21] In *The Recognitions,* the "analysis" so many of the minor characters undergo is always the butt of a joke or target for some gibe. In a comic anticipation of Bettelheim's work on fairy tales, one character is even writing a psychoanalytic study of Mother Goose. But judging from his more serious treatment of character, one can hazard to think that Gaddis would appreciate an approach like Lacan's that doesn't presume the ego's stability at the outset and that "returns" to Freud's interest in language and literature as privileged domains of insight through his notion that the "symbolic order is constituent for the subject." Any novelist so obviously oriented toward presenting character in and through speech habits would probably have to find Lacan's theory attractive. Yet these rather superficial commonalities remain interesting only insofar as they point toward similarities at the more crucial level of structure.

The Missing Subject: "The self who could do more"

The most crucial key for disengaging the novel's basic structure is the peculiar logic that governs the relationship between the protagonist, Wyatt Gwyon, and the multitude of characters who populate the social space through which he moves. As Wyatt disappears in the course of the narrative, actually going nameless for some seven hundred pages, he comes to exemplify both the "sense of something lost" that so many of the characters feel, and some better version of themselves, a "self who could do more." This aspect of *The Recognitions* is clarified and reinforced by several bits of dialogue between various characters that point self-interpretively toward the text itself. The most important occurs when Wyatt explains to Valentine how he sometimes feels:

—Like . . . as though I were reading a novel, yes. And then, reading it, but the
hero fails to appear, fails to be working out some plan of comedy or, disaster?
All the materials are there, yes. The sounds, the images, telephones and telephone numbers? The ships and subways, the . . . the . . .
—The half-known people, Valentine interrupted easily,—who miss the subways and lose each other's telephone numbers? Cavorting about dressed in
the absurd costumes of the author's chaotic imagination, talking about each
other . . .
—Yes, while I wait. I wait. Where is he? Listen, he's there all the time. None
of them moves, but it reflects him, none of them . . . reacts, but to react with
him, none of them hates but to hate with him, to hate him, and loving . . .
none of them loves, but, loving. . . . (263)

Now, not only does Wyatt occupy the place of the "hero" in *The Recognitions,* but he also fails to appear, both in the sense that he drops out
of sight for most of the other characters and fails to fulfill the expectations
which have been set up through his identification with a number of
figures in Western myth and cultural history. But though he doesn't
successfully fill the roles of a modern Faust, heroic artist, martyred saint,
or nomadic quester en route to personal salvation, he does make it
possible for these patterns to appear in outline. In this, he functions as
a kind of tracer, cutting a line that traverses the multifarious activities of
the other characters, and also mirroring their own emptiness and lack of
significance. Gaddis himself, in "Notes" from which he allowed Peter
Koenig to quote, stresses the psychological dimension of this aspect of
the novel. Since Wyatt embodies the "spirit" the other characters have
lost, his loss of name symbolizes the loss of that part of themselves that
would enable them to act more heroically, or at least more authentically.
Gaddis further explains:

> There are troubles with pronouns, especially "he," in those scenes which, when
> at all extended, the no-hero—that is Wyatt, becomes lost or confused. To a
> strong degree this should be so, as, with Valentine (and all the others, but
> pointedly Basil Valentine) he, the no-hero or not-yet-hero, is what the other
> person might be: in Valentine's case, the self-who-can-do-more, the creative
> self if it had not been killed by the other, in Valentine's case, Reason, in
> Brown's case, material gain; in Otto's case, vanity and ambition; in Stanley's
> case, the Church; in Anselm's case, religion, &c. &c.[22]

For all of the important characters, in fact—we could also add Gwyon,
Esther, Esme, Sinisterra, and Ludy to those Gaddis cities—Wyatt is both
the "self who could do more" and the signifier of that lost self.

Wyatt thus possesses a complex, double role in the novel, since he functions both as a character in his own right and as a symbolic agent unifying the narrative. Yet his double role is no simple allegorical device. For the latter could hardly account for the peculiarity that, as a character, Wyatt is at once excessive and lacking: as the protagonist of the central narrative, he presents a surplus of signifiers, as the number of roles or positions he occupies in various patterns indicates, but on the level of the signified, he is always "missing from his place," as Lacan says of a symbolic object, and his absence becomes more significant than his presence.[23] At the same time, all the significant characters are defined in relation to him, or echo him in some way. In this, Wyatt functions as what in French structuralist theory is called the *case vide* or "empty slot" —a symbolic object that traverses a field and in so doing manifests or precipitates a structure formed as elements in the field crystallize into positions defined by their relations to the object.

As an excessive signifier, Wyatt elicits—indeed, defines—desire, but it is a desire he cannot or will not fulfill, for he has always moved elsewhere. In various ways, he kindles and then refuses to fulfill the desires of Aunt May, the Reverend Gwyon, Esther, Otto, Brown, Valentine, Esme, Sinisterra, and Ludy. In fact, we can trace the novel's plot in terms of this movement of desire, as Wyatt assumes different positions and then refuses or fails to fulfill the corresponding role, whether as Protestant minister, initiate son, husband, artist, counterfeiter, co-conspirator, lover, penitent, or madman. In every case, Wyatt opts out or fades away, a refusal or "absence" that is presented in its schematic essentials in his last encounter with Ludy, where the exchange echoes all the previous encounters, and Wyatt's final words recapitulate the pattern:

—You and I . . . [Ludy says]
—No, there's no more you and I, Stephen [Wyatt] said withdrawing uphill slowly, empty-handed. (900)

From the evidence of the narrative alone, it is difficult to say whether Wyatt is here refusing a gesture of beseeching complicity, and hence a kind of relationship, or simply refusing an identity of any sort (just as the phrase "empty-handed" may be read in either of two ways: he has released the bird, symbolically disburdened himself of his mother's spirit, and thereby found release himself, or he has reached a state of final impoverishment and dispossession). On close inspection, Wyatt's various interactions with the other characters seem hardly motivated at all: they simply repeat this basic pattern, which becomes somewhat enigmatic in the absence of a compelling psychological explanation for his behavior. We might simply say that Wyatt is neither willful nor perverse, but literally "not all there." Yet, however this gap or syncope is to be interpreted psychologically (and the novel allows for several possibilities), the fact of this gap remains and, hence, the feeling of a necessary incompletion.

In his relations with the other characters, then, Wyatt always plays a rather special role. This is particularly evident in his passing dialogues with them, where we never have the impression of two people talking who are alien or closed off from one another. Here again, the effect recalls one special to Dostoevsky. Bakhtin observes that "Dostoevsky always introduces two characters in such a way that each of them is intimately connected with the interior voice of the other. . . . The profound essential bond, or, to express it otherwise, the partial coincidence of one character's word with the interior secret word of the other is an indispensable element in all of Dostoevsky's most important dialogues."[24] In the case of Wyatt, this special psychic link or affinity is manifest particularly in his dialogues with Esther, Brown, and Valentine, even though it seldom attains the kind of hypnotic fascination that we regularly find in Dostoevsky's novels. Perhaps Stavrogin, that profound "absence" at the center of *The Possessed,* offers a more precise parallel to Wyatt, since he too assumes a structural function.

Which brings us to the other salient aspect of Wyatt's identity: the peculiar fact that in the course of the novel he is associated with a series of names or signifiers—Clement of Rome, Faust, Raymond Lully, John Huss, Hugo van der Goes, and others—whose signified is never actualized in his own person in a series of corresponding acts. Again, we observe an excess in the signifying series and a corresponding lack at the level of the signified. In both cases—in Wyatt's relation to other characters and in his identification with various mythic and cultural figures—we witness the same disequilibrium between two series, between (in structuralist terms) a mobile *case vide* and a continually displaced *occupant sans place.* But now, thanks to structuralist theory, we can see that it is precisely this disequilibrium between an excess in the signifying series and a lack in the signified series that defines the novel's structure and indicates how the novel's elliptic and inconclusive narrative is predicated on Wyatt's "absent" centrality. In contrast to a traditional novel, where the actions of the protagonist define the narrative, *The Recognitions* is shaped by the protagonist's *failure* to coincide with himself and to fulfill any of his allotted roles. The narrative will trace this absence or gap, at the same time showing how it is reflected or dispersed in the activities of other characters. But though Wyatt has no fixed place *in* the narrative, he is hardly tangential to it either; on the contrary, as both a nameless presence and an overnamed absence, he both sets it going and causes it to reverberate into the activities of others. Neither an antihero nor a hero of the absurd, he is rather that stranger entity that Gilles Deleuze calls a hero of the structure: "Neither God nor man, neither personal nor universal, he is without identity, made up of non-personal individuations and pre-individual singularities."[25]

But what exactly does this mean? For one thing, Deleuze's notion of a "hero of the structure" provides a very precise explanation of Wyatt's "intensity," which is clearly his most distinguishing and important trait as a character. In psychological terms, Wyatt is "intense" in the sense that everything he does and says is charged with affect and significance; he is the character most able to bring about a response in others and to elicit the reader's serious attention; his speech, though stammering and often incomplete, is always charged with import. But more significant, Wyatt's intensity is also the effect of a structural "difference"; indeed, his most fundamental role in the novel is to refer one series of differences to another series of differences. What makes him a signifier of loss also enables him to serve a positive function as a "differentiator," since it is *through* him that the two series described above communicate, and that "difference" in a new and positive sense is distributed throughout the novel. For as we have just seen, Wyatt occupies a slot in both series, but that slot always falls absent, causing a perpetual displacement in the series. Thus, "Wyatt" is actually a locus of cross-references, his identity deriving solely from our awareness of differences between items in the series. He elicits, in short, a kind of differential perception. Furthermore, by making the two divergent and heterogeneous series resonate (it is essential to note that they never converge), Wyatt becomes what Deleuze calls a "dark precursor" in an intensive system. Through his "difference"—and the reversal, doublings, echoes, reflections, and transversal movements that ripple out from it—Wyatt sets the novel reverberating as a textual machine.

The Novel as Intensive System

These notions are novel enough to require further elaboration. To illustrate how a work of fiction may constitute an "intensive system," let us consider the doubtlessly more familiar example of Virginia Woolf's novels. In *Mrs. Dalloway* and *To the Lighthouse,* a transcendent, authorial point of view is abandoned for a series of immanent perspectives. Commenting on a passage taken from *To the Lighthouse,* Erich Auerbach writes that "this [lack of a definable point of view] goes so far that there actually seems to be no viewpoint at all outside the novel from which the people and events within it are observed, any more than there seems to be an objective reality apart from what it is in the consciousness of the characters."[26] Following Auerbach, other critics have gone on to speak of a breakdown of the subject-object dichotomy and of the dissolution of the borders of consciousness. But to speak of a breakdown presupposes that the unifying and constituent acts of a transcendent authorial consciousness—subtended, philosophically speaking, by something like Husserl's transcendental ego—have failed or are no longer operating.

These negative or regressive assumptions do not apply, however, to *The Waves,* where point of view and its subversion no longer form the basis of the fiction. Instead, the characters Bernard, Neville, Louis, Jinny, Rhoda, Suzanne, and Percival are constituted as individuations within a larger and more encompassing vibratory movement called "the waves." The waves play a role comparable to the "wind" in Charlotte Brontë's *Wuthering Heights:* it constitutes an impersonal force that sweeps through everything in a movement whose amplitude and rhythm vary in time. Whether wind or wave, this force is a purely immanent one, having neither origin nor end, *arché* nor *telos.* Within the immanent field that it defines—what Deleuze will later designate as the "plane of immanence" —character is only an affective, individuated state of an anonymous force. Thus, in *The Waves,* the characters consist mainly of packets of sensation, affective states or "tropisms" (to borrow Nathalie Sarraute's useful term), and interrelated movements that make of their lives a multiplicity and state of becoming not reducible to discrete centers of consciousness that open out onto an objective world. Each character's name designates a different configuration of these states, and a different set of correlations among physical, psychological, and social elements. Percival, whose name harks back to the hero of medieval romance, seems at first to unite the group, inasmuch as he comprehends the largest number of interrelations. He is also the most conventional of the characters, inhabits the public world most completely, and is even something of a hero. Fairly early in the narrative, however, he dies. Yet as the waves carry the others away from one another at different rates, his absence sets into motion another wave, which establishes a rhythmic communication among them all. Like Wyatt in *The Recognitions,* Percival thus functions as a lost hero whose absence has a palpable effect and resonates through the lives of the others. Like Wyatt, he too adumbrates a "self who could do more," although apparently he is not that self. He only makes visible something that would not appear without him, yet only appears with his own disappearance or absence.

Freud's theory of the phantasm (or phantasy, as the term is usually translated),[27] which Deleuze takes as one particular instance of an intensive system, provides another useful illustration. As is well known, an important turning point in the development of psychoanalysis occurred when Freud realized that the stories of childhood seduction that his patients related to him were not always literally true, in the sense that they did not actually occur, but were phantasies that were recalled as memories. Freud then postulated that the memories were produced by unconscious psychological mechanisms activated by traumatic repetition: when a series of childhood memories was stirred in the unconscious by a series of adult experiences that in some way echoed them, the phantasy was the result. The purpose of these phantasies masquerading as memories was to make "inaccessible the memory from which the symptoms have been generated," which usually turned out to be an Oedipal desire.[28]

Deleuze insists that it is the repetition that brings both the phantasy and the childhood event into play, and that it is difficult moreover to account for the period of delay or time lapse between the infantile scene, supposedly originary, and its effect, which takes place at a distance in an adult scene that in some way resembles and "derives" from it. (This, of course, is the famous problem of *Nachträglichkeit* or "retroactivity" produced by an event that brings into existence a first or prior event that it will be said to repeat.) Deleuze reformulates the problem as one involving a resonance between two series, but not between an infant series and an adult series. The childhood event is not part of the first "real" series but rather the "dark precursor" that establishes communication between two more basic series: the one formed by the adults we knew as children, and the other formed by the adults we are with other adults and other children. With respect to these two series, the individual subject is completely decentered, in accordance with a truly *inter*subjective unconscious. This decentering is illustrated with an example taken from Proust's *À la recherche du temps perdu:* the narrator's love for his mother when he is a child is the "agent of communication" between the two adult series, that of Swann's love for Odette and that of his own grown-up love for Albertine; in both, there is "the same secret, the eternal displacement, the eternal disguise of the captive that indicates as well the point where the series coexist in the intersubjective unconscious."[29]

In Deleuze's account, the childhood event is no longer delayed—it *is* the delay, a pure form of time that makes the before and after coexist. When Freud says that the phantasy may be the ultimate reality, thus implying something that goes beyond the series, we ought not conclude that the childhood scene is unreal or imaginary but rather that the empirical condition of succession in time gives way in the phantasy to the coexistence of two series, that of the adult we will be with the adults that we "have been." The child is the dark precursor of the adult, but this "event" occurs in the phantasy, or rather, the phantasy *is* the event. What is originary in the phantasy, therefore, is not one series in relation to another, but the "difference" of the series; the phantasy is precisely what enables us to refer one series of differences to another. Furthermore, since no order of succession can be established in the unconscious, where the various series all coexist, no one series can be considered as originary in relation to another that would "derive" from it; the model/copy paradigm in fact no longer applies. Hence, the phantasy (or phantasm) is a simulacrum and not a "bad" copy of a copy: it forms a differential or intensive system comprised of divergent but resonant series by means of a dark precursor which goes beyond them all in a "forced movement."

Freud's theory of the phantasy is an especially good example because it clarifies several difficult points. First, it doesn't deny that from the individual subject's point of view the two "original" series—one infantile and pregenital, the other genital and postpubescent—succeed one another in time. What it denies is that the phantasy or "meaning-event" that causes the two to resonate can be understood in these terms. In fact, in psychoanalysis, the meaning and the event cannot be distinguished: the event or phantasm *is* the meaning, since it alone allows us to articulate the series into a meaningful set of relations. Freud's *Totem and Taboo* (especially the chapter "The Return of Totemism and Childhood"), as well as his other writings on the "primal scene," constitutes an important theory of the event in this sense, but for our purposes, his case study of the Rat Man provides the most convenient example. Freud shows that at the heart of the Rat Man's phantasy there lurked an overwhelming feeling of debt, and that a debt was exactly what linked his trauma with an early episode in his father's life. A resonance between two divergent series, one paternal and the other filial, both involving a debt, a friend, a rich woman, and a poor woman was thus established. In both series, the relations between elements are determined as a function of their position in regard to the debt. These relations thus comprise evidence of a structure founded not on a temporal progression or order, but rather on a repetition whose terms are always displaced or disguised. Since the structure repeats itself across or "through" the subject, it can be said that the place of the structure is the intersubjective unconscious. It is intersubjective because reducible to neither an individual nor a collective unconscious.[30]

As different as they are, Woolf's novel and Freud's theory of the phantasy are both instances of an intensive system. In the latter case, the intensive system accounts for the workings of psychic reality as a structure of the intersubjective unconscious, while in the former, it describes narrative relations as purely immanent to a series of individuating rhythms called waves—hence, the rightness of calling *The Waves* a "poetic" novel. In *The Recognitions,* the intensive system comes about when the simulacra which produce the "reversal" of the Platonic perspective begin to resonate, echo, and cross one another. This "reversal" in which original and copy "re-appear" as resonant simulacra and phantasms is thus the novel's central and most consequential event, and must be envisioned as catastrophic in the literal sense of a radical overturning. Everything in the novel, from its depiction of an "upside-down" carnival world to its dialogical mode of signification, follows from it. This, of course, includes the novel's portrayal of character, which now must be regarded specifically in these terms.

A Differentiator of Differences

Let us first recall that, following the overturning of Platonism, the simulacrum is now no longer perceived as a degraded copy of a copy but instead as the internalization of a positive difference. Before this overthrow, difference can only be thought negatively, in the reflected light of relations of identity, sameness, and similarity founded upon the sovereignty of the Idea. That is, difference itself can only appear secondarily, in the shadows of deviance and discrepancy, as an undesirable threat to the exemplary sameness of the self-identical model and the imitative similarity of the copy that closely resembles it. But as Deleuze shows, Plato establishes this model-copy distinction only in order to found and justify another one—between copies and simulacra (or "good" images and "bad")—and thus to save, justify, and select out the "good" images or copies in the name of the self-identical model and by means of their interior resemblance to it. But what if this "model" only comes to exist in the process of selection and is established only in a belated act of induction from the copy that is purportedly true to it? This would mean that the model was produced as an aftereffect and hypostatized by Plato as the origin.

To reverse Platonism, therefore, the simulacrum must be given its due, and considered "for itself." Above all, this means reestablishing the ontological primacy of "difference." Denying all models, unless it be the impossible "model of the other," a model of difference from which only internalized differences would follow (but in what sense would it then be a "model"?), the simulacrum lives on difference. For if the copy or "good" image is centered on the model, and the model on the Idea (through Plato's theory of participation), then the simulacrum decenters the series, causing divergences that lead to chaos—or rather, as Deleuze prefers to call it, to a "chaosmos" of free and decentered differences whose only "law" is Nietzsche's doctrine of eternal return. This doctrine itself should be interpreted in the light of the overturning of Platonism; indeed, it can only be read intelligibly in this perspective. We may infer as much from the fact that the doctrine is presented twice in *Thus Spake Zarathustra*: once when Zarathustra is sick, when he complains that his doctrine has been reduced to the terrifying banality of a cyclic return—"the eternal return of the same," and again when it becomes the ultimate object of affirmation.[31] Two perspectives: one reactive and the other affirmative. But what is affirmed in the eternal return? It can only be "difference"—the value Nietzsche prized above all others. The eternal return of the same, or a ceaseless displacement and decentering into a purely novel difference? There can only be one affirmative interpretation:

the eternal return as repetition producing difference and singularity by constantly decentering every series and increasing their divergence. According to this reading, everything returns except the essences and laws that would impose a simple, mechanical, non-deviant re-production. Platonism can return, it does so all the time, but only as a species of reactive thought, as a will to recenter and align the series, to reestablish essence, and to deny difference as a primary ontological category. Thus, the question becomes: Repetition as the return of the same, or difference disguised as the same? Repetition as mechanical reproduction, or symbolic and intersubjective resonance? Good images faithful to the Idea, or simulacra composed of decentered differences and disguised repetitions?

But the "return of the simulacra" does more than undermine these age-old metaphysical questions: it also threatens to bring ruin upon the foundations of representation. For simulacra by their very nature circumvent the demands of identity, resemblance, analogy, and opposition, or the basic principles upon which representation is built. The simulacrum does not "represent" anything; through its disguises, displacements and decenterings, it only produces effects. Yet sometimes, these effects are of identity, resemblance, or analogy. Such effects must be seen as secondary, however, as by-products only incidental to the more basic phenomenon of repetition. In other words, it is not a matter of posing repetition against representation but, again, of reversing the relationship, of seeing representation as a secondary effect of something more primary. This is what happens when repetition is foregrounded and begins to operate directly on the surface of a representation. Then representation as such is menaced and begins to give way to what Deleuze calls a "theater of repetitions," where one encounters "pure forces, dynamic lines in space that act on the spirit without intermediaries and that unite it directly to nature and history, a language that speaks before words, gestures that are elaborated before bodies are organized, masks before faces, spectors and fantoms before persons—the whole apparatus of repetition as a terrible power."[32]

The Recognitions trembles at the threshold of this "chaosmos," beckoning toward it and holding it at bay at one and the same time. As a representation, it is poised ambivalently between two radically different articulations (and hence, implied readings) of the world. The chief means by which the novel "knows itself" in such terms, as I have suggested, is through a dialogic that sustains its fundamental ambivalence, visible in its "repetition" of prior representations and thus in its ambiguous status as a literary construction. This ambivalence turns on the reversal from model and copy to simulacrum and phantasm that sweeps through the novel and constitutes its most singular "event." Furthermore, as I shall now show more fully, the protagonist Wyatt Gwyon acts as the chief figure in this event by ushering it in as its "dark precursor." Thus Wyatt not only gives the narrative its complex unity but also, as an agent of reversal, sets the novel to work as an intensive system. Wyatt, in short, is the novel's most important simulacrum, and the reversal he brings about is enacted most visibly in his presentation as a character.

On the literal level of the narrative, Wyatt is a lost son, husband, artist, friend, minister, and most importantly, a lost hero. The peculiar pathos of his position is that he has to be one of these things in some sense before he can be lost, he has to assert himself in these various roles before he can be said to fail, and yet this is precisely what is always in question. At the same time, Wyatt is associated with a series of important cultural figures. To be sure, these associations also suggest a symbolist reading of the novel, in the same way that *Ulysses* is generally taken to be a symbolist work. Accordingly, Wyatt may be seen as a symbolic Clement traversing the modern waste land in search of spiritual truth and authenticity, and similarly, as a symbolic Faust—a gifted, creative soul whose energy can find no positive realization unless he is tempted by a devil figure and can redeem himself. He is also like Hugo van der Goes, whose religious convictions are menaced by madness, and Raymond Lully, John Huss, Peer Gynt, Calderón's Segismund, and still others (like Saint Stephen or Ulysses) alluded to in the text. As a self-evidently modernist work of fiction, *The Recognitions* presumes a style of reading in relation to this series of shifting analogies. In this symbolist perspective, each of these figures would provide an analogy in terms of which the reader is to view Wyatt in his various roles and activities. However, given the inadequacies and failures of Wyatt's life, if read this way, the novel can only appear as ironic, as registering a set of discrepancies between the ideal and the real, the heroic and the banal, the mythic and the modern. Wyatt must therefore appear as a degraded copy or repetition of a series of heroic originals, and the novel as an illustration of the impossibility and pathos of such a figure in the modern world.

Yet such a reading only partially accounts for *The Recognitions*'s complexity. First of all, the analogies on which it depends are always incomplete and transitory. If Wyatt is Faust, then Otto is a comic Wagner and Brown a rather incompetent and paternalistic Mephistopheles. Esme becomes an unlikely Gretchen; she is, in fact, associated with *Das Ewig-Weibliche*. Yet not only are these identifications transitory in the narrative as a whole, but they also seem deformed and out of kilter when the novel is compared, say, to Goethe's drama, and with little or no ironic effect. These identifications only echo the "original" in a faint reverberation. But they also raise obvious questions: In the Faust pattern, what role does Esther assume, and if Valentine is Gretchen's brother, how are we to account for the glaring discrepancy between the portrayal of the two in the drama and novel? In fact, it would be easy to show that for each of the cultural figures alluded to, the corresponding pattern as it is realized in the novel is so "deviant" and fragmentary that it raises more questions than can be resolved by appealing to the suggestive reticence of a symbolist practice. And while it is interesting and even significant that the patterns are sometimes "layered" as sedimentations, as in the instance of the Clement and Faust narratives, just as often, as in the case of Faust and van der Goes, or John Huss and Raymond Lully, the associations seem contradictory or arbitrary as a cluster and form no coherent pattern. But the larger, central question is how to account for this very excess, this mania for cultural allusion and supplementary analogy, and the attendant fact that the patterns have little more than a local and transitory significance.

There is also a second problem: even upon a casual reading, Wyatt appears as the site of radical textual discontinuities and possible incoherences (as in the stream-of-consciousness section), which can be recuperated and justified at the level of representation only with great difficulty. Of course, his fading and delirious consciousness and the "syncoped" and incomplete nature of his experience can be "explained" by referring to his drinking and madness. Or, reading less literally, it can be viewed as symptomatic of or motivating on a psychological plane the textual disturbances caused by the continual telescoping, grafting, and crossing of different texts within *The Recognitions*. The discontinuities in Wyatt's consciousness could then be seen as registering, while at the same time "suturing" or stitching up the discontinuities of the text. But again, the problem is not so much the wrongness as the incompleteness of this interpretation. To view Wyatt's behavior as a mere "textual effect" in this sense is both to miss or obscure his underlying functional role in the novel and to foreclose on the radical form of subjectivity he traces.

These problems appear as such only because of an inadequate conception of the novel's structure. In my reading, Wyatt is not to be taken as some modern version of Clement or Faust—as a degraded copy of a heroic original—for it is precisely this kind of relationship that the novel has thrown into doubt or reversed. If anything, "original" and "copy" now cohabit in a new space of simultaneity, with no ontological priority attached to either. In this new modernist space, as Edward W. Said has described it, "relations of complementarity, adjacency, correlation, and correspondence" are explored, and repetition is what underlies their deployment. In relation to *Ulysses,* Said's primary example, the action is treated as a "concurrence of parallel moments" rather than as a succession, and this proves further to be a way of "living through" at the narrative level the problems of paternity and filiality expressed at the thematic. Thus Said, by way of Nietzsche's "subversion of genealogical thought," formulates a more satisfactory explanation of what Joseph Frank calls "spatial form":

> For Joyce and for Nietzsche, the order of creativity is the perception and the enactment of simultaneity, the redistribution of events in numerous random or parallel series, as well as the general abrogation of the dynastic tie. This is less a matter of representing simultaneity than it is a matter of treating simultaneity—say one very complex day rather than a series of days—as the medium or the space of representation.[33]

This notion of structure as a serial redistribution is even more explicit in Deleuze's comments on *Ulysses,* which he describes as a novel that establishes a relationship between two series—one signifying Bloom, the other whose signified would be Ulysses—by means of multiple forms which comprise "an archeology of narrative modes, a system of correspondence between numbers, a prodigious use of esoteric words, a method of question-response, [and] the institution of thought-streams or trains of multiple thought."[34]

These formulations provide the specific context in which the reversal in *The Recognitions* must also be read. The "space of simultaneity" is simply the space created by this reversal and in which a multiplicity of relationships now unfold. But in contrast to *Ulysses,* the heterogeneous series in *The Recognitions* communicate not through a panoply of formal devices but through the central character, Wyatt Gwyon.

In short, I am arguing that only when Wyatt is perceived as a simulacrum, rather than a debased copy of a heroic "original," be it Clement, Faust, Raymond Lully, John Huss, or Hugo van der Goes, can his role in the novel as well as its textual peculiarities be properly understood. Having neither identity nor origin in a previously established essence or idea, the simulacrum comprehends a difference in itself which is articulated in relation to two or more heterogeneous and divergent series on which it "plays" and makes resonate. As a result, its resemblance to anything prior, as well as any priority of distinction between model and copy, original and imitation, is problematized and thrown into question. We have already seen that Wyatt has no proper identity: he can only be defined in relation to a shifting series of differences, which in turn refer to other differences articulated in the novel. In short, we can't identify him in positive terms. Of course, it could be said that he *is* a counterfeiter, but such an "identity" only covers over other destabilizations, especially in regard to the peculiar status of his forgeries. But finally, Wyatt can only be defined satisfactorily as a simulacrum comprehending multiple and heterogeneous series. The two most immediately evident series are: (1) son, Protestant minister, husband, artist, friend, counterfeiter, criminal, and madman; (2) Clement, Raymond Lully, John Huss, Faust, Hugo van der Goes, Segismund, Saint Stephen, Ulysses, Prester John, the Reverend Gilbert Sullivan, and Han van Meegeren. We could also add a third list composed of the strange or esoteric expressions he utters: *homo* or *homoi, gettato a mare,* "maybe we are fished for," "another blue day," and so forth. The lists show that the series often blur categories and do not derive from or exemplify any single model or essence, though admittedly most in the second list are in some way heroic. There are also subtle and interesting confusions. "Clement" refers here both to the Clement of the *Clementine Recognitions,* who is a fictional character, and to Clement of Rome (a confusion the novel itself encourages in order to provoke a subtle "mis-recognition"). "Faust," of course, is already a composite identity deriving from historical, literary, and mythic sources. The "Reverend Gilbert Sullivan" is obviously fictitious, a humorous allusion to the British comic opera partnership of Gilbert and Sullivan. In contrast, Han van Meegeren is generally assumed to be the "real life" person upon whom Wyatt was modeled, since there are many parallels between the two.[35]

Now the important thing—to repeat a fundamental point—is that Wyatt doesn't fulfill any of these roles or identities. As a simulacrum, he only "simulates" them. As name, character, and textual figure, "Wyatt" is what brings these various roles and identities together, constitutes them as a series, and makes them resonate, but without any convergence. Since the series are related not through identity but through difference, Wyatt's re-enactment of these roles must henceforth be conceived as a repetition in the Nietzschean or Deleuzian sense, that is, as a displacement (and disguise) that decenters the series into a novel redistribution. If, therefore, it is his repeated *absence* that causes the various series to communicate, it is his *difference* that decenters the series into a new context of multiple relationships in which causality and sequence yield to the logic of the simulacrum.

Thus, Wyatt may be said to be "difference" itself, as it is figured in the novel, or difference in personae as it articulates a principle of individuation and intersubjectivity that always goes beyond itself into an undetermined future at the same time that it "complicates" the past (in Giordano Bruno's sense of *complicatio*) into a different shape and new set of relationships. Wyatt therefore marks a point where an older set of codes (and hence, interpretive strategies) are outstripped in a reversal that entails a positive redistribution of "difference," albeit with a certain ambiguity. Near the end of the novel, he himself insists that we redefine the past by "living through" the present, a remark that is at once empty and full of significance in the context of the subjectivity he traces. Like the Nietzschean Over-man, Wyatt is a self-overcoming subject whose only enduring shape or definition is a question mark, and who will assume many of the names of history in his voyage of intensity.[36]

Wyatt's role in relation to the novel's dialogic may now be more fully specified. In a phrase, he serves as a differentiator of differences. First, and most simply, if his "difference" is read negatively, as an ironic discrepancy in accordance with the Platonic paradigm, then we commit ourselves to a symbolist reading of the novel as a whole.[37] On the other hand, his "difference" can be read positively. But this entails a "reversal" that will echo and ramify throughout the novel because of Wyatt's special structural position. This reversal, in turn, demands a very different reading, one that I have developed in relation to a Deleuzian intensive system. According to this second reading, Wyatt will be seen as a simulacrum and the "dark precursor" who propagates or distributes difference throughout the novel by ushering in and adumbrating the reversal that constitutes its central event. That *The Recognitions* can elicit both of these readings, that it articulates at one and the same time the condition that make both possible, is of course a consequence of its dialogic structure.

The Character System

Having indicated how Wyatt functions in relation to the other characters as the dark precursor in an intensive system, I must now show how these other characters are to be viewed within the "reversed" perspective such a system implies. As Deleuze conceives it, an intensive system is populated with undeveloped subjects and passive selves: "They are passive selves because they are undistinguishable from the contemplation of couplings and resonances; undeveloped subjects because they suffer or support the dynamisms [of the system]."[38] Hence, the subject cannot be disengaged from the system of which it is part and which enjoys a structural priority; as in Lacanian psychoanalytic theory (upon which Deleuze draws), the subject is an "optical effect of structure." At the same time, the "couplings" and "resonances" produce entirely new and unforeseen combinations, so that each individuation is a "throw of the dice." Note also that such a system is the obverse of a representational system like the traditional nineteenth-century novel, wherein characters are foregrounded as fully independent, psychologically coherent entities, while the systems which make this possible—social, legal, and psychological, not to mention the conventions of representation itself—remain in the background, often assumed without question. What is perhaps most remarkable about an "intensive system," however, is that it privileges neither a founding and central subject that would deploy meanings in self-constitutive acts nor a set of essential objects that would offer points of convergence for the recognition of forms and attributes. In short, an intensive system doesn't pose subjects against objects but sees both as produced by an underlying play of forces related in terms of difference and repetition. In an interesting essay on *The Recognitions,* Stephen-Paul Martin shows how "Gaddis's people are repeatedly overwhelmed by the intrusion of external forces and often seem to exist only as vehicles through which nonhuman energies manifest themselves."[39] Without being able to explain it, Martin draws attention to a feature of the novel that the intensive system *can* account for, simply because it doesn't define the human subject in opposition to such external forces.

Deleuze argues that it is only superficially that the subject is a unified structure of meanings at all. Beneath the surface of bodies, there lies a field (which he refers to variously as an abyss, ocean, or chaos) where multiple forces encounter one another and mixtures form out of disparate parts. The way in which these forces within the bodies' depths emerge on the surface to produce zones of intensity is enormously complex and, for our purposes, need not be of concern. Suffice it to say that such basic activities as eating, talking, thinking, and sex are each a different way that relationships between the corporal depths, the body's surface, and its projections and sublimations are established and maintained. The most important of these relationships are those brought about through the agency of the *phantasm,* which insures that series of partial objects and activities form on a surface or along partial surfaces. The body as a centered organism with its articulated and structured parts presupposes this action of the phantasm; indeed, the phantasm is what makes the body an assemblage of adjoining zones of intensity which can then be structured. As a purely "surface effect," the phantasm has for its topological function to serve as a zone of contact between the interior and exterior. Thus, it forms an interface where inside and outside unfold on a single plane and where "subjective" and "objective" are not yet distinguishable. Moreover, as a consequence of this unique position, the phantasm is subject to a double causality: on the one hand, to those external and internal causes that produce it in depth, and on the other, to the "quasi-causes" that work on the surface and insure its communication with other phantasms.

This psychoanalytic topography will help clarify the formation and behavior of the characters in *The Recognitions.* Instead of bodies over whose surfaces various phantasms play, let us consider the domain of the symbolic, by which is meant not only the unconscious structure of language but the whole network of existing cultural codes and representations, clichés, images, and *semes* available for articulation into meaningful utterances. Imagine now that *The Recognitions* constitutes a zone of more or less continuous surfaces on which a number of "characters" emerge and crystallize out of this symbolic domain. These characters have only a nominal or phantasmic identity, for they are singular points or singularities, united or, better yet, "constellated" under a name or signifier that designates not a unity but many heterogeneous series.[40] The more items in the series that correspond to the singularity, the more complex the character. Every character so constituted is a simulacrum: there is no prior "original" which the character would represent, in the sense of copy or imitate, nor any essence or single identity that would unify the series. Instead, each character is composed of two or more heterogeneous series that communicate through the *name* and produce an effect of resonance and textual crossing. In this sense, the proper name in Gaddis's fiction designates not so much a subject as something happening among a set of terms or elements. Compared to characters in more traditional fiction, those in *The Recognitions* appear therefore to have been relocated and redefined on a textual surface. Yet it is not merely a textual surface as generally understood but rather a surface of pure events or a plane where phantasms communicate. The phantasms in which the characters are caught up are what appear to Martin as the "intrusion of external forces" and "nonhuman energies."

Esme may serve as one example. Her name, first of all, forms part of a series of names in the novel that all begin with "E": Esther, Edna Mims, Eileen, and Ellenore. This series recalls and resonates with another series of names beginning with "E" (Eileen Vance, Emma, EC) in Joyce's *A Portrait of the Artist as a Young Man*. (Since Otto has affairs with the first three on the list—the last entry, incidentally, refers to the heroine in Benjamin Constant's novel *Adolphe,* which Otto carries around without ever reading—a satiric comparison with Stephen Dedalus may be subtly implied.) The name "Esme" also evokes the character Esme in J. D. Salinger's story, "For Esme—With Love and Squalor." Thus, many contemporary readers may see in Gaddis's Esme a different but comparable ratio of innocence and sophistication. In Chapter Two, I remarked that, at Esme's first appearance in the novel, she is perceived by different characters variously as a drug addict, "schiz," model, whore, and mother. We can now see that each one of these facets of her identity connects a different series of associations and events. For example, she is a mother in the literal sense, though her child never appears in the novel (strangely, its birth constitutes a gap or hiatus in her life); she is associated with Wyatt's mother, Camilla, in several ways (she models for him when he attempts to complete his mother's portrait, and she takes Camilla's Byzantine earrings); and she "appears" as the Virgin Mary in several paintings of the Annunciation that Waytt forges. Her image forms another series:

her "simulacra" assail Stanley on the voyage to Rome, her image as a "succubus" obsesses Anselm, and the image of her face in Wyatt's forgeries elicits comment from many characters. Esme's vocation as a poet not only brings her into contact with Brown (as a publisher), but also connects a series of verse passages quoted in the novel: her parody of a nursery rhyme, her imitation of Pope's satiric verse, her poem about innocence bespoiled, and the passage she transcribes from memory from Rilke's *Duino Elegy*. The Rilke passage, in turn, connects a series of extreme psychic states: mystical self-absorption and discontinuity, heroin addiction, and schizophrenic breakdown. I already noted that Esme is associated through Wyatt with Goethe's Gretchen (and also with Marlowe's Helen). Similarly, she is identified with Senta in *The Flying Dutchman* and Solveig in Ibsen's *Peer Gynt*. Her relation to these figures is not mimetic or analogical but rather constitutes yet another series that she comprehends and decenters as a simulacrum.

Though the terms of her "construction" may sound odd at first, Esme is not wholly unlike a conventional fictional character; however, what she "does" in the novel is not separable from the networks of meaning she both articulates and sets resonating, though she remains unaware of them. Even within the narrative, her effects are more important than her acts; in fact, the latter turn out to be quite *in*effectual, while the former have a phantasmic power. And like Wyatt, her identity arises out of differences that we perceive in the disparate series that resonate "under" her name. In the light of the reversal he adumbrates, we see her not only as a fictional character with attributes indicated by these various associations but also as a cluster of singular points produced, like an " optical effect," by the play of difference and repetition which redistributes these series in this particular way. "Esme" is simply the name of this effect. And again, this is not a mere textual device, even though it occurs by means of textual relationships. On the contrary, this is the way identity must be seen once we are freed from the constraints of Platonism, which by imposing unity, makes the work of difference unrecognizable.

Deleuze spells out in a sentence what this reversal entails at the level of the individual subject: "What appears in the phantasm is the movement by which the self opens itself onto a surface and frees the pre-individual, impersonal, a-cosmic singularities that it imprisons."[41] In *The Recognitions,* where the "return of the simulacra" and the resonances among them produce the phantasms and, hence, the reversal I have described as the novel's central event, such a "release of singularities" occurs as an essential aspect of the novel's presentation of character. No longer perceivable as the representation of a discrete and autonomous person, each character now appears as a locus of singularities, with each singularity corresponding to a series that, in turn, expands through associative chains until it reaches a neighboring singularity. In this way, the text constitutes a "field" of singularities. But if each singularity corresponds to a differential relationship articulated by the series, it manifests itself as a singularized state of being (moral, psychological, physical) or affectivity (sadness, anguish, joy), in either case as a point or node around which relations between characters condense or reverse themselves. Singularities are therefore never reducible to a single character's expression or attributes, or to a "psychology." Moreover, like the differential relationships to which they correspond, they are forever redistributed and displaced throughout an intersubjective structure. But though undefinable within the bounds of individual persons, the characters can nevertheless be apprehended immediately. Esme's singularity, for example, is evident from her first appearance in the novel:

> Looking out at nothing, her lips silent and almost smiling while the rest chattered, her body still where everyone else shifted, conscious only in herself while all the others were only self-conscious. Alone on the couch, and alone in the room like the woman in that painting whose beauty cannot be assailed, whose presence cannot be discounted by turning one's back, but her silence draws him to turn again, uncertain whether to question or answer. (193)

What we see in Esme's relationships with the other characters is not only her childlike, haunting beauty but also a fundamental impassivity that constitutes her most striking singularity. The latter proves fatal to Stanley and Otto, who both seek to impose on her patterns of coherence—she appears to one as innocent and to the other as depraved—in order that she, in turn, will recognize their own desires. Only Wyatt, who seeks no such recognition, is able to "move" her. Yet when Wyatt reveals that he is only interested in her "image" and not in her as a "person," it is too much for her fragile sense of self, which she begins to view from the "outside" in a schizoid manner. Later, when she mistakes the drowned Spanish sailor for Wyatt, her impassivity breaks down entirely into a hysterical religious quest that leads to her absurd death. In the first instance, the phantasm moves *through* her, effecting others; in the second, she is caught up in a phantasm that moves through others.

Taken as a group, the characters in *The Recognitions* may be said to constitute a field of singularities distributed in different constellations which don't always or necessarily allow a "three-dimensional" projection into the depth of an assumed world, as in the case of "round" characters, and thus conform to the usual expectations regarding their unity and boundaries. But because a simulacrum also simulates identity, as understood in the customary sense, the illusion of depth is sometimes present, though it is not always uniform. It should be unnecessary to emphasize that this presentation of character challenges the often stated (and reductive) opposition between novels that provide a full and "faithful" imitation of characters, which are assumed by convention to exist independently in a world remarkably like (or unlike) our own, and those that present flat figures on a surface having no more reality than the patterns they trace. In *The Recognitions,* as in much pre-and post-realist fiction, the characters don't seem to "live" outside the fiction they are part of, but are inextricable from the representational system and fabric of themes and motifs in which they are articulated. Yet this does not mean that they are puppets manipulated according to the author's designs, as is often assumed with such fiction. Although produced on a surface formed by mechanisms that operate by repetition, displacement, disguise, and decentering, Gaddis's characters are not mere fictional devices that can be described and accounted for as "narrative functions" or *actants,* as in the respective structuralist analyses of V. Propp and A. J. Greimas. While the latter may account very well for a narrative structure, they have little to say about the impact of the characters or their effects within the narrative.[42]

If the characters in *The Recognitions* can be viewed as a "release of singularities" on a plane of immanence that articulates a textual surface, as I sketched above, then the signs of breakdown and disintegration of their personal identities must be regarded in a double light, which I can now summarize. On the one hand, *The Recognitions* appears to be a symbolist novel with a vast collection of characters ranging from flat stereotypes to more complex portraits rich in symbolic association. A salient tendency among them all is to undergo some kind of psychological breakdown—hence the widespread feelings of instability and malaise, depression and hysteria. Moreover, the thematic emphasis on an encroaching entropy and decadence underscores the general realization that older roles and models are exhausted and that they no longer provide any vitality and coherence. This perspective, in essence, suggests that the contemporary individual subject has disintegrated into a collection of "tics," obsessions, types, and role models that, like Humpty Dumpty, can never be put back together again. On the other hand, there are clear signs in the novel of a completely different conception of character, one more in accord with the principle of carnival. In this second view, human identity is something donned, as a mask (persona) or disguise, or results from a position taken up and held in a preexistent symbolic network. In such a network of relations, *who* you are counts much less than *where* you are. Identity so conceived is relational and, therefore, more shifting and fluid; it is defined by slots in a structure and surface configurations producing "intensities," not underlying essences implying continuity over time and solidity in depth.

In *The Recognitions,* these two conceptions of character operate simultaneously. In at least one instance, when Wyatt escapes from the Use-Me ladies disguised as the Reverend Gilbert Sullivan, which occurs, significantly, just after his father has revealed to him that he is a priest of Mithra and not a Protestant reverend, we witness a reversal or shift from the first to the second in a character's act. For the most part, the two conceptions coexist throughout, even though they have fundamentally different underlying assumptions. In a word, they operate dialogically. But how is this dialogic presentation of character to be conceived in relation to the "return of the simulacra" and the reversal that comes as the novel's central event? To answer this question, the typology of characters extrapolated earlier must now be reformulated.

In Chapter Two, I discussed the characters as if they were presented rather conventionally, but only because it was necessary in order to summarize the novel's main narrative developments and its carnivalesque themes. Even so, in instances like Valentine and Brown (or Anselm in Chapter One), it was impossible not to acknowledge and illustrate to some extent how these characters also function textually or participate in textual events; their formation and their "acts" as characters are so clearly motivated by textual rather than representational factors that these aspects could not be overlooked. As I have just indicated, Wyatt and Esme also function in this way. These characters, and Gwyon and Camilla could just as well be added to the group, are now to be understood as simulacra, but in the positive, post-Christian sense that follows from the overturning of Platonism. To say that they are simulacra in this sense, and that they can be properly understood only as such, is to say that they somehow forward or propagate this reversal from model and copy to simulacra and phantasm. In short, they are not simply counterfeits, nor can their behavior be accounted for simply in terms of *in*authenticity. Even without Deleuze's theory, it is clear that they demand a more complex reading than any such monological approach can provide. Reverend Gwyon, for example, is obviously a counterfeit Protestant minister, and his sermons barely mask his real spiritual preoccupations. In the light of his own research, however, Protestantism itself begins to appear as something of a counterfeit religion and a betrayal of true religious mystery. But this reversal is not sustained by Gwyon's worship of the sun as a priest of Mithra either, which appears in turn as the hothouse obsession of a religious scholar run amok. Yet, in spite of the obvious fact that the Reverend is not the "real thing" in either case, there is a compelling force to his psychic journey through the layers of Western religion. His phantasy of a return to the origins of religious mystery in ritual and sacrifice has a resonance and intensity that go well beyond the parameters of individual identity. And similarly in regard to the other characters of the first type; resonance and intensity, not authenticity, are the criteria that must be applied to them.

But if authenticity as a criterion of value is dropped or suspended, as it must be with the reversal of values that the novel is adumbrating, how then are we to respond to the second type, the fakes and counterfeits described earlier? To what extent do resonance and intensity apply to these characters?

Otto in particular provides a revealing focus for these questions. On the one hand, he is obviously a "simulacrum," or "part of a series of which there is no original," as another character asserts. But Otto is not a simulacrum in the Deleuzian sense. For though there seems to be no "original" of which he would be the copy, as a character he is inconceivable apart from their interplay. Far from throwing into doubt the Platonic paradigm, Otto confirms it with his every act, which is always accompanied by a gaze into the mirror. For insofar as Otto is always modeling himself on some ego-ideal or elevated, "interesting" image, he illustrates the instability and collapse into narcissism of the Platonic system. That his models turn out to be "bad" models or simulacra themselves is, of course, what generates much of the comedy. That, and the fact that Otto himself is a "bad" image or copy, since for all his posing and attempts at image projection, the effect is always comically unconvincing. (And the same must also be said, *mutatis mutandis,* for Sinisterra's comically inept efforts at counterfeiting money.) It seems fitting then that Otto should be the son of Mr. Pivner, who as the novel's "mass man" presents a kind of zero degree of individuality or a locus of generalities rather than a cluster of singularities. But Otto also comprehends several series which include mythic and literary figures. Again, would this not make him a simulacrum in the Deleuzian sense? The problem is that the series do not diverge, and thereby allow the possibility of resonance, but always converge in Otto's mirror image. His narcissism, therefore, leads to a comic replication of the same and a repeated denial of difference, even though his every effort to project an image creates it. In psychoanalytic terms: by always seeking recognition in his mirror reflection, Otto remains forever caught within this imaginary order.

Curiously, this desire for recognition also distinguishes the first type in the typology from the rest of the characters like Otto. For one reason or another, in one way or another, all in the second group are seeking recognition. Esther, Benny, Max, even Sinisterra, who wants to see his work reviewed again in *The National Counterfeit Detector*—all are anxious to have their identities recognized, even though, or perhaps because, there is something suspect about them. It is as if in *The Recognitions* the seeking of recognition itself becomes a suspicious act, a sign of inner inadequacy and instability, and finally a symptom of social dysfunction. These characters must ceaselessly repeat or copy one another in an effort to maintain stability and contact and to move ahead in the world. Ironically, the more they deny difference, the more they produce it, and in this denial, recognition is reduced to an automatism. Max, the successful artist whose art appears to be avant-garde while actually only fulfilling clichéd expectations, or Ludy, the popular novelist whose platitudinous writing is filled with stereotypes of sensitivity, provide examples of "recognition" reduced to this trivial level. The easy agreement between the French critic Crèmer and Max in regard to the latter's show in Paris illustrates how aesthetic recognition has collapsed into a form of economic and social exchange. Significantly, Crèmer's statement that he considers his own work a "disciplined nostalgia for the things I umm ...might have done" (670) echoes Wyatt's earlier pronouncement that criticism must be informed by a "disciplined nostalgia," and so indicates the debasement of this ideal.

In their various activities in the social, aesthetic, and religious realms, the characters of the second type continually seek to forge an identity by appealing to what is "recognizable" in the most obvious ways. But in seeking stereotypical recognitions, they also reveal the inadequacy of the model and its inherent limitations. Paradoxically, they too propagate difference but, in failing to participate in the novel's reversal of values, insist that these differences be perceived negatively and, thus, confirm the Platonic model. Like Otto, they appear as "bad" images or simulacra in the Platonic sense. In relation to the novel's reversal, therefore, they can only be viewed as a "reactive" type.

In summary, when the characters in *The Recognitions* are perceived as simulacra, they present themselves under two aspects in relation to the novel's "reversal": either as "bad" images or false pretenders in the Platonic sense, or as simulacra in the positive sense espoused by Deleuze. In the first perspective, they appear as fakes or counterfeits: in one way or another, they lack authenticity. In the second or reversed Deleuzian perspective, the characters fall into two types: the positive or affirmative simulacra—those who further the reversal and who can only be appreciated in their positivity in relation to it—and the negative or "reactive" simulacra—those who have only a symptomatic relation to the reversal and who still assert or depend upon the original/copy paradigm for their definition. For the sake of completeness, a third category might be added to designate those characters who exist only as anonymous voices and who represent a zero degree of simulation. A further distinction is that those of the second type are always seeking recognition, in contrast to those of the first type whose lives are "experimental" and who figure difference in and for itself. The opposition here, as the Nietzschean echoes suggest, has nothing to do with moral categories. From the perspective of conventional morality, Valentine would probably elicit condemnation, or at least a negative response, whereas Esther and Sinisterra would no doubt be viewed more sympathetically. As in much twentieth-century fiction, a "moral response" to these characters is inappropriate until redefined in relation to the novel's reversal of values.

A final example will illustrate some of these interrelations between the novel's subject and system. In relation to the latter, Stanley and Anselm form a particularly interesting pair. Since they often appear together, in tandem, to a certain extent they form a "pseudo-couple" whose dialogues constitute a ministructure that functions almost independently of what is going on around them. If considered as a splinter group, they also demonstrate how the religious impulse takes opposing form in their ongoing *agon:* in Anselm, it assumes a particularly intense form of satire, while in Stanley, it reveals itself as a tendency toward idolatry most obviously visible in his persistent effort to link art with the Catholic church. Yet in view of the novel's other mode of presentation of character—as singularities that correspond to resonant but divergent series—this grouping appears too restrictive and short-circuits other associations. So while Stanley and Anselm may be conceived as a dramatization of two warring impulses—toward the sublimated and the physical, respectively—in the manner of Dostoevsky or Dickens, such a critical view can only be the first step in analyzing their overall significance in the novel.

The limitations of this framework become evident as soon as Anselm and Stanley are viewed as simulacra. Anselm can easily be described in terms of several heterogeneous and divergent series by expanding the information I have already provided. One series (call it the cultural series), is composed of particularly incompatible figures: Origen, St. Anselm, Diogenes, Kirilov (from Dostoevsky's *The Possessed*), and Thomas Merton (whose "real" life Anselm's fictional one parodies). And, like Wyatt, Anselm decenters the series into a new context, thereby producing a novel configuration. As we saw earlier (see page 82), Anselm also "reflects" Wyatt in an interesting textual way. This relationship can now be rewritten more specifically at the level of the narrative in his relations with the Viareggio crowd: Anselm appears to function as a faint echo of Wyatt. He too is a lost spirit tracing a path through the activities of others, and reflecting the emptiness or "lack" in their preoccupations. Anselm also disappears and, like Wyatt, later withdraws into a monastery, or at least that is the rumor. Whatever the case, Anselm never reappears in person but has been displaced by his published confessions, which surface in book form as his representative and provoke the same kind of effects (on Bildow and Stanley, for example) as he did formerly in his own person.

Stanley, by comparison, seems almost a conventional novelistic character. As an artist and Catholic, he is sincere, dedicated, and "authentic." His quirky habits and peculiar obsessions only make him appear that much more of an individual. Nevertheless, he is clearly a "reactive" type, and nowhere is this more visible than in his concern with art and the way it reflects social reality. Of all the characters in the novel, Stanley is the most obsessed with fragmentation. For him, the fragmentation of experience is "the modern disease," as he explains to Agnes Deigh:

> —That's what it is, a disease, you can't live like we do without catching it. Because we get time given to us in fragments, that's the only way we know it. Finally we can't even conceive of a continuum of time. Every fragment exists by itself, and that's why we live among palimpsests, because finally all the work should fit into one whole, and express an entire perfect action, as Aristotle says, and it's impossible now, it's impossible, because of the breakage, there are pieces everywhere.... (616)

Since Stanley conceives art in reaction to this sense of fragmentation, he can see the present as a context for art only in terms of degeneration and degradation:

> How could Bach have accomplished all that he did? and Palestrina? the Gabrielis? and what of the organ concerti of Corelli? Those were the men whose work he admired beyond all else in his life, for they had touched the origins of design with recognition. And how? with music written for the Church. Not written with obsessions of copyright foremost; not written to be played by men in worn dinner jackets, sung by girls in sequins, involved in wage disputes and radio rights, recording rights, union rights; not written to be issued through a skull-sized plastic box plugged into the wall as background for seductions and the funny-papers, for arguments over automobiles, personalities, shirt sizes, cocktails, the flub-a-dub of a lonely girl washing her girdle; not written to be punctuated by recommendations for headache remedies, stomach appeasers, detergents, hair oil ... O God! dove sei Fenestrula? (322)

In Stanley's view, the work of art created today, the organ concerto that he is composing, for instance, must therefore deny time and historical contingency through its formal perfection: "finished to perfection... every transition and movement in the pattern over and against itself and within itself proof against time" (323). Such an aesthetic "law," with its massive denials, exacts a great price, no less than the life of the artist, and this is something Stanley too seems to know: "Every piece of created work is the tomb of its creator," he thinks to himself late in the novel. So, in a fundamental and characteristic irony, Stanley's aesthetic project, resonant with the overtones of modernism, carries him to his death in the late medieval cathedral at Fenestrula. That a medieval church and not the New York subway collapses upon him is both an ironic confirmation of his fear of entombment and a black comic reminder of the quixotism of his aesthetic ideal.

Now, it is precisely Stanley's persistent attempt to link fragmentation and degradation to the modern loss of transcendent authority, particularly that of the Church, that continually draws Anselm's ire. In the following typical exchange, Stanley speaks first:

> —But . . . even Voltaire could see that some transcendent judgment is necessary, because nothing is self-sufficient, even art, and when art isn't an expression of something higher, when it isn't *invested* you might say, it breaks up into fragments that don't have any meaning and don't have any . . .
> —You sound like Simon Magus, *invested*, for Christ sake, Anselm said, putting a dirty hand on Stanley's shoulder.—Why don't you go see his heart, they've got it in the Bibliothèque Nationale. You might understand him. By osmosis.
> —Simon Magus? Stanley said, turning, confused.
> —Voltaire, for Christ sake. He patted Stanley on the shoulder.—How's your crack, Stanley, he asked him. Two people turned, raising eyebrows in shocked interest. Agnes Deigh pretended to be looking for something in her large pocketbook.
> —Why, what . . .
> —The crack in your ceiling, what do you think I mean. (617)

Here, Stanley's attempt to discuss a serious issue is derailed by Anselm into a whirl of confusing assertions, digressive and deflationary asides, and sexual innuendo. However, in the novel as a whole, the recurring confrontation between them becomes more than the perpetual conflict of differing points of view as the two come to "figure" contrasting modes of satire and irony. As in the passage above, Stanley is constantly invoking a transcendent authority that will sustain him and give meaning to the spiritual yearnings he seeks to express in his organ concerto. But Anselm sees that implicit in Stanley's appeal is a denial of the here and now, particularly of the body's sexual claims. Stanley's "organ" concerto thus takes on an unconscious, libidinal association, as the pun implies. Furthermore, Stanley's obsession with fragments has a resonance of its own and connects with other fragments in the novel: the fragments of Wyatt's paintings he keeps as material proof of his forgeries, the body parts scattered throughout the novel, and the various textual fragments as well. Nevertheless, for Stanley, the work of art stands over and against the fragments and palimpsests that make up modern life. Viewed as an "idol," art has its own "law" that reflects "down" upon the shortcomings of life. Yet it is precisely Stanley's effort to deny and transcend "life among the palimpsests" through his art that leads to his death.

It has been said that the satirist attacks the weaknesses and temptations in others that are really within himself, thereby at once gratifying and punishing his own vices.[43] So, by attacking Stanley's spiritual yearnings, Anselm both exercises and blasphemes against his own similar desires. In general, his attitude recalls Swift's credo that everything spiritual and valuable has a gross and revolting parody, very similar to it, with the same name, but with the proviso that the "parody" has now become the reality. As Anselm himself says, "God has become a melodramatic device" (458). Yet Anselm's own view does not adequately clarify the link between his satire and his evident regression.

Anselm appears as a regressive figure in several ways: he insists on crawling around on all fours at parties in a parody of a religious ritual—the *ritu quadrupedis,* he calls it—and he eventually emasculates himself, thus expressing a desire to return to a pregenital stage. He is also obsessed with body parts, particularly those of the lower body. In psychoanalytic terms, satire is an art of regression and desublimation that involves a double movement: for every sexual regression on the body's surface, there is also a regression into the body's depths through the alimentary and digestive tract. For every outward burst of the satiric voice, as it emits its obscene and abusive words, there is a movement down to the cloacal depths and excremental source where words are not yet detached from material body parts. This phantasmatic movement gives the satiric words their terrible wounding force: they strike the target's body as if they were lumps of feces. (The euphemism " mudslinging" still retains something of this idea.) Whether or not all satire is linked to this particular phantasy, in Anselm's case it undoubtedly is: the two components are voiced in the obscene words (like "succubus") he directs at Esme and, in the insulting, abusive words he directs at Stanley.

The intense interaction between Stanley and Anselm is thus revealed to be a site where phantasms communicate, and death, dismemberment, and fragmentation are the terms of their resonance. Stanley's concern with art and the Catholic Church, with transcendence and its "law," obeys a simple logic: the greater his spiritual yearning, the more fragmentary "life at the surface" appears. As the novel's principal character seeking transcendence, he thus figures an ironic perspective. Opposing this movement "upward," Anselm pursues a reversal that will carry him downward beyond the body's sexual surface and into its depths, a regression that becomes both the condition and source of his satire.

Such considerations lead inevitably beyond the bounds of the characters' individual identities and into the complexities of literary representation, thus beyond the domain of the novel's "subject and system" as they have been defined here. In the next chapter, I want to explore still further the consequences of the reversal from model and copy to simulacrum and phantasm which I have argued is *The Recognitions*'s central event, by focusing primarily on the consequences of this reversal for the novel's generic identity.

Chapter 4

The Becoming-Simulacrum of the Novel

> These serio-comical genres [Socratic dialogues and Menip-
> pean satires] were the first authentic and essential step in
> the evolution of the novel as the genre of becoming.…
> Precisely what is this novelistic spirit in the serio-comical
> genres, and on what basis do we claim them as the first step
> in the development of the novel? It is this: contemporary
> reality serves as their subject, and—even more important—it
> is the starting point for understanding, evaluating and for-
> mulating such genres.
>
> —Mikhail Bakhtin, "Epic and Novel"

In its concern both to represent a world and at the same time to register prior wordings or textualizations of it, *The Recognitions* encompasses two very different kinds of novel: on the one hand, it is an extended contemporary Menippean satire directed against everything sham, fake, and imitative—artworks, ideas, identities, products, even languages—in the nascently consumerist, mass-media–directed American society of the 1950s; on the other hand, it is an encyclopedic, self-consciously modernist epic teeming with textual allusions and mythical echoes in the pattern of Joyce's *Ulysses* and Lowry's *Under the Volcano*. Moreover, in its elaborate working out of the counterfeit theme on representational and textual levels, where the opposition between model and copy, original and imitation, real and fictional are continually played out (and perhaps finally dissolved), *The Recognitions* comprises a vast "anatomy" of every possible "recognition-effect" and anticipates postmodern fiction's critique of representation through its implicit foregrounding of textuality in a potentially endless display of re-articulations. But perhaps the simplest way to state the case for this Janus-faced work is to say that it effects a "generic reversal" from the novel as usually conceived to what Mikhail Bakhtin calls a polyphonic, fully "dialogical" work of fiction.[1]

Indeed, by demonstrating that the novel's most distinctive feature is not its *mimesis* but its incorporation of various forms of speech and social discourse (its "heteroglossia" and linguistic "stratification"), Bakhtin's theory of the novel proves particularly useful for the study not only of Gaddis's novel but of much postmodern fiction, which has come to rely less and less on *mimesis* as its primary end and justification without however relinquishing its claim to engage with contemporary "reality."[2] But while Bakhtin's notions of "double-voicing," "heteroglossia," and "novelization" offer a more useful vantage point from which to consider the language and transformations of "source material" in *The Recognitions,* they are not specific enough to account for the full range of effects that issue from Gaddis's deployment of forgery and counterfeiting as "fictional techniques." As we shall see, these latter result in a peculiar textual logic that brings about not only a "generic reversal" but a proliferation of simulacra that theories of intertextuality alone cannot account for. In what follows, I shall suggest that this aspect of *The Recognitions* should be finally understood in relation to the becoming-simulacrum of the novel itself as a generic form.

Double-voicing

Let us begin with what Bakhtin calls "double-voicing," which he finds to be a primary means of heteroglossia in the novel. Bakhtin defines a "double-voiced" utterance as one directed both toward an object in ordinary speech and toward another or different voicing of the object. The author of a double-voiced discourse appropriates the utterance of another *as* the utterance of another and uses it "for his own purposes by inserting a new semantic intention into a discourse which already has, and which retains, an intention of its own."[3] The reader will thus perceive both the "original" or first version and the second simultaneously, in a kind of palimpsest effect. The most obvious examples are parody and stylization, but any kind of imitation or pastiche, when perceived as such, functions in this way.

In these terms, virtually the entire text of *The Recognitions* appears to be "double-voiced." Before examining specific instances, I want to extend Bakhtin's notion to situations where there are intentional deceptions in the text's voicing. For example, both plagiarism and forgery are instances of a "doubling denied": plagiarism denies and hides the first or original speaker of an utterance by attributing it to a second speaker; forgery denies a second speaker's doubling of an utterance by falsely attributing it to a first. Forgery resembles parody, of course, in that it foregrounds aspects of an "original" that are generally regarded as characteristic. Furthermore—and Bakhtin insists that this is a feature of all double-voiced speech—in both forgery and parody not only do we find an interaction between two speech acts or inscriptions, but that interaction is designed to be heard and interpreted by a third person, whose own process of active reception is anticipated and directed.

The position of this person is not necessarily privileged however. In *The Recognitions,* the central character, Wyatt Gwyon, emphasizing the care that goes into his own forgeries, points out that forgers usually perceive and consequently imitate an original in the style of their own period. Thus, earlier forgeries appear as obvious to later generations, who can see in them the stylization of the earlier period. Later viewers usually take this evidence of an earlier deception as a sign of their own critical acumen, yet it would be more logical to conclude that an "original" can never be perceived in its own terms, *qua* original, but only relationally; paradoxically, the original only becomes "original" retroactively when copied or imitated. Similarly, and according to the same logic, Wyatt's statement becomes "double-voiced" only if and when we perceive it as a "new semantic orientation" of a prior utterance in the novel; as it stands, his statement is simply echoed by the observations of Frank Sinisterra, another artistic counterfeiter (mostly of U.S. currency), that no imitation can be perfect since something of the counterfeiter always sticks or shows itself. Though not strictly speaking "double-voiced," Wyatt's statement *is* however double-referenced, since it applies self-referentially both to the text we are reading and to referents "inside" the novel.

Let us consider an unmistakable instance of "double-voicing" which also has thematic significance for Gaddis's novel as a whole. In Part I, Otto reports hearing a story about the recent discovery of a genuine Titian painting. (The passage is quoted earlier on page 22.) In the account, an art expert detected a bad forgery of a Titian and then scraped off the canvas's surface, revealing a fairly good but conventional nineteenth-century painting underneath. The expert then probed further and discovered a real Titian underneath the second painting. Now the reader already knows that this story "originated" with Wyatt, whom Otto often imitates and for whom the story has a special significance, since he uses it to justify his own practice of forgery, and that furthermore much hinges thematically on the difference between Otto's comic plagiarisms and the much more interesting forgeries that Wyatt produces. But it also turns out, *mirabile dictu,* that the Titian story is true, in the sense that it actually occurred. According to Peter Koenig, Gaddis read about the incident in the newspapers and felt compelled to insert it into his novel, even though it had already gone to the printer. For Koenig, who reads *The Recognitions* as an "epic of missed recognitions in a world of counterfeits," the incident simply illustrates a corollary: that underneath layers of counterfeits and fakes the genuine or original lies hidden.[4]

It seems evident that the "double-voicing" of this "true story" is closely related to what we might call its "citability," or its apparent significance for both author and a specific reader/critic, in addition to the characters. Let us linger for a moment on the fact that the incident was transposed from the newspapers. Koenig indicates that Gaddis "relied heavily" on newspapers for his material, especially the *New York Daily News*. In an unpublished prefatory note (which Koenig quotes in part) Gaddis evinces a concern for two effects resulting from this practice: first, that readers would "recognize" in his novel incidents they have read about in the newspapers ("Regular readers . . . may feel the sudden blurt of familiarity with certain situations that arise in the following pages"); and secondly, that those readers who are not familiar with these newspaper reports will think these incidents grotesque and exaggerated beyond reality and will therefore credit him with "an imagination of infernal consequences." Gaddis goes on to say, presumably in his own defense, that "no single imagination is competently aberant [*sic*] to conceive of the abundance of phantastical horror which exists on all sides as reality."[5] Thus, for some readers familiar with the *New York Daily News*, the incident may even appear to be doubly "double-voiced." In any case, what makes the incident "citable" to the author is the very collapse it suggests between the fictional and the real, between his own authorial imagination and the products of contemporary culture, whereas for at least one reader (Koenig), the incident is "citable" precisely because it re-establishes and even grounds this opposition in a "real" event.

Not all of the effects of "double-voicing" in *The Recognitions* involve such complications in how they are to be "recognized." Often the re-current parody is relatively straightforward, as in the case of the poem Esme sends Recktall Brown which begins:

> Sweet Nora Winebisquit bedewed with sleep
> Swept down through sooted flues of chimney-
>   sweep.
> And where? she cried, can be the sceptered rod

That men call Recktall Brown, and I call god.
(349)

And so it goes for twenty-three more lines, in perfect imitation of Pope's mock-heroic style. The "source" of this imitation is, of course, easy to recognize (even so, Pope is mentioned by name at least three times in the novel, on pages 202, 242, and 600). More often, however, parodies of great lines by "the masters" are in no way acknowledged. To describe the city of Paris, the narrator deflects Enobarbus's description of Cleopatra in Shakespeare's *Antony and Cleopatra* to "age had not withered her, nor custom staled her infinite vulgarity" (63). Wyatt (here called Stephen) parodies Macbeth's famous line— "Yes, who would have thought the old man to have had so much blood in him . . . ?" (897)—when Ludy falls and cuts his hand. In fact, well over thirty lines from Shakespeare's plays are echoed in the novel. T. S. Eliot's poetry is also frequently targeted for parody (Koenig reports that originally Gaddis intended to parody every line in Eliot's *Four Quartets*). However, in Eliot's lines, although to some extent this is true of Shakespeare's as well, we begin to notice that instead of straight parody often the lines have been simply "lifted" and incorporated into the text, as the following examples illustrate: "Winter thawed into sodden spring, cruel April and depraved May reared and fell behind" (42); "she found herself clutching their fragments, attempting again with this shabby equipment her raid on the inarticulate" (299); "Saint Paul would have us redeem time; but if present and past are both present in time future, and that future contained in time past, there is no redemption but one" (160). Such stolen lines or "disguised quotations" abound, particularly at the level of the phrase: "distracted from distraction by distraction" (202) evokes a passage from Eliot; "a cool million" (399) Nathanael West's novel.

Such extensive incorporation of imitated and disguised quotations, like the newspaper material, produces a tessellated surface on which every relationship between "original" and imitation, copy and counterfeit (or plagiarism), is ceaselessly played out. It seems evident, moreover, that it was precisely the desire to work out the counterfeit theme on the textual level—in addition to the narrative and thematic—that led Gaddis to "double-voicing" as a constant fictional strategy. Of course, such a strategy inevitably impels the alert reader to suspect every voicing to be double, every passage or scene to be plagiarized or composed of disguised quotations and, therefore, to wonder how and where the "authentic" might be "recognized." At the same time, such a question appears immediately problematic in relation to the novel's represented events, as the oppositions that underlie the novel's basic themes—original/imitation, copy/counterfeit, self/other, intellectual/physical, sacred/profane—become reversible: original paintings turn out to be copies; forgeries, genuine works of art; quests for knowledge and art, the masks of sexual and social obsession; and all human acts, interchangeable.

This dissolution of the novel's basic oppositions, of course, has important consequences for its formal identity. As conventional novelistic logic gives way more and more to a logic of masquerade and carnival, a process of transformation seems underway, but one that by its very nature soon outstrips authorial intent and control. I am suggesting, in short, that textual forgery or the carrying of the counterfeit theme into the writing of the novel's texture both motivated and became the chief means for ushering in a fundamental mutation in the novel's form. For at a certain point in reading *The Recognitions,* the innocence of representation can no longer be supposed, even momentarily, and the author can no longer be viewed as a "confidence man," challenging the reader to recognize his plagiarisms and literary forgeries. Instead, the reader himself or herself must now join in the production of a new textual space. To adopt Roland Barthes's terms, in *The Recognitions* we are led to participate in a transformation from a literary "work" conceived as unique, organic, autotelic, and authored, in the sense of filiated to the writer as father and creator, to an "already written" and constructed "text," endlessly open and produced by the reader, who inserts it into a network of recurrent but perpetually deferred sigifications.[6]

Textuality and the Space of the Phantasm

Evidence of this textual transformation is symptomatically visible in Gaddis's selection and appropriation of "scholarly" source material. Thanks to Koenig's research and Stephen Moore's indispensable *A Reader's Guide to The Recognitions,* we can see that traces of Gaddis's erudition, like the literary parodies and plagiarisms, are embedded everywhere in the text as "disguised quotations" and textual allusions. Reverend Gwyon's statement about Christianity's victory over Mithraism (57), for example, is lifted practically verbatim out of W. J. Phythian-Adams's study *Mithraism.* Similarly, Valentine's comparison of the contemporary art world to Chancellor Rolin's court in fifteenth-century Flanders (especially on pages 689–690) draws heavily from Huizinga's *The Waning of the Middle Ages*.[7] Many incidents and anecdotes relating to the early history of Christianity that pepper the text are culled from F. C. Conybeare's *Myth, Magic and Morals: A Study of Christian Origins*. As a case in point, in one of Wyatt's delirious speeches, he refers to the attempt by Aristobulus, a Hellenized Jew of Alexandria, to prove that Pythagoras, Socrates, Plato, Homer, and Hesiod all plagiarized their wisdom from Moses, a charge Conybeare discusses in some detail.[8] Earlier in the same passage, Wyatt plays with the word "exhomologesis"; by combining it with "jesuit" he produces "exhomolojesuis":

> In Spain Ignatius' militant limp and Xavier 4'6" exhomolojesuis abhor the shedding of blood, and the Inquisitor De Arbues describes Love ex hac Petri cathedrâ without raising a Welt. (392)

As Conybeare explains, "exhomologesis" was a rite invented by Pope Calixtus (about 218 A.D.) in order to circumvent the early puritanical Christian belief that mortal sin committed after baptism could not be expiated. The rite of exhomologesis—of outright confession—repeats the rite of baptism with all formalities except the use of water. Since the Jesuits in turn made confession even easier, the portmanteau word encapsulates a process of institutional accommodation. Another of Gaddis's "sources" of erudition, George P. Marsh's *Mediaeval and Modern Saints and Miracles,* illuminates the second half of the quoted sentence. According to Marsh, De Arbues, the Inquisitor of Aragon from 1442 to 1485, was reported "to have been eminently successful in inventing methods of torture which inflicted the keenest agony on the victim without a wound or even breaking the skin."[9] Hence, this "description of Love" ironically directs our attention to Christianity's more unsavory "methods," with the pun on *Welt* (German for "world") deflating its otherworldly aspirations.

More, of course, could be said about this passage, as well as about the hundreds of other similarly obscure and esoteric passages that fill *The Recognitions.* But there is a general point to be made. Conybeare's study attempts to demonstrate that Christianity owes more to the "hallucinations and transcendental fancies" of Paul than to the teachings of Jesus. Marsh's work is an exposé of Catholic superstition and displays a strong anti-Jesuit bias, often heaping ridicule on the saints' lives and religious marvels that it reports. These two books thus give some indication of the kind of scholarly research Gaddis sought out and used: that which delights in pointing up heresies and false beliefs and takes controversial or eccentric attitudes toward common cultural assumptions. Gaddis also tends to play off one scholar against another or combine "sources" eccentrically. For example, like Joyce, Eliot, and Yeats, he seems to have been influenced by Frazer's *Golden Bough,* and fascinated by the numerous parallels between primitive ritual and contemporary behavior. But as Moore reveals, Gaddis also draws material from Andrew Lang's *Magic and Religion,* which attempted to refute many of Frazer's ideas, thus setting one scholar against another in a "dialogized" relationship.[10] Another important "source" was Robert Graves's *The White Goddess,* which refers erroneously to the *Clementine Recognitions* as a novel popularizing the belief of the Gnostic Clementines. When we add Diogenes Laertius's *Lives and Opinions of Eminent Philosophers,* Carl G. Jung's interpretation of alchemy in the Faust myth (in *The Integration of the Personality*), and Laurence Dwight Smith's *Counterfeiting: Crime Against the People* to the sources already mentioned, we can more readily grasp Gaddis's tendency to assemble material that will "carnivalize" knowledge through its very process of selection and combination.[11]

While Koenig is uncritical of Gaddis's scholarly sources, Moore admits that they are, "to varying degrees, problematic," Marsh and Conybeare in particular being "somewhat dated and iconoclastic." We are therefore admonished to "separate the wheat from the chaff, an act of discrimination Gaddis did not always perform" and to "remember that Gaddis's borrowings fulfilled only artistic needs, and that he wrote not an encyclopedia but a novel."[12] But while Moore's spadework is immensely helpful, he has failed to perceive the full significance of Gaddis's use of such source material and scholarship. The novel's "encyclopedism" (or "topicality" in Bakhtin's terminology) should first be seen as a basic feature of Menippean satire, evident in modern fiction beginning with Flaubert's *Bouvard et Pécuchet.*[13] Even more pertinent is the novel's contemporary realization of a literary space articulated as a network formed by books of the past, or a "bibliosystem," as Edward W. Said has called it.[14] Yet Gaddis's novel does not simply reactivate traditional, esoteric, and journalistic "sources" in a modern literary text. There is something more interesting at work.

In his essay on Flaubert's *La Tentation de Saint Antoine* entitled "The

Fantasia of the Library," Michel Foucault has commented on the book's capacity as an object to create a system of references that feeds off of while also revivifying a domain of knowledge shaped not by rhetorical or pragmatic concerns but by the library as space and institution. Foucault emphasizes that this domain is less an enclosure or fictional alternative to the depiction of external reality than the creation of a "new imaginative space." Hence, the "imaginary is not formed in opposition to reality as its denial or compensation; it grows among signs, from book to book, in the interstice of repetitions and commentaries; it is born and takes shape in the interval between books."[5] More important, this "interval" created through citation, allusion, and textual reference is in no way neutral or inert, for the imaginative space opened up by the kind of erudition Foucault describes is a scholar's phantasmagoria, teeming with phantasms. Foucault is thus interested in that point, so well illustrated by Flaubert's Saint Anthony, where the lights of scholarly knowledge reverse into the sandstorms of hallucination, where intellectual rigor and precision give way to the fantastic, and the book disappears into the maw of monstrous spectacles that only books at that time could generate. In *La Tentation,* for example, the whole world of pre-Christian gods and religion is swallowed up only to reappear as hallucinated figures of horror and desire.

In *The Recognitions,* many of the main characters—the Reverend Gwyon, Wyatt, Anselm, and even Stanley—are subject to this intellectual delirium in which the border between knowledge and hallucination gives way. Perhaps the most vivid short example, however, is encapsulated in the fate of Mr. Farisy, who shares a room with the Reverend at the Happymount asylum. Before his breakdown, Farisy had been appointed by the Congregation of the Sacred Rites at the Vatican to investigate early methods of crucifixion:

> As a scientist, Mr. Farisy had always relied on empirical methods, and found no reason to abandon them now: twenty arms were delivered to his laboratory. He nailed each right hand, and each left wrist, to the wall, and attached mobile weights driven by a system of bellows which he'd removed from a player piano, to simulate the rising and falling motions of the breathing human being. Then he set the thing in motion: weights rose and fell; wood creaked; flesh tore; bones split; and something snapped in Mr. Farisy's head. (713)

Farisy now dreams of a crucifixion on a mountaintop, but the victim's flesh gives way as Farisy tries over and over again to raise him higher, in a grotesque travesty of transcendence. We last see Farisy, who has secreted a hammer and nails under his mattress, trying to convince the Reverend to allow himself to be crucified to the door of their room.

One may well wonder about the relation between Farisy's macabre phantasy and the authentic pursuit of knowledge. His "machine" for producing knowledge is based on scientific principle, yet the result is not a credible scientific experiment but a horrifying simulacrum. Scientific method, mechanical relationships, the human body and its simulation, as well as a penal practice symbolically important for Christianity, have all been connected together in such a way so as to produce something having no relationship to any of these. Furthermore, the passage resonates with a whole series of missing or ineffectual arms mentioned throughout the novel: the arm missing from Ignatius of Loyola's reliquary, the statue of Saint John the Baptist in Brown's collection that has lost an arm, the fake arm hanging in Frank Sinisterra's closet, and of course, Otto's counterfeit wounded arm. And there is another dimension to this unlikely event, for Koenig reports that the experiment was actually performed, and then featured on a television program called "In Search Of." (The "conclusion" of the experiment was that nails were indeed driven through the wrists in Roman crucifixions.)

The example is also typical in that knowledge and the quest for truth and authenticity in *The Recognitions* are often subverted by madness, hallucination and delirium, most vividly in the depictions of Gwyon, Wyatt, and Anselm, but in local examples everywhere. For both Plato and Deleuze, the proliferation of simulacra is intimately related to the process of "going mad" (*devenir fou*), and in Wyatt's and the Reverend's deliria, which hyperbolically jumble and consume the past, we see this effect actualized at the level of a character's experience. By violently recycling a heterogeneous mix of Western religion, mythology, and art, their rambling and abstruse speeches dislocate and decontextualize parts of the literary and cultural tradition into textual "vortices." Moreover, the cultural fragments, citations, and references that make up these highly wrought dispersions constitute especially visible points of impurity and heterogeneity in the novel's discourse, since they can only be partially "integrated" through the psychological associations of the characters or through the analogies these allusions imply. At the same time, elements from these textual clusters form into heterogeneous series and chains of signifiers that traverse the text "at an angle," producing textual crossover and "resonance" effects.

Consider, in this regard, one instance of Wyatt "talking" to Valentine:

Did you hear? how they were chopping time up into fragments with their race to get through it? Otherwise it wouldn't matter. But Christ! racing, the question really is, homo- or homoi-, who's who, what I mean is, who wins? Christ or the tortoise? If God's watching, . . . Christ! listen, O my sweet Gold! why were we born so beautiful? That's why we're here, an alchemist and a priest, without blemishes, you and I. It's true? You've never seen a cross-eyed priest? an ordained amputee? No, never! By all that's ugly, it's done! He sat, pinching up folds on the back of his hand.—Now, remember? Who was it, "gettato a mare," remember? an anchor tied to his neck? and thrown, caught by Kelpies and martyred, remember? in the celestial sea. Here, maybe we're fished for. (382)

As an exchange between characters the passage conveys very little. Only by a strained analogy can we think of Valentine and Wyatt as an alchemist and a priest, although Wyatt's theological obsessions do hold the passage together. Yet we cannot help but notice that the themes and signifiers evident—the fragment, homo- or homoi-, gold, body mutilation, drowning, the celestial sea, and fishing—are also picked up and redistributed in a variety of other situations and textual events in the novel: the drowning of a sailor who resembles Wyatt, the amputation of Stanley's mother's leg, or the discussion of Picasso's *Night Fishing at Antibes,* to mention only a few.

Wyatt's delirious "talk" thus also functions as a simulacrum, gathering up only to disperse a complex of textual strands. The resulting "textuality" is very unlike the kind of fragmentation and juxtaposition found in Pound's or Eliot's poetry, however, and seems closer to the art of assemblage, where techniques of collage and montage are used to transfer bits and pieces of "culture" to new settings and configurations rather than to recreate an archetypal one. Though Wyatt's aesthetic theory is based on an archetypal, Platonic sense of repetition, textual repetition here functions in the Nietzschean sense, establishing "difference" by displacing and decentering textual parts into an unpredictable "chaosmos." Yet this is not merely a textual effect: in his last appearance in the novel, after Ludy encounters him scraping the surface of a Titian painting at the Spanish monastery, Wyatt lyrically affirms the necessity of "living through" what have proved to be his own decenterings.

Let us trace the successive appearances of a more extended literary simulacrum. At Max Schling's cocktail party in Part I, Max reveals the plot of his own unfinished novel to an unidentified interlocutor who has been complaining that the only perceptive chapter in the novel she has just read "is where the boy discovers he is queer." His own novel, Max replies, is "slightly reminiscent of Djuna Barnes," but then his summary crudely undercuts any perceptible similarity: "A man is told that his girl is a lesbian, so he makes himself up as a girl and goes to a party where she'll be. He makes advances to her, she accepts, and he throws off his disguise and rapes her . . ." (188). Sometime later, Otto tries to interest Brown in his play, which has already been refused by the literary agent Agnes Deigh, who complained that it sounded "too familiar," though no one in her office could say exactly why. When Otto abashedly admits that they intimated he had plagiarized it, Brown briskly hands him Max's just published novel, *Wild Gousse Chase,* as an example of a book completely "lifted" from another but with enough changes to make it legally publishable. "So you picked up a few things here and there for yours, what the hell? What hasn't been written before? You take something good, change it around a little and it's still good" (350). Such is Brown's paternalistic advice to Otto. Later, Max's book turns up again as the topic of another party conversation. An unidentified person remarks to Don Bildow that he's read the manuscript and that Bildow appears in it, although the "real" situation has been reversed:

> A character named Hawthorn, and I swear it's you, just about the time you were mixed up with that same blond, except he's got her having you psychoanalyzed just like she had him analyzed when he was trying to get rid of her and couldn't because she was paying for the analysis, so he's got this character that I swear is you screwed up like this with her. You could sue that wise bastard. (609)

It is difficult to make out how these various versions of purportedly the same book correspond. Taken separately, however, each version echoes something in *The Recognitions.* The first version recalls the "drag" party in Harlem, and Esme's androgyny. Brown's advice to Otto applies of course to much of the material in Gaddis's novel. That Max has substituted Bildow's personal life for his own in his novel is not only funny, but also oddly interesting when we recall that the situation described also applies directly to Agnes Deigh and her first husband. The title of Max's novel, *Wild Gousse Chase,* indicates that it is presumably a rip-off of Rex Warner's novel *The Wild Goose Chase,* published in 1937, although Max's novel doesn't sound much like Warner's expressionist allegory about political power. Since *gousse* is French for lesbian, Max's plagiary seems to have taken a very different direction. Altogether, then, the novel's multiple nonrepresentational relationships make it a prime candidate for consideration as a simulacrum: it is less a "likeness"—an image of life or an imitation of another book—than an array of deformed analogies that comprise divergent but resonant series of items and resemblances.

In many essential respects, *The Recognitions* works on a larger scale the way Max's *Wild Gousse Chase* does in miniature.[16] Alerted by the obvious textual references most readers will see how fragments of the stories of Clement of Rome and Faust are echoed in Gaddis's novel, and how we distort the latter if we attempt to read it in any strictly analogous manner. Many other literary works—novels by Dostoevsky, Joyce, and Gide as well as Ibsen's *Peer Gynt* and Dante's *Inferno*—enter similarly into the novel's composition. In addition, there are references to books whose existence is suspect (*Toilet Training and Democracy*, *Can Freaks Make Love?*, *Our Contraceptive Society*), books which the characters are reading (*Walden*, *Uncle Tom's Cabin*, *How to Win Friends and Influence People*), books which are being plagiarized (*Imitation of Christ*, *The Duino Elegies*), and books which are simply the object of stray references. In fact, Gaddis's novel illustrates almost every possible relationship between a book and "the world," from ironic parallel and deflated analogy to grotesque or travestied realization. Books are also put to every possible use: in addition to being written, published, and read, they are discussed, reviewed, quoted, memorized, psychoanalyzed, autographed, used to disguise other books, and displayed as signs of sophistication. This very excess of references, correspondences, and uses obviously works against the privileging of any particular book as the model or source that might provide an authoritative analogy or interpretive key to *The Recognitions*.

To take a simple example, Somerset Maugham is mentioned by an unidentified character passing in the street (262), and later, his novel *The Razor's Edge* appears at Esther's cocktail party in the hands of Mr. Feddle, as he stands outside the bathroom door (he has probably or is about to counterfeit the author's autograph, as is his habit at parties). Why is our attention drawn to this novel in particular? In an essay on *The Recognitions*, David Madden mentions Maugham's novel as a "middlebrow parallel to Gaddis's novel," presumably because both involve a young American's quest for spiritual values in Europe (which, incidentally, Maugham's hero finds only in Indian mysticism), and the general resemblances between the characters (Wyatt and Larry, Valentine and

Elliot Templeton, Esme and Sophie).[17] What is striking, however, is the way the similarity between Gaddis's novel and Maugham's is perverted within the text when Anselm takes Gwyon's razor from Esther's bathroom and (about seven pages after the mention of Maugham's novel) emasculates himself with it. Yet what initially appears to be only a bizarre, minor detail actually provides evidence of a constant textual process at work in *The Recognitions:* the way in which repeated elements are displaced so as to pervert or parody an implicit analogy. In other instances, as in the example of the "Crotcher" episode or Janet's giving herself to a bull, a "phantasmatic logic" generates unforeseen events by recombining signifiers in unexpected ways which subvert the logic of novelistic representation.

In addition to the series of books, the many references to popular and classical music both testify to the great variety in which cultural references function and provide examples of similar textual effects. Characters listen to and often discuss such classical composers as Handel (predictably, of course, his "plagiaries" are a topic), Mozart, Mendelssohn, Palestrina, and Purcell. Snatches from popular songs circulating through the streets and cafés or overheard at parties also provide incongruous and comic juxtapositions. These songs range from the immediately recognizable, like Cole Porter's "Let's Do it" or "Return to Sorrento," which is always playing at the Café Viareggio, to the more esoteric "Yes We Have No Bananas," a popular hit in 1923 that was copied from Handel's *Messiah,* or the suggestively salacious "I'm Going Down to Dutch Siam's" and "I'm a Little Piece of Leather." But the most apparently significant are the recurrent references to opera: Mozart's *Don Giovanni,* Verdi's *Aïda,* Gluck's *Orfeo,* Wagner's *Ring* and *The Flying Dutchman,* and Puccini's *La Tosca.* Since this last opera concerns a young painter, we might expect the references to signal that scenes or situations in Gaddis's novel are to be read analogously, a device Joyce employs to great effect in *Ulysses.* Yet looking at individual instances (on pages 91, 92, 393, 394, 446, 520, 683), we discover that this is usually not the case. Actually, most of the allusions refer to Tosca's two arias in Act 2, just before and then after she stabs the police chief Scarpia, who promises to release her lover in return for sexual favors but then has him executed instead. These musical highlights punctuate the novel's scenes and exchanges between characters not analogically, which would suggest a mimetic correspondence between two sets of represented events, but as "moments of intensity" from another discourse that sometimes seem to determine events in *The Recognitions*. For example, early in the novel, Wyatt is listening to *La Tosca* on the radio when Esther returns to their apartment. As they begin to talk about Picasso's *Night Fishing at Antibes,* he suddenly asks if Tosca's "kiss" (by which he means her stabbing of Scarpia after he betrays her) is not "reality." Later, in the novel's last reference to the opera, as Wyatt bends over Brown's dead body after the latter has fallen fatally from the stairhead, he murmurs a few lines from the part where Tosca thinks her lover is only playing dead, after what was supposed to be only a mock execution: "Il sangue? ti soffoca il sangue? O yes, ecco an artista . . ." (683). But here, Wyatt's response seems peculiarly misplaced, since the situation is in no way analogous to that of the opera. However, soon after this moment, when Valentine begins to insist on their future collaboration in a new forgery ring, Wyatt suddenly stabs him repeatedly with the penknife he has taken from Brown's body. Thus, even though the situations are hardly analogous, Wyatt's stabbing of Valentine in effect repeats Tosca's stabbing of Scarpia. One might even say that these fleeting references to the opera function as motivational links at the level of representation, but they function through difference, not similarity.

Like much of the novel, the scene proliferates with references to various works of Western culture. Much earlier, when Wyatt makes his pact with Brown to paint forgeries, he is clearly identified with Faust and Brown with his tempter Mephistopheles. Here, the identification is repeated when a pompous member of the Royal Academy of Art refers to the shin guards of the armor Brown dons as the "false calves" of Mephistopheles. But more important, Wyatt's stabbing of Valentine recalls Faust's swordfight and mortal wounding of Gretchen's brother Valentin in Goethe's *Faust* (Part II, lines 3620–3775), and thus seems doubly entwined with or motivated by textual allusions. And there are other associations as well. Wyatt thinks of Brown as the Frog King in the Grimm fairy tale and the Troll King in Ibsen's *Peer Gynt,* and mumbles allusions to both in this scene. Even Valentine refers to Brown as "the ugly venemous toad with the precious jewel in its head," a line culled from Shakespeare's *As You Like It*. The penknife Wyatt uses to stab Valentine recalls the penknife in a verse from the children's rhyme "There was a man of double deed," which fascinates Wyatt and which he recites earlier (99). As the scene progresses, we are also reminded of the constantly changing music in the background: "a vapid tenor, widely known and loved, wound *Silent Night* round his throat, and strangled on it, into the brackish laughter again, and then from the north Beethoven's *Missa Solemnis* emerged, commenced to fill the place, and was gone into jazz, *When the Saints Go Marching In*" (683).

These multiple allusions are typical of how "the space of representation" in *The Recognitions* is saturated with cultural references, some being fairly well "hidden" while others obtrude rather ostentatiously. In fact, the more we look at any given scene the more we discover how many elements appearing elsewhere in the novel have been incorporated and how the scene has been constructed as a mosaic of quotations, references, and allusions to the cultural past, with the total effect of such textual mosaics greatly exceeding anything that "double-voicing" and "disguised quotation" could account for. Rather, it is as if *The Recognitions* had been consciously elaborated according to a basic principle of intertextuality— that "every text is the absorption and transformation of a multiplicity of other texts."[18] In a general sense, this seems true enough. In writing the novel, Gaddis has obviously transposed and "rewritten" fragments from many texts, the *Clementine Recognitions* and *Faust* among others, thus generating a literary structure that achieves "visibility" only in relation to other literary structures. Yet, on this view, these intertextual traces cannot be seen to function ironically by highlighting the discrepancy between the "original" and the deformed or counterfeit version (the "imitation"), as in Koenig's (and Moore's) reading (i.e., "underneath layers of counterfeits and fakes the genuine or original lies hidden"), for the logic of intertexuality disallows the privileging of any single text as the origin or more authentic version. As Jonathan Culler succinctly puts it: "there are no moments of authority and points of origin except those which are retrospectively designated as origins and which, therefore, can be shown to derive from the series for which they are constituted as origin."[19] Yet Culler also shows that intertextuality, while useful in revealing signification's condition of possibility, "becomes less a name for a work's relation to particular prior texts than a designation of its participation in the discursive space of a culture." Thus, if Koenig's thematic reading doesn't go far enough and leaves too much to be accounted for at the textual level, intertextuality as a general theory is not specific enough to tell us much about the variety of textual appropriations and transformations that make up Gaddis's novel, and what they might mean. What is missing is a third term or concept that will mediate between the two and bring them into some kind of meaningful relationship. And that is exactly the role fulfilled by the simulacra.

The Boundaries of Representation

Before pursuing this idea, let us first look at two examples of how representational boundaries are put into play in *The Recognitions*. In the novel's representation of a short dramatic scene and a specific place, we shall notice that a kind of contamination or leakage from one "literary" space to another is always at work. As a consequence, the boundary line that "ought to run between the text and what seems to lie beyond its fringes, what is classed as the real," as Jacques Derrida puts it, is continuously "complicated."[20] This, in turn, raises the question of how this "complication" is to be considered in relation to the novel's self-referential textuality.

The first example is the rather simple scene in which Valentine and Wyatt, having just left Brown's apartment, share a cab downtown. Their conversation has centered on topics that reflect on the novel itself, such as the function of the hero in the novel and the interplay between accident and design. When the cab nearly runs over a pedestrian (whom we recognize as the hapless Mr. Pivner), Valentine begins to berate the cab driver. Wyatt suddenly exclaims that Valentine really hates people, to which Valentine replies: "They're the same, the ones who construct their own disasters so skillfully, in accord with their ignorant nature, and then call it accident" (264). When Wyatt repeats the charge, Valentine only adds "Emerson's advice" : "We are advised to treat other people as though they were real . . . because, perhaps they are." In response, Wyatt suddenly begs off from their dining engagement and says goodbye. Valentine, his sophistication unruffled, replies: "Not goodbye . . . People don't say goodbye anymore. You look up and they're gone, missing. You hear of them, in a country with exotic postage stamps, or dead at sea" (264). Valentine quickly catches another cab, inside of which he discovers that he has mistakenly carried off Wyatt's copy of Thoreau's writings. There he finds the following passage underlined by Wyatt: *"What you seek in vain for, half your life, one day you come full upon, all the family at dinner. You seek it like a dream, and as you find it, you become its prey"* (265). The scene concludes as Valentine looks up to see that he has arrived at his front door.

In a manner similar to what Gregory Bateson calls a metalogue, the scene seems to illustrate the very things that are being discussed, to offer simultaneously an example of and commentary upon itself.[21] What is particularly noticeable is the rather complicated interplay between literary allusions, exchanges between the characters, and the action depicted within the scene. All appear to be motivating one another in such a complex reciprocity—the discussion "calling up" the event, the event evoking literary quotation, which in turn evokes another, these allusions all functioning as an exchange between characters—that the boundary between the illustration and the illustrated, the representation and the represented, is constantly blurred. Pivner, the "idiot" Valentine refers to in the altercation with the cab driver, does indeed seem to construct his own disasters, which visit him in the form of accidents. At the same time, Wyatt is right: Valentine hates people, perhaps because they are "real" in a way that he is not. And is it an accident that Wyatt leaves behind his copy of Thoreau, with Thoreau's own response to another piece of Emerson's advice underlined? Whether intended or not, the underlined passage has an anticipatory relevance, for Valentine does indeed seek Wyatt in vain, and later will become his "prey" when Wyatt stabs him. Finally, Valentine's remarks about people disappearing, as with his earlier remarks about the hero of a novel, turn out to be literally true in the novel we are reading: they apply to Otto, who disappears in an exotic country, and to Wyatt's symbolic surrogate, who drowns in a shipwreck.

The second example concerns the depiction of the monastery in Spain where the Reverend Gwyon at the beginning of the novel and Wyatt at its end both spend a few days. We can observe immediately that, on the one hand, enough physical and historical detail is furnished to produce what Barthes calls *l'effet du réel*, but on the other hand, clusters of other details constantly threaten to collapse the novel's referential illusion in the interest of humor and textual play.[22]

The somewhat unlikely name of the monastery, *Real Monasterio de Nuestra Señora de la Otra Vez* ("Royal Monastery of Our Lady of Another [or Second] Time") ambiguously suggests a repetition, which makes the reference to the Virgin Mary or indeed to any saint appear troubling. Though now a Franciscan monastery, the heterogeneity of its physical appearance reflects a history rife with heresy and eccentric behavior:

> When the great monastery was finished, with turreted walls, parapets, cren-elations, machicolations, bartizans, a harrowing variety of domes and spires

in staggering Romanesque, Byzantine effulgence, and Gothic run riot in mullioned windows, window tracings, and an immense rose window whose foliations were so elaborate that it was never finished with glass, the brothers were brought forth and tried for heresy. (9)

The "brothers" refers to the unnamed order who built the monastery and who were "extinguished" upon its completion in the fourteenth century. The order was so guilt-ridden, and its measures of atonement so stringent, that "those who came through alive were a source of embarassment to lax groups of religious [*sic*] who coddled themselves with occasional food and sleep" (9). But the official reason for their eradication, the narrator explains, was over a matter settled at the Council of Nicaea (which they missed): whether Jesus was *Homoousian* or *Homoiousian,* of one substance or like substance. The order chose the latter— "as a happier word than its tubular alternative (no one gave them a chance at *Heteroousian*)"—and their fate was sealed in a diphthong. Of the Fransciscans who took over the monastery, three individuals are mentioned: Brother Ambrosio, Abbot Shekinah (a convert), and Fr. Eulalio. Their names are rather unlikely, as are the "legends" associated with each of them. Fr. Eulalio, for example, "a thriving lunatic of eighty-six who was castigating himself for unChristian pride at having all the vowels in his name, and greatly revered for his continuous weeping, went blind in an ecstasy of such howling proportions that his canonization was assured" (10).

When Gwyon appears at the monastery, he is admitted as a Protestant "curiosity" but then denounced as a heretic when one of the brothers observes him through a keyhole administering the Eucharist to himself. He is defended however by Fr. Manomuerta, the organist (whose name of course means "dead hand"), who convinces the others that "there is some of Christ in him." During Wyatt's stay at the monastery as a kind of penitent, the monastery and Franciscans recede somewhat into the background as our attention is focused instead on Wyatt's encounter with Ludy, the "distinguished" but obviously mediocre writer. Only Fr. Eulalio's namesake is singled out, no doubt because of his curious obsession with typewriters and the humor that results when he brings Ludy an entire suitcase full of photographs of them.

Gaddis's depiction of the monastery thus treads a thin line between a credible representation of an actual place and an elaborate joke. Stephen Moore reports that its name is a fictitious replacement for the Real

Monasterio de Guadalupe in Estremadura, where Gaddis stayed from 1949 to 1950, and many of the details suggestive of the surrounding landscape and general "feeling" of the place carry an authentic ring. At the same time, certain details (such as those itemized above) strain credibility, as if Gaddis were deliberately pushing the reader to the point just this side of a guffaw and shake of the head. There is also a noticeable "textual effect" resulting from a playing with signifiers. As a young man, Wyatt was also obsessed with the question of *homoousian* or *homoiousian*. According to the novel's phantasmatic or textual logic, this interest is simply one manifestation of a generalized interest in homosexuality and being "queer" in different contexts. "Ambrosio" (a cognate of ambrosia, the food of the gods) and "Shekinah" (which in Hebrew means "the visible glory of the Lord") are, of course, completely unlikely names for Franciscan monks, but "Eulalio" is even odder. Although we can decompose it into the Greek *eu-* (meaning well) and *lalia* or *lalein* (meaning to babble), it actually sounds like a portmanteau word compounded of "echolalia" and "eulogia." The first means to echo repeatedly and idiotically, but the second has a more complex meaning. In the early Christian church, it originally referred to the Eucharist and, later, to those elements of the eucharist sent to the sick or from one bishop to another as a symbol of Christian love and fellowship and then, still later, to the unconsecrated bread not used in the communion service, but blessed and given as a substitute for the Eucharist to the noncommunicants. When we ponder the fact of Eulalio's presence (as his father's later echo?) near the end of the novel, and the parody of the Communion that occurs when Wyatt unwittingly eats bread made from dough mixed with his father's ashes, "ingredients" which have been sent by one preacher to another, these signifiers no longer seem arbitrary but suddenly link up in a rebus or dream logic not unlike the signifying chains in the "Crotcher" episode.

Perhaps not too much should be made of this textual effect, although other commentators have also noted the resemblance between the monastery and the novel we are reading. In any case, the "monastery" marks one site—Gwyon's "parsonage" another—where signifiers tend to clot or cross one another, thereby anticipating or even dictating later actions and events. Interestingly, these places in the text where networks of signifiers become clearly visible also mark the limit points of Wyatt's appearance in the narrative.

These two examples, in that they more or less suspend the representational function in the interest of self-reflexivity and textual play, may also suggest a rather restricted view of textuality in *The Recognitions*, inasmuch as they may imply a privileged perspective or frame in which these various textual effects could be gathered into a unity of purpose and hence be seen to articulate a unified textual system. That is, given so many clear signs of the novel's preoccupation with the making and reception of art, its sources, "origin in design," materials, and traditions, shouldn't we consider its textuality primarily in regard to the tradition of the modern novel as a self-conscious and self-reflexive text, concerned above all with its own self-elaboration and/or self-(de)construction? In Jean Ricardou's theorizing on the *nouveau roman* and Paul De Man's notion that modern literature is always self-deconstructive—to cite two recent examples—this kind of explicitly textual practice entails a specific interpretation of the modern (or postmodern) literary work.[23] Can *The Recognitions* also be read in such terms?

Before answering, I should first acknowledge that the theory of post-modernist writing as a self-reproducing "text" also accomplishes a complete reversal of the mimetic theory, or fiction understood as a credible representation of the world. In this view, a work of fiction does not so much reflect the world through the intermediary of a fictional narrative as use the world as a pre-text or "ground" to narrate or dramatize the story of the text's own genesis and self-generation. Applied to *The Recognitions*, the theory would suggest that Wyatt's failure to become an artist is only a prelude and necessary condition to his becoming a success as a forger of old master paintings of the Renaissance, and that his "story" in turn is only an allegory of *The Recognitions*'s necessary failure as a conventional novel in order that it can become a successful "forgery" and intertextually generated modernist text. Wyatt's story would therefore amount to a partially disguised account of the novel's own process of composition. Just as he achieves a special kind of distinction by forging works of art that are more significant than the "originals" of his contemporaries, so Gaddis's novel, by counterfeiting the *Clementine Recognitions*, *Faust*, and numerous other classics, would also achieve its status as a (post)modernist work of art. As the "true" story of the Titian found underneath the forgeries would suggest, the layering of texts in *The Recognitions*, like the layering in Wyatt's paintings produced by a memory that goes "way back" to the "origins of design," would have to be seen *through* in order that we arrive at and "recognize" the origin(al) beneath the "counterfeit" surface. Yet the fact that the origin(al) is absent (it doesn't matter whether it is only "outside" the novel or doesn't in fact exist) means that it will have to be endlessly supplemented—that is, added to while indefinitely deferred through a referential relationship—as in the story of the newly discovered Titian or in Wyatt's exclamation, "Thank God there was gold to forge!" The play within the text produced by the proliferation of counterfeits therefore exemplifies what Derrida calls "the movement of supplementarity," which makes up or stands in for this deficiency at the origin.[24] What makes Gaddis's novel distinctive is that the field of its play is truly encyclopedic and encompasses many different levels of reference and areas of knowledge. Nevertheless, according to this textual reading, we would still have to see all its multifarious details, insofar as they participate in this play (i.e., become part of the text), as finally self-referential, as they articulate this process of textual self-generation and its endless dis-play of oppositions.

But what are we to make of the novel's obvious satire, which takes up a good portion of its content? Since satire generally depends upon pre-existent values and directs our attention toward the activities represented, in this case to tourism and mass culture's degrading reproductions of high culture, wouldn't it resist being subsumed in this logic of self-representation? Not necessarily—in fact, such satire is just as surely inscribed in this logic. Everything satirized is only a ludicrous or comic repetition of something treated seriously in the main plot: Otto and Sinisterra are satirized versions of Wyatt as the artist as counterfeiter; tourism is a degraded travesty of the spiritually enriching voyage; popular culture, at least in consumer society, is always a crude reproduction, a bad copy of a copy of a copy. Far from working against textuality, these satiric instances only present other versions of its logic in a "low mimetic" mode. What appears at first as a dialectic between book and world is really only the mirror play of good and bad copies, of images that replicate in endless series. Mimesis and the Platonic theory of iconic harmony has not been jettisoned, only internalized more completely.

In these terms, however, the allegorical reading itself becomes subject to reversal at another, "higher" level of interpretation. One might wonder, for example, if this internalization of literary devices and compositional strategies in the service of the text's own self-generation doesn't simply reproduce in "literary" terms the logic of consumer capitalism, according to which everything must be reproduced as a version of itself.

This logic necessarily dictates the suspension of all reference (including use value and the gold standard) in the "differential" play of a structural law of value. Ironically, then, the novel would achieve its autonomy and attain self-determination at the very moment when most of society falls under the totalizing rationale of the commodity form and generalized exchange. Such a "de-intensification" of difference in the novel would then be compensated by a hypervalorization of its formal values.[25]

Whether or not such an argument, which can only be sketched here, appears convincing, one may wonder if the deconstructive or allegorical reading does not finally deny the multiplicity and heterogeneity so insistently present in *The Recognitions*. It opens up the novel to textual play but, at the same time, circumscribes this play within the field of language. Joseph Riddel, having performed a deconstructive reading of several of Poe's stories, suggests however that this is not so much a true opposition as a "play" between two metaphorical conceptions of the text:

> What is called "modern" narrative exposes the fiction of the origin by exploiting the fissure in the mausoleum, library or pyramid [all important figures in Poe's stories] which has concealed this absence; but it performs this operation only by laboriously constructing a house upon the flawed structure of the old house. Its deconstructions produce an allegory of construction, an always doubled creative/resolvant text. This does not lead to an open text that is the reversal and displacement of the closed text, but instead produces a play between those two metaphors. The modern text is no more open than closed, but it is always interpreted as one or the other, as tending toward one or the other.[26]

Insofar as *The Recognitions* also exposes "the fiction of the origin," Riddel's formulations seem applicable. By playing out the copy/counterfeit motif, *The Recognitions* also becomes a "doubled creative/resolvant text," and thus subject to the allegorical, deconstructive reading. At the same time, the proliferation of simulacra resonating through the novel which makes this textual reading possible also complicates and, to a certain extent, even disqualifies it. In these terms, the question of the opening and closing of *The Recognitions* as "text" may be answered on a double register: working against the closure of representation is the novel's intertextuality and the play of its signifiers, but working against the deconstructive reading of the novel as an allegory of its own self-elaboration are the dispersive simulacra and their ramifying series, which in their textual heterogeneity resist the kind of self-referentiality on which this allegorical reading depends. I must insist on this last point because, as we shall soon see, the process of textual self-generation in *The Recognitions* is only one aspect of its participation in what Bakhtin calls the novel as a genre of becoming.

The Novel as Simulacrum

In one sense, of course, all works of fiction are simulacra— "distorted" representations of a nonexistent "original." But I have given the term a much stronger meaning: as a simulacrum, *The Recognitions* "simulates" an external reality but, at the same time, throws into question the original/imitation or model/copy paradigm. For Gaddis's novel, like postmodern fiction in general, such a paradigm, although reduced in importance in the modernist aesthetic of visionary and iconic revelation, has now become profoundly problematic in a cultural space in which the opposition between "originals" and "imitations" no longer governs representation. In any case, to say that a novel is a simulacrum implies that in some way it reproduces the conventions of the novel without actually being a novel. This is what Jean-Paul Sartre seemed to have had in mind when he alluded to the appearance of "anti-novels" by Vladimir Nabokov and Evelyn Waugh in his "Preface" to Nathalie Sarraute's *A Portrait of a Man Unknown,* which he wrote about the time Gaddis was writing *The Recognitions.* Sartre remarks:

> These anti-novels maintain the appearance and outlines of the ordinary novel; they are works of the imagination with fictitious characters, whose story they tell. But this is done only the better to deceive us; their aim is to make use of the novel in order to challenge the novel, to destroy it before our very eyes while seeming to construct it, to write the novel of a novel unwritten and unwritable.[27]

And, in a later interview, Sartre also mentions the "false novels" of Witold Gombrowicz:

> There also exist novels of another kind [*genre*], the false novels like those of Gombrowicz, which are a sort of infernal machine. Gombrowicz has an excellent knowledge of psychoanalysis, Marxism and many other things, but he maintains a skeptical attitude, so well in fact that he constructs objects which destroy themselves in the very act of their construction.[28]

In these comments, Sartre catches a glimpse of what will become a postmodernist strategy but then falls back into an ironic or modernist viewpoint, since he takes the "anti-novel" or false novel to be merely a model (or allegory) of self-destruction: reflecting on the novel form from within, the anti-novel reproduces it only as an act of ironic self-cancellation. Unable to see the anti-novel in anything but negative terms, Sartre fails to grasp the peculiar logic of the simulacrum.[29]

To clarify what is at stake, Sartre's remarks may be contrasted with what I take to be the postmodernist view of Gilles Deleuze. In *Différence et répétition,* where the subversion of representation is a central issue, Deleuze shows how the simulacrum as a specific structure of differences pertains to the modern novel. Significantly, Deleuze also takes a novel by Gombrowicz as a primary example. Deleuze finds that in the latter's *Cosmos:*

> Two series of heterogeneous differences (one of hanging objects and another of mouths) seek to be put into communication through diverse signs, until the institution of a dark precursor (the murder of the cat), which acts here as the differentiator of their differences, as meaning, incarnated however in an absurd representation, but starting from which dynamicisms will be released, events will be produced in the cosmos system, which will find their final issue in the death instinct overflowing the series.[30]

Cosmos thus functions as what Umberto Eco calls an "open work," but instead of a layering or superimposition of several divergent narratives, Deleuze discovers two different series of divergent but reverberating signifiers that communicate "within the heart of chaos." Because its structure is based not on iconic resemblance but on two series of communicating differences, Gombrowicz's novel must be considered a simulacrum.

Following Deleuze's discussion of the "overturning of Platonism," I have argued that the multitude of copies, counterfeits, and simulacra in *The Recognitions* could be understood in two different ways: as Platonic or archetypal repetitions in which identity is maintained or lost, as in the "bad" copies (i.e., counterfeit or sham items), or as Nietzschean repetitions in which identity is no longer predicated on "originality" or "authenticity" but must be conceived as a "self-difference" defined only in relation to other differences. Into the first category fall the plethora of shams and fakes that crowd the novel and that we "recognize" as such; into the second, the simulacra composed of heterogeneous series that achieve unity or coherence not at the level of representation but as structures of difference communicating through the "resonance effect." From the main character himself and the simulacra he forges to the many objects, words, representations, and "narratives" embedded in the text, these simulacra all somehow subvert the logic of identity or analogy and thereby "figure" a reversal of the Platonic perspective based upon this logic. In these terms, the reversal of perspective that intertextuality entails in Culler's description above must now be seen as conditioned by a deeper or more profound reversal (of which it seems to be one instance): the overturning of Platonic assumptions and the reinstatement of the simulacrum as a structure of differences.

To the extent that *The Recognitions* as a whole is fissured by a prolif-erating series of heterogeneous items that work against its coherence as a mimetic representation, it too tends to become a simulacrum. Indeed, *The Recognitions's* obvious generic impurity obliges us from the very outset to question any simple notion of model. While Gaddis appears to have started out to write a modernist "art novel" about art "in the age of mechanical reproduction," his theme (forgery and the counterfeit) and compositional strategies ("double-voicing," repetition and doubling, polyphonic dialogues, long digressions into encyclopedic farragoes, and magpie compilations) led to a very mixed narrative form, one that while variously resembling the anatomy, Menippean satire, and what Bakhtin calls the polyphonic novel, doesn't correspond to any single literary "model." Even Joyce's *Ulysses,* which *The Recognitions* resembles in many ways, cannot be said to be a model, for Gaddis's novel exhibits too many significant differences: it repeats a "romantic" rather than a classical myth, lacks the stylistic variety and systematic elaboration of correspondences, and has a more fragmented narrative line (which includes a parody of the symbolic father-son crossing in *Ulysses*). And similarly with other books that *The Recognitions* resembles. Like Otto's play, in fact, Gaddis' novel often sounds very "familiar"; but unlike the play, it achieves a singularity by consciously evoking and then subverting all specific resem-blances. And like Wyatt's "forgeries," which are not copies of any "orig-inal" but bathe in the full ethos of the art of an earlier epoch, *The Recognitions* is a "forgery" of a modernist classic that calls into question the very notion of a literary "original."

As a simulacrum of the novel, *The Recognitions* fully maintains the novel's outward conventions and compositional strategies. In traditional deployment, we find plot, character, and theme; the maintenance of narrative sequence, illusion and closure; and effects like satire, parody, and irony. These are things we "re-cognize," since the repetition of elements is subordinated to a logic of representation which sustains identity and continuity, even though there may be and usually are significant deviations. At the same time, there are other effects—black humor, delirium, a nonsensical textual logic—which we can not "re-cognize" but only "encounter" or observe, since these effects are produced by a repetition of elements in which a displacement or a nonrepresentational logic, as in the telescoping of words, images, and narrative fragments into serial relationships, articulate structures of difference not founded on analogy and identity. Yet these two contrasting kinds of effects occur side-by-side, issuing from a dialogical structure that encompasses both.

In short, the same "dialogic" founded on the Platonic model/copy paradigm and its simultaneous overturning that determines the novel's thematic presentation and texture also operates at the level of the novel's overall composition. The interweaving religio-aesthetic dialogue between Wyatt and Valentine, which of course exhibits significant similarities with Plato's Socratic dialogues, provides one instance of how this dialogic manifests itself as an essential generic feature. But a more compelling case can be made by showing in a final example how the dialogic entails that we read the *The Recognitions* in two ways, that is, as both novel and "text." This final example will also allow me to suggest how Bakhtin's concept of "novelization" makes their integration possible.

One recurrent device Gaddis employs for satiric purposes is the incongruous simile. For example, when several characters attend the "drag" party in Harlem, the narrator draws out an analogy between the party and earlier festivals:

> There was, in fact, a religious aura about this festival, religious that is in the sense of devotion, adoration, celebration of deity, before religion became confused with systems of ethics and morality, to become a sore affliction upon the very things it had once exalted. Quite as festive, these halls, as the Dionysian processions in which Greek boys dressed as women carried the ithyphalli through the streets, amid sounds of rejoicing from all sexes present, and all were; glorious age of the shrine of Hercules at Coos, where the priests dressed in feminine attire; the shrine of Venus at Cyprus, where men in women's clothes could spot women immediately, for they wore men's clothes. (311)

And so it goes for another full page. But what starts as an anthropological foray, unearthing unexpected connections and hidden analogies between an ancient and a contemporary social gathering, is comically exploded with the last parallel: "So even now, under a potted palm with silver fronds, a youth making a solemn avowal held another youth by that part where early Hebrews placed their hands when taking oaths, for it represented Jahveh" (312).

The passage borrows heavily from Frazer, while not being exactly a "disguised quotation," imitation, or plagiary. In any case, the incongruity in the comparison it draws between an earlier and "authentic" ritual practice and an episode from contemporary life generates the humor: festivals which formerly celebrated and insured procreation now find their humorous echo in a homosexual love feast. Thematically, the passage is also entwined with a series of satiric conflations or equivalences: the male sexual organ, homosexuality, writing, and counterfeit money. The young men referred to in the passage are "members" of Agnes Deigh's entourage whom she "collected" while working as a literary agent. In the novel, writers are always suspected of being "queer," and Otto, living on the fringe of Agnes's circle, is not only suspected of being queer but frequently holds his play, which he carries in a leather case, between his legs. When he loses the play, he goes to Agnes's office in the hope that she has found it. Soon afterwards, he has dinner with Frank Sinisterra, believing mistakenly that this counterfeiter is his father. When Sinisterra gives him a bag of counterfeit money, which he refers to as "the queer," Otto holds the bag "pressed against his parts" (554). Later, in order to account for his sudden wealth, Otto tells his friends that he has sold his play.

Nothing in this economy of "counterfeit" exchanges poses any problem for interpretation; to the contrary, the satire depends upon this pattern of clearly recognizable analogies. However, what starts as satire also modulates into something else on a different track or line. On the same evening as the "festival," Otto and Ed Feasley steal an amputated leg from a hospital refuse can and carry it through the streets, before finally leaving it to rot on a subway seat. In one sense, the episode obviously burlesques the ancient ritual of Greek boys carrying ithyphalli through the streets, as a descriptive detail suddenly generates a scene in the novel. But it also illustrates what Mathew Winston calls "grotesque black humor," which is to be distinguished from "absurd black humor" because of its obsession with the human body, particularly with "the ways in which it can be distorted, separated into its component parts, mutilated and abused."[31]

There are many incidents of such grotesque black humor in the novel—

Farisy's experiment, Wyatt's consumption of his father's ashes (prefigured when he acquires the name "Stephen Ashe"), and Mr. Pivner's lobotomy. Even more important, through the circulation of body parts in the novel, these various incidents all participate in a "phantasmatic movement" that resonates through other simulacra in the novel. Significantly, this circulation does not symbolically reconstitute a textual "full body"; instead, the divergence and dispersion of the resonant series which make up the simulacra work against even such a symbolic closure.

Because these simulacra are intrinsically "openended," they function as an important means by which "novelization" occurs in *The Recognitions*. In his later essays, Bakhtin gives the name "novel" to those anticanonical forces working within a literary system that mark its limits and make its conventional constraints visible, while also pushing beyond them. He thus sees the "novel" less as a definable genre than as a site where interacting tendencies within the various social languages of a period are staged and played out. In the same general way, Bakhtin uses the term "novelization" to refer to the process by which literary genres become more open and flexible, and capable of incorporating "extraliterary heteroglossia and the 'novelistic' layers of literary language." As a result of this process, genres are "dialogized, permeated with laughter, irony, humor, and elements of self-parody." But most important, they achieve a "semantic openendedness, a living contact with unfinished, still-evolving contemporary reality (the openended present)."[32]

It is in this sense that the simulacra "novelize" much of the heterogeneous material in *The Recognitions*. For if parody, satire, and double-voicing are used to fictionalize the "raw" and "already formed" material of cultural life, the simulacra that traverse this material set it resonating in structures of serial relationships not bound or defined by oppositions such as original/imitation, real/counterfeit, or true/fictional. Just as the most obvious literary "models" for *The Recognitions*—the *Clementine Recognitions*, Goethe's *Faust*, Dante's *Inferno*, Joyce's *A Portrait of the Artist* and *Ulysses*, and Gide's *The Counterfeiters*—are internalized and "decentered" into a series of intertextual referents, so all the various items incorporated into the novel—paintings, books, operas, and popular songs; body parts and assorted objects; events from mythic, literary, journalistic, and "topical" sources; quotations from the cultural past; languages, expressions, and representations from advertising, tourism, art history, theology, science, mysticism, and church history—are also caught up and articulated in various divergent series that "communicate" through the simulacra. As in Gombrowicz's *Cosmos*, these resonating heterogeneous series communicate through difference—not iconic resemblance—and thus move across or through thematic oppositions like real/counterfeit. In so doing, the simulacra they form insure that the "real" and the "fictional" never harden into an antithetical opposition, which would thereby allow the novel to close off iconically to the outside as a strictly bounded representation.

Instead, a multiplicity of possible relationships always remains open. As each reader brings its various elements into resonant play, he or she is caught up too in another series. For finally, it is a property of the simulacrum to include in itself the differential point of view by including the observer. According to Plato, the simulacrum implies large dimensions, depths, and distances which the observer cannot master; in fact, it is because the observer cannot master them that he or she experiences the effect of resemblance. But because "simulacra are constructions which include the angle of the observer," he or she becomes part of the simulacrum, which in turn is further transformed by his or her point of view.[33] In the space of this continual disparity, described by Plato in the *Philebus* as an "unlimited becoming," a ceaseless proliferation of difference thwarts the eternal repetition of the same.

To be sure, this tendency within *The Recognitions* is not unlimited, nor could it ever be. Working within and against the novel's mimetic function, the "becoming of simulacra" is ultimately restrained and framed by the demands of representation. Yet in the dialogic interplay between a mimesis and a becoming-simulacrum, Gaddis's novel achieves its own singular identity. Only by means of such a dialogic can it both draw upon a set of thematic oppositions (original/imitation, authentic/counterfeit) for the purpose of satire and, at the same time, dissolve those oppositions in the interest of articulating a new configuration of literary, artistic, philosophical, and social referents.

This configuration suggests the end of art conceived in separation and autonomy, or as a project for individual salvation in the age of mass-media reproduction. One critic, Kathleen Lathrop, has written that *The Recognitions* satirizes the "impotence, decadence, vulgarity, and perversion of popular culture."[34] But what needs to be added is that this is because in popular culture the most mechanical repetitions of modern life become prominently visible in its degraded plots and images. In the last pages of *Différence et répétition,* Deleuze argues that "the more our everyday life appears standardized, stereotyped, and submitted to the accelerated reproduction of consumer objects, the more art must engage with it and wrench from it this small difference that works somewhere else and simultaneously at other levels of repetition, and even to make the two extreme series resonate, the one of consumer habits and the other of the instincts of death and destruction."[35] This ambition, it seems to me, describes Gaddis's achievement in *The Recognitions.* In the "small difference" articulated by Wyatt's forgeries, delirious dissolution, and the many absurdities of a social world defined by false identities, sham productions, and simulated desires, the two series reverberate with a critical force; not a negative force, but an overflow, an excess, a breaking down of boundaries and "literary" oppositions in a becoming-simulacra that finally entails the becoming of the novel itself as a generic form.

Chapter 5

Toward Postmodern Fiction

> The postmodern would be that which, in the modern, puts
> forward the unpresentable in the representation itself; that
> which denies itself the solace of good forms, the consensus
> of a taste which would make it possible to share collectively
> the nostalgia for the unattainable; that which searches for
> new presentations, not in order to enjoy them but in order
> to impart a stronger sense of the unpresentable. A post-
> modern artist and writer is in the position of the philoso-
> pher: the text he writes, the work he produces are not in
> principle governed by pre-established rules, and they cannot
> be judged according to a determining judgment, by apply-
> ing familiar categories to the text or to the work. Those
> rules and categories are what the work of art itself is look-
> ing for. The artist and the writer, then, are working with-
> out rules in order to formulate what *will have been done.*
>
> —Jean-François Lyotard, *The Postmodern Condition*

Lyotard's definition of the postmodern has the virtue of isolating what
is often considered to be most fundamental to postmodern art and literature: its questioning of the limits of representation by focusing attention on what is "unpresentable" in representation. Since notions of
the subject and of subjectivity have been tied to particular forms of
representation at least since Descartes, it makes sense that as an emerging
critical term, "postmodernism" should also designate the questioning
and even radical dissolution of the individual subject as it too has been
generally represented since the Renaissance. Of course, the term is not
always or even often used in this specific sense. Just as concepts like
the "subject" or "representation" are frequently employed in a variety of
ways, with their meanings shifting from context to context, so "postmodernism" has also been variously employed to denote the present technological, postindustrial era, the new artistic period style succeeding
modernism, and even the contemporary cultural paradigm or *epistēmē*.
In the more restricted domain of literary history, the term has been used
increasingly to refer to the radically disjunctive, antirealistic and later
explicitly "textual" writing that began to appear in the 1950s and early
1960s and which continues to appear to the present day.

In previous chapters, I have indicated how *The Recognitions* participates in this emergent postmodernism by giving free play to forces working within or underneath representation that are not reducible to its logic and that visibly destabilize both the writing and written subject, the author as transcendent unity as well as his fictive creations. However, to insert *The Recognitions* and Gaddis's subsequent novels more fully into the postmodern context, as I now wish to do, it will not be necessary to arm myself with a full-scale or complete definition of postmodernism, especially since this would require a rather detailed account of the term's ongoing evolution since its first appearance.¹ Rather, the importance of postmodernism here is that it urges us to go beyond such features as "loss of self," black humor, widespread parody, and self-reflexivity, which would all be important in situating *The Recognitions* in its historical context, toward an attempt to define the putatively more fundamental reconfiguration of which they would be the visible herald or surface manifestation. Since these features signal a hemorrhaging of credibility with regard to traditional literary representation and the kind of centered subjectivity it entails, they may also mark the site where heretofore "un-presentable" differences might be seen to emerge. If postmodernism does indeed constitute a rupture with the modernist epistēmē and its foundations in "analytico-referential" discourse, these are the signs by which we might expect to recognize its appearance in contemporary fiction.²

The Break with Mimesis in American Fiction

Though stylistically varied, much of the writing of the 1950s and 1960s bears testimony to and sometimes even accepts the instability or fragmentation of what was usually called the "self." The first literary critic to explore this tendency in detail was Wylie Sypher, in a study called *Loss of Self in Modern Literature and Art* published in 1962. Sypher employs the word "modern" rather than "postmodern," but his examples (Beckett, the Beats, the *nouveau roman*) and his general frame of reference (Heidegger, modern science and art, non-Aristotelian logic) indicate that he is primarily concerned with works that no longer fit within the modernist paradigm. Nowhere is this clearer than in his last chapter, bearing the symptomatic title, "The Anonymous Self: A Defensive Humanism." Surveying the nihilism, despair, and meaningless absurdity of 1950s art as exemplified in the work of Beckett, Ionesco, and Dubuffet, Sypher nevertheless clings stubbornly to an admittedly no longer vital humanist perspective within which the "self," having been stripped of its creative powers in the new totalitarian, technological era, is reduced to a fragile subjectivity now only capable of acknowleging its complete alienation. In this tenuous affirmation, moreover, Sypher was only following the pattern evident in American writers of his own generation, writers like Saul Bellow, J. D. Salinger, Norman Mailer, Bernard Malamud (especially in *The Assistant*), and Lionel Trilling, who all found in "neo-realistic" narrative forms an adequate vehicle for their explorations of an existential crisis of the self in post–World War II America.[3]

Significantly, Sypher found support for his "defensive humanism" in the writings of Sartre and Camus. But if these French philosopher-novelists butted against meaninglessness and absurdity as the limit and condition of individual human experience, their successors, the structuralists, might be said to have found in "nonsense" a creative principle, insofar as structuralism demonstrates that "meaning" does not originate in the individual's intentional act but is always produced out of nonsense and its perpetual displacement in a preexistent and underlying system or structure.[4] Similarly, in the early 1960s, a new generation of American writers led by Heller, Nabokov, Barth, and Pynchon found in absurdity and black humor a new creative principle. By decentering characters in relation to fictional and historical structures within which the individual was a continually displaced position (rather than a substantial entity), these writers began to move away from the mimetic and humanist assumptions that had governed the traditional novel since its inception. One clear indication of the change is that "character" in their novels most often appears as a mask or persona in a textual theater of repetitions and displacements. In Heller's *Catch-22*, for example, the characters are defined completely in relation to the structure of "paper fictions" generated by the military bureacracy and have no existence outside it. In this sense, "Sweden" is both a utopian realm of escape and the novel's tenuous reference to an "outside" or unstructured exteriority. Nabokov's *Lolita* reveals a more complex relational structure in the series of masks composed of John Ray–Humbert Humbert–Clare Quilty– "Nabokov" (this last entry referring to the author's self-referential appearance in the afterword). In relation to this series, Lolita is both the only "real" character (in the older sense) and the most explicit occasion for textual play as the sublimation of erotic desire. In Barth's *The Sot-Weed Factor* and Pynchon's

V., this type of serial structure composed of characters-as-masks is carried to even more complex elaborations, since it is articulated onto the fabric of history in a series of narrativized historical fictions. Thus, Burlingame's various "disguises" or Stencil's "impersonations" are not simply parodic mirrorings of the novelist as historian but also draw attention to the way in which every history is a construction embedded in and relying upon the fiction-making process.

The recognizable break with realistic fiction initiated by the Byzantine, picaresque plots and obviously fictive personae of the historical parody novel was even more pronounced in the surreal and fragmentary fiction published at this time by Hawks and Burroughs, where the "reality" of the characters was defined in terms of entropic, disintegrating landscapes constructed out of memory, dream, and hallucination, and language, as much as anything else, was the real subject. Hawks has gone as far as to say that when he started writing he thought of plot and character as the "enemy"; for Burroughs, it was "the word" itself, approachable only in writing conceived as a recording of mental processes produced through his cut-up, fold-in textual manipulations.[5] In their fractured and nightmarish fictions, not only were mimetic assumptions rejected, but the disordering and irrational forces of primary or unconscious processes began to assume a constitutive role in the generation of the literary text.

Overall, then, the "postmodernist breakthrough"—if indeed we can speak about it as such—seems to have necessitated the complete abandonment of humanism, not so much as a collection of abstract notions about "man" as a specific set of assumptions about what governed the production and structure (and therefore meaning, value, and function) of a literary work. In short, the fictional structures adumbrated in these novels of the late 1950s and early 1960s are no longer intelligible as individual structures of intentional "meaning" articulated within a descriptive representation of social reality; if anything, they embed themselves within the more anonymous structures—or within what has come to be conceived as the endless "text"—of culture, language, and the unconscious.

To be sure, such structures were first revealed in modernist explorations. As Freud showed in his case study of Dora, Dora elaborates her own role and repeats her love for her father only in relation to the roles assumed by those around her (K, Madame K, the governess), and the roles that she herself assumes in relation to these others. Yet Freud can only view this kind of decentered structure negatively, since it becomes visible only in and through the symptomology of hysteria. For modern novelists like Joyce, Woolf, Lawrence, or Mann, this kind of splintering of the ego into diverse roles led toward or was part of the apprehension of a mythic and more integrated self. While it may have been true that character as defined in modernist fiction often tends to dissolve into a "stream of atomized experiences, a kind of novelistic *pointillism,*" as Irving Howe describes it, the modern novelist's intention was always to create a newly complex, centered consciousness, open to new modes of being and perception.[6] Thus, even when the modernists intended to expand notions of individual identity to include larger frames of reference which were mythic or archetypal, they never questioned the idea or desirability of identity itself.

The passage from this modernist conception of an expanded individual identity to the postmodernist one of a decentered structure in which the individual is only a locus of transindividual singularities and intensities would seem therefore to involve an acceptance of fragmentation and dissolution of ego boundaries, or at least a more positive exploration of what were formerly taken to be signs of personality breakdown and even schizophrenia.[7] However, to state the case so baldly implies an illusionary or fictional view of the "self," as if it could be abstracted from the structures which make it possible. But as we saw in Chapter Three, no such subject is conceivable outside a structured system of articulations, and this is certainly the assumption of the novels cited above. Yet, undeniably, among many contemporary novelists there is a noticeable tendency at the level of representation to want to get at least one character out of this system, even at the price of his or her sanity or identity. In this perspective, Wyatt's dissolution and disappearance in *The Recognitions* may be taken as a paradigmatic instance which is repeated in countless other examples of postmodern American fiction.[8]

If we ask ourselves what kind of "world" such a structure supports or gives rise to and from which such characters desire to escape, we begin to see why the term "black humor," though never sharply defined, gained such rapid and widespread appeal in the early 1960s, when reviewers, critics, and novelists alike began describing the new fiction and sensibility. For whether the term was used to denote a specific tonal range or stylistic effect, it always implied a certain state of the world, a world gone awry and arbitrary, somehow out of control and proliferating with absurdities

to the point where it no longer seemed susceptible to rational understanding or even manageable within a humanist framework. Thus, it was
quickly agreed that black humor was "beyond satire," since the latter
assumed or depended upon stable, shared values and at least the possibility of social rectification. Many writers like Bruce Jay Friedman (in
the Introduction to his anthology *Black Humor*) emphasized that black
humor had something to do with the "fading line between fantasy and
reality" in modern life, and it is significant that the most telling examples
were drawn from the newspapers and television. Friedman himself goes
as far as to assert that *The New York Times* "is the source and fountain
and bible of black humor."[9] Similarly, Philip Roth zeroes in on the mass
media in his essay "Writing American Fiction," published in 1961. Roth
relates how the newspaper reportage of the murder of two girls in Chicago explodes into a three-ring circus of absurdly burgeoning "media
events," as the victims' mother, the accused, and his mother all become
celebrities in a manner that quickly exceeded the novelist's own standards
of verisimilitude. Roth's point is that the novelist's more modest inventions can hardly compete in an age in which everyday American reality
constantly surpasses "credibility" and even presidential candidates are
"believable" only in literary terms, as caricatures and satirical types.[10] In
fact, it is precisely this discrepancy that will push writers to such extremes
of Menippean satire as Robert Coover's *The Public Burning*, in which
Richard Nixon appears as a delirious narrator and major character.

The need to situate the move toward greater self-referentiality in postmodern fiction within this new historical context of the mass media's
power to define "reality" would therefore seem inevitable. For if "experience" in the contemporary world presents itself to the novelist as
either "unrepresentable" because always already mediated by too many
"fictions" of one sort or another, what could seem more logical than an
increased self-referentiality within fiction itself, which would now differ
from the world of "real" experience precisely by proclaiming or laying
bare its own artifice and "constructed" nature. In fact, self-reflexivity
in postmodern fiction almost always functions politically, as a refusal
of two kinds of complicity: first, with a certain *image* of society that
novelistic representation automatically conveys by not admitting chaos,
disorder, fragmentation, and dislocation except within the larger, ra-
tionalized frame of novelistic conventions; and second, with an *image* of
language as a transparent signifying system adequate to or commensurate

with the expression of the needs and desires of unified subjects. In an era that witnessed the complete erosion of credibility and coherence in official discourse and the multiplication of differences within and among subjects, self-reflexivity indeed appeared necessary if the novel was to establish its own credibility and claim of relevance.

If modernist self-referentiality served primarily as a means of defining the artwork through spatial form or a purely formal type of closure (the work as autotelic artifact or "well-wrought urn"), postmodern self-reflexivity operates either negatively, as in Sartre's example of the "anti-novel," or critically, as ironic de-definition or self-deconstruction. Pursuing this line of thinking, some critics have therefore defined postmodernism as a move beyond modernist skepticism to a full-fledged ontological and epistemological doubt about language's capacity to signify the real.[11] For the novelists themselves, however, this doubt has obviously not been a cause for despair but a justification for taking full advantage of the dissolving boundaries between the fictional and the real in a new mode of writing usually designated as "fabulation."[12] Fabulation may be defined as a narrative strategy or means of storytelling that does not anchor itself in a transcription of social reality that would guarantee its "truth," but instead refers to another narrative authority or version of events which in turn refers to yet another source. Thus, in a series of nested narratives or embedded versions of events, a whole set of fictions is put into play, and credibility, probability, and the value of a particular fiction—rather than "truth" itself—define what is at stake. Since it does not rely upon mimesis (and therefore the distinction between the fictional and the real) as its primary end and justification, fabulation quickly became a means by which writers could engage with issues in a context in which "events" as represented by the mass media were automatically phantasmatic, and public space became more and more populated with simulacra which could not be discredited by reference to any widely agreed upon or certifiable notion of "reality."

In this perspective, the widespread and intensive use of parody encountered in the emergent postmodern fiction of the 1950s and early 1960s does not simply concern literary precincts alone, since it prefigures this disturbance in the relation of language to reality as a whole. While local parody operates on a clearly delimited segment of the literary surface (as in Joyce's specific parodies in *Ulysses*), widespread or generalized parody (as in Nabokov's *Lolita* and *Pale Fire*) begins to suggest that every representation is only a highly artificial construction whose relationship to actuality may be *only* parodic, or constitute a kind of linguistic "counterfeit." As both fictional strategy and theme, the counterfeit could thus be said to operate as a hinge between the expanded mimetic impulses of modernist fiction and what will later be called postmodernist "textualization."

As we have seen, *The Recognitions* not only stands at this turning point but enacts this very transformation. In fully working out the tendency of widespread parody to give way to "disguised quotation" and textual counterfeiting at several levels, Gaddis's novel participates in a shift in imaginative mode that we now take to be an essential sign of postmodern fiction. In his study *The Counterfeiters,* Hugh Kenner tried to pinpoint this shift in similar terms: "Nearly fifty years after *Ulysses,* juxtaposition has wholly given way to counterfeiting, in a world of image-duplicators; parody to quotation, in a world of nonfictional fiction; classicizing to eclectic connoisseurship, in a world that has turned into one huge *musée sans murs.*"[33] For Kenner, who does not seem to have read Gaddis, Beckett and Warhol have the same signal value for contemporary culture as Pound, Eliot, and Joyce had for the modernist culture of fifty years ago. Kenner deftly demonstrates how our current technological power to construct or synthesize automated processes (the computer as a simulation of the brain) ultimately derives from the culture's obsessive working out of empirical and rational imperatives, which in turn calls out for satirical countermeasures. However, rather than pursue connections between the present highly technological culture and the postmodern artistic strategies of counterfeiting, "phosphorescent quotation," and eclectic connoisseurship, he is distracted by affinities with the English satirists of the eighteenth century (1690–1740) and fails to theorize the mutation from modernism to postmodernism to which he so elegantly draws our attention.

Like many American literary critics writing in the 1960s, Kenner sensed profound cultural changes underway that he could not or did not care to theorize. And although much has been written about postmodernism since then, there is still very little consensus—apart from the general feeling that modernism is now receding into the past—about how it should be defined and analyzed. In this respect, it is significant that while postmodernism as an evolving literary term has been current since the 1960s, as a term designating a larger shift in the arts and Western culture as a whole, it began to be frequently used only *after* or in conjunction with the discussion of new ideas deriving from structualist and poststructuralist theory in the 1970s and 1980s.[14] This point is important for my contention that it is only from within the current postmodern context that we can really begin to read *The Recognitions,* as well as understand why the novel remained largely unrecognized for over twenty years. While Gaddis's first novel manifests the same configuration of features evident in the 1950s and 1960s fiction briefly remarked upon above, it also turns or tropes upon the counterfeit motif in a way that could only assume full significance retroactively, that is, after postmodernism had become a theoretical template for perceiving cultural change. But the inverse may also be true: *The Recognitions* can direct our attention toward what is or should be of signal importance for any theory of postmodernism.

The Recognitions and Postmodern Theory

Let us begin with the premise that there may be a structural or intrinsic reason for much of the current confusion and disagreement about postmodernism. Lyotard, for example, in the passage cited earlier, calls the postmodern that within the modern that cannot be presented: "Postmodernism thus understood is not modernism at its end but in the nascent state, and this state is constant."[15] In these terms, the relationship between modernism and postmodernism would be neither one of continuity, stable opposition, nor paradigm shift (as would be the case in some kind of period break or historical *coupure*). Perhaps postmodernism may be even better conceived as an instance of *Nachträglichkeit:* it comes after modernism in the sense of a belated supplement that reactivates elements of modernism which, in the institutionalization of the latter, have been excluded, repressed, or marginalized.[16] As both an artistic and critical enterprise, therefore, postmodernism demands a reordering and reassessment of modernism, and especially of the latter's claim "to make it new." The experience of *Nachträglichkeit,* of deferred and retroactive action, entails a very different sense of temporality and precludes the possibility of "originating" an event or even understanding it in the self-contained moment of its occurrence. If modernist art privileges the ecstatic fullness of a visionary moment or frames the present against the mythic time of archetypal recurrence, postmodernist art moves toward the decentered repetitions of an endless temporality, as in Beckett's fiction, or the multiplicity of bifurcating virtual times, as in Borges's story "The Garden of Forking Paths."

Another way to formulate this difference in the postmodern literary configuration is to say that postmodern works must create not only their own precursors, as Borges said of Kafka, but also the conditions to which they are in some way a response. That is, these conditions are no longer simply "given" as part of some new experience the artist seeks to render "firsthand." Rather, what he or she confronts is a preselected set of representations that give rise to problems in and of themselves; in other words, postmodernist works depart from a set of cultural representations which they must assume and critique even as they reframe or (re)produce them. (Hence, the importance of pop art as the first sign of postmodernism in the visual arts.) Of course, every representation does this to some extent: every visual representation restructures the visual field in relation to prior representations; every written text is a rewriting of prior written texts. But in postmodernist works, this operation is explicitly foregrounded or thematized, so that prior representations, rather than "lived experience," become the primary material focus, and the "work" itself consists of this continual process of restructuration. The necessity of *Nachträglichkeit*—of deferred action—thus applies not so much to the new contents of experience as it does to the form(s) in which it occurs.

The Recognitions is an exemplary case in point. As a Janus-faced novel standing at the threshold of the postmodern reconfiguration, it reactivates the Faust myth, but not as a centering archetype of Western experience operating according to the modernist "mythic method"; instead, it functions as a desedimented element in a series of textual decenterings and displacements that allows an unrepresentable "difference" to emerge and resonate with other "differences" in other series.[17] More profoundly, *The Recognitions* points to what can now be postulated as the most important conceptual shift underlying the postmodern reconfiguration: the reversal of the Platonic heritage and the counter assertion of the logic of the simulacrum. As we have seen, this reversal resonates through the novel as a special kind of "event" in the Deleuzian sense, a phantasm-event that completely escapes the logic of representation and liberates "difference" as a pure intensity. And it is precisely in this production of textual singularities that the novel presents the "unpresentable," as Lyotard calls it, and thus articulates the postmodern within the modern.

In these terms, Gaddis's *The Recognitions* can legitimately lay claim to being the first American "postmodern" novel. But perhaps more important, it suggests that "the postmodern condition" may be described more specifically as a situation in which "originals" no longer automatically assume primacy over copies, or a model over its image.[18] In an environment defined more and more by the new information technologies of consumer society, we have become increasingly aware of how difficult it is to separate the meaning and effect of a current "event" from its "reportage" or representation and of how the contemporary world is saturated with "copies" without originals, grafts and replications which cannot be reduced to a point of origin or explained by their source. The "reversal" of the Platonic paradigm begins however when we give up the search for the "truth" beneath appearances or the "real" before its distorting appropriation, transmission, and/or re-presentation, and attempt to think the relationship between original and copy, model and image, in a new way.

One such way follows from the Nietzschean attempt taken up by the French poststructuralist philosophers to complete the overturning of the Platonic heritage based on relations of identity and similitude. Above all, this means thinking through the logic of the simulacrum, since it is precisely the simulacrum—as understood in the anti-Platonic sense—that most directly calls into question the hegemony of representation by reversing the latter's degradation of difference. As Deleuze clearly demonstrates, by giving ontological priority to identity, representation necessarily summits difference to the "quadruple links" of a mediation by which it is effectually repressed and degraded or reduced to contradictory, negative status, as in Hegelian philsophy.[19] Now it is precisely this lost and reduced "difference" —variously conceptualized by Jacques Derrida, Jean Baudrillard, and many feminist writers, in addition to Deleuze himself—that defines what is at stake today in contemporary poststructuralist writing: it is what they all seek to reinstate and affirm in positive terms.[20] However differently they define their theoretical projects, these poststructuralist thinkers all take this anti-Platonic "difference" to be primary, both ontologically and politically. Indeed, its current theorization may very well mark the final overthrow of Platonism initiated by Nietzsche and inaugurate the full conceptualization of the postmodern era.

Taking up the Heideggerian theme of ontological difference, Jacques

Derrida has initiated a new theorization of writing itself (*écriture*) as a simulacrum. That is, writing does not re-present a speech whose "originating" presence in the thought or consciousness of a speaker would be the guarantee of its transcendent meaning; instead, writing is conceived as a differential structure of traces without origin in which spacing (and therefore deferral and divergence, the two meanings of *différence* in French) is demonstrated to be the condition for the assertion of any meaning whatsoever. Derrida invents the neologism or graphic sign *différance* (distinguishable only on the page from the French word *différence*) to show that meaning is never fully present in a representational system but only results from the constant interplay of differential signifiers. As the difference of difference, "differance" is neither a word nor a concept but a simulacrum-concept. In fact, in order to show how such essentially "undecidable" terms as *pharmakon,* "supplement," or "hymen" operate in the respective texts of Plato, Rousseau, and Mallarmé, Derrida must invent a whole series of such simulacrum-concepts—"trace," "gram," "archi-trace"—which allow him to sketch out "on another scene" (the scene of writing) the movement by which a text comes into being and can never remain identical to itself.[21] Although Derrida's deconstructive method of reading has no doubt had its greatest impact on contemporary literary theory and philosophy, it also corresponds to an important strand of postmodern writing that operates directly at the level of language as a graphic signifying system, as in various fictional works by Walter Abish, Raymond Federman, Ronald Sukenick, Steve Katz, and others.

Jean Baudrillard, on the other hand, pushes much further in the direction taken earlier by Hugh Kenner (both, incidentally, were strongly influenced by Marshall McLuhan). In a postmodern perspective, Baudrillard might be said to have literalized the reversal of Platonism, since for him the "real" is simply what can be constructed in order to guarantee the authenticity of our representations, or rather our "simulations." Baudrillard argues that we have passed from an order based on the production of identical objects according to a model of resemblance to a free-floating order of "simulacra" (copies without originals) in which codes at another level generate structural differences in an indeterminate and aleatory process. What, for example, is the exact relationship of the genetic code in DNA to the life substance it somehow informs? The essence of Baudrillard's theory can be quickly grasped by considering his postulation of four successive stages of the image:

it is the reflection of a basic reality
it masks and perverts a basic reality
it masks the absence of a basic reality
it bears no relation to any reality (it is a pure simulacrum)[22]

In this last stage, the image (or simulacrum) no longer points back to a referent that would guarantee its intelligibility. Instead, it operates in a system of coded differences that play on an earlier system which now provides a kind of fantom referential domain. For example, in his early work, Baudrillard showed that the value of mass-produced consumer objects had nothing to do with their material reality but derived from a sign system in which referential values (like status) function only as structural differences. And the same is true of theory itself: in current theoretical discourse the Marxist political revolution or the Freudian unconscious provides only a pseudoreferential domain for theories that "float" like currency on the world market and assume value only in relation to other theoretical discourses.

Baudrillard takes Disneyland as a revelation of our current entangled orders of simulation. Its simulacra and phantasms—the Pirates, the Frontier, Future World—no doubt function ideologically, as "a digest of the American way of life, a panegyric to American values, [an] idealized tranposition of a contradictory reality" (24). But it also conceals the fact that America itself is the *real* Disneyland, just as modern prisons conceal the fact that the social fabric itself, in its "banal omnipresence," has become carceral: "Disneyland is presented as an imaginary order in order to make us believe that the rest is real, when in fact all of Los Angeles and the America surrounding it are no longer real, but of the order of the hyperreal and of simulation. It is no longer a question of a false representation of reality (ideology), but of concealing the fact that the real is no longer real, and thus of saving the reality principle" (25). This last stage of the image, in which conventional representation is everywhere engulfed by simulation—for Baudrillard, the state of contemporary American culture—operates according to a logic of "hyperreality" which seeks to make everything "more real than the real." Photorealist artwork, in which the painter appears to copy a photograph in order to reproduce some aspect of our objective world with meticulous accuracy, conveys the eery sense of hyperreality that Baudrillard seeks to describe. Although his theory takes off from the same point (the reversal of Platonism) upon which *The Recognitions* turns, it obviously goes far beyond the kind of simulation found in Gaddis's novel. Its primary usefulness in the post-modern literary context lies in the way it illuminates the hyperrealist and neosurrealist fiction of the 1980s represented by such writers as Frederick Barthelme, Steve Erickson, William Gibson, and Ted Mooney.

In the theory of Gilles Deleuze, on the other hand, there can be no neo-Hegelian succession of self-contained stages of the image (or of representation), as Baudrillard proposes; such schemes only serve to perpetuate the illusion of an earlier and less mediated (or fictionalized) social arrangement. In contrast to the sense of "reality loss" that animates Baudrillard's work, Deleuze's recent work argues that the "real" is always construed according to the way in which the flux of "desire" is produced, channeled, and coded in a specific type of social field. More specifically, "desire" is governed by different "semiotic regimes" that operate in conjunction with various material or nondiscursive arrangements—a specifically defined territory, a set of tools or technologies, the possible ways that bodies can interact.[23] For Deleuze, literature therefore is less a representation than a mapping of how desire operates in a specific social configuration. Of greatest interest is writing that is "rhizomatic" and which escapes those structures of desire that only reflect the hierarchical, bipolar organization of repressive social structures. In fact, it is only in the pursuit of the rhizomatic wanderings of desire that the writer is able to invent a verbal assemblage (*agencement*) out of the assemblages which created him or her.[24] In this extension of Bergson's concept of multiplicity to new arrangements between words and things, Deleuze's work provides a philosophic parallel to the large and excessive novels of information overload and rhizomatic proliferation published in the 1970s and which were prefigured in many ways by Gaddis's *The Recognitions*. Not surprisingly, then, this strand of postmodern fiction—exemplified most conspicuously by Thomas Pynchon's *Gravity's Rainbow,* Joseph McElroy's *Lookout Cartridge,* and Don DeLillo's *Ratner's Star*—would also include Gaddis's later novels *JR* and *Carpenter's Gothic.* These last two novels function more explicitly as postmodern fictions than *The Recognitions,* which to a large extent is still constrained by the exigencies of representation. I want to conclude therefore with a more detailed account of the terms in which these later novels must be read.

JR: Deterritorialized Speech and the Flux of Capital

If *The Recognitions* plays out and ultimately subverts the copy/counterfeit opposition in its articulation of the logic of the simulacrum, it is not surprising that Gaddis's second novel *JR,* published in 1975, should seek to discover new fictional terms, terms that are appropriate, as one perceptive reader of Gaddis has put it, to an age of "credit and credibility" rather than of belief.[25] The new terms point not to another "novel as simulacrum" but to the novel as "paper empire." This phrase compactly describes both the novel *JR* and its central subject, which is the meteoric growth and collapse of a financial holding company, the JR Family of Companies, headed by a tenaciously greedy eleven-year-old who simply follows the instructions of his elders after his sixth-grade class visits a Wall Street investment firm. The crucial point of the novel, however, is *not* that the JR Family of Companies is a mere paper empire, or a simulacrum mimicking those sturdier, more serious firms that populate Wall Street and of which Governor Cates's investment firm is both prime example and JR's "model." This kind of opposition no longer holds, in the sense that the difference between JR's company and Cates's is not a generative one for the novel, as is the difference between copy and simulacrum in *The Recognitions.* Rather, what is at stake in *JR* manifests itself first as a formal or even technical problem: how is the chaos and flux produced by the paper empires of contemporary finance to be rendered in a prose fiction novel, which is, of course, both another kind of paper empire and its antithesis?

First of all, in order to portray the dizzying effects of Wall Street machinations and the disorders of a purely commercial culture on the novel's characters, Gaddis completely dispenses with narrative and plunges the reader into a postmodern "novelistic space" composed almost entirely of fragmented conversations, interrupted mutterings and stammerings, delirious harangues and jargoned doublespeak. In fact, since the medium of the novel is almost totally reduced to recorded speech, the result might be more accurately designated as a transcribed acoustic collage. That is, the novel collages the discourses of advertising, big business, politics, and public relations, the slang of school kids and street people, the ruminations of drunken intellectual and failed artists, the bitter reproaches of divorcing couples and lovers in turmoil, thereby making these registered "sounds" barely distinguishable from the general background noise of our multimedia environment.[26]

With broken, fragmented speech serving as the novel's primary compositional element, its de-narrativized structure can strive for an almost seamless montage effect. As one reader has noted, all is flow—money, finance capital, video images, water, conversation, a radio playing, one scene or character impinging on another.[27] But in thus seeking to render the flux and flow of contemporary life, *JR* takes great risks, both in its method and "message(s)." As we are whirled from one node of connection to another—from an old family house in Long Island to a local school, then to the local bank, then to a Wall Street investment firm, and finally to an upper Eastside apartment—it becomes clear that no overriding, stabilizing speech will be heard, indeed *could* be heard, since no identifiable consciousness could be in control or take it all in. For the novel relentlessly demonstrates that it is not production or intelligible purpose but the ceaseless movement and proliferation of useless information and objects that define our world.

Unlike *The Recognitions,* then, *JR* makes no attempt to maintain even the outward conventions of the traditional novel. To be sure, there are characters caught up in events whose actions and responses we take an interest in and begin to follow. But this is made exceedingly difficult by the novel's manner of presentation. Not only has the ostensible author disappeared, but so have even the minimal authorial functions: speakers are usually not identified except by "tics" and idiosyncrasies of speech; shifts from one scene to another are only indicated briefly in lyrical and oblique ways. Furthermore, both time and sequences of action must always be inferred by the reader, with no chapter breaks to help. As a consequence, *JR* often exceeds even the most difficult and recalcitrant of modernist fiction in its demands on the reader. But while it is true that the reader must learn to identify voices, (re)construct fictional situations and supply some meaningful context simply in order to "read" the novel, he or she soon discovers significant patterns of coherence. But with one "structuralist" qualification: in this elaborately self-coded "open work" that teaches the reader how to read it, form and content, order and disorder, discourse and reality can only be defined in relation to one another.

In an early scene set in a Long Island school, the science teacher Jack Gibbs is lecturing to the kids on the concept of entropy:

—All right let's have order here, order . . . ! he'd reached the [television] set himself and snapped it into darkness.—Put on the lights there now. Before we go any further here, has it ever occurred to any of you that all this is simply one grand misunderstanding? Since you're not here to learn anything, but to be taught so you can pass these tests, knowledge has to be organized so it can be taught, and it has to be reduced to information so it can be organized do you follow that? In other words this leads you to assume that organization is an inherent property of the knowledge itself, and that disorder and chaos are simply irrelevant forces that threaten it from outside. In fact it's exactly the opposite. Order is simply a thin, perilous condition we try to impose on the basic reality of chaos . . . ."[28]

These assertions suggest, of course, that the processes of reading and writing—classroom activities usually displaced at this school by "video instruction"—should also be construed as "perilous condition[s] we try to impose on the basic reality of chaos." Gibbs's later references to Norbert Wiener and information theory pick up this central thematic concern, but it is his delirious speech that most effectively emphasizes how human communication itself is the most fragile attempt to impose order:

read Wiener on communication, more complicated the message more God damned chance for errors, take a few years of marriage such a God damned complex of messages going both ways can't get a God damned thing across, God damned much entropy going on say good morning she's got a God damned headache thinks you don't give a God damn how she feels, ask her how she feels she thinks you just want to get laid, try that she says it's the only God damn thing you take seriously about her puts you out of business and goes running around like the God damned Israelis waving the top half of the double boiler have to tell everybody they're right. God damned Arabs mad as hell sitting there with the bottom half pretend you take them seriously only thing you want is their God damned oil . . . . (403)

As in the cocktail party chatter in *The Recognitions,* most of the dialogue in *JR* fails as communication, usually because the speakers talk at cross-purposes and can neither order their thoughts nor complete their sentences. Of course, many characters are simply mouthpieces of some type of professional or bureaucratic dysfunction. For example, the utterances of Mr. Whiteback, who is both the school principal *and* president of the local bank, always stall in jargoned redundancy: "—In terms of tangibilitating the full utilization potential of in-school television . . ." (39) is his inept attempt to justify the use of audiovisual equipment. But Whiteback's reliance upon bureaucratic jibberish, a tendency Gibbs will later parody (47), hardly conceals the fact that he and his cronies, which include a local congressional assemblyman, are using the school as a clearing house for "home ec" and other educational equipment for their own profit. In Whiteback's office, the telephones for both school and bank business "rant" incessantly, and usually there are three and four conversations going on simultaneously. To complicate matters further, exchanges between characters on the telephone are always literally one-sided, in the sense that only half of the conversation is reported. In this way, the reader is made intensely aware of the extent to which he or she is being forced to "fill-in" and make sense out of information that is partial, confused, and often highly redundant.

Reducing the authorial function to a recording apparatus also enables Gaddis to foreground the importance of the "communication model" in relation to novelistic forms. In the perspective of information theory, traditional novelistic conventions appear as forms of organization that only seem "inherent" to life (or to knowledge, as in Gibbs's assertion above). This naturalistic attitude appears not only naive but inadequate for the contemporary novelist who senses that the "information" in our own environment does not fit into and cannot be conveyed by these forms. A basic premise of information theory is that the more complex the message, the greater its improbability and the more work the receiver must do to decipher it. *JR* actualizes this assumption through its very manner of presentation, leaving it to the reader to discover meaning and significance within what is apparently only noise and redundancy. Consequently, as one critic has shown, reading the novel amounts to acting against "the entropy of the text, [by] tying together speech acts that, in terms of their direction and manner of presentation, tend to disperse, wander, dissipate, dwindle, disappear."[29]

This postmodern shift of the burden of textual coherence to the reader may require some justification. Even the sympathetic reader wants to know if there really is "a story" here that needs to be told in this manner and what will finally make the novel worth the time invested. Of course, this second question contains an implicit irony, since the novel itself is so directly concerned with the worth or value of information. In these terms, moreover, the black-humor vision *JR* projects is as much the inevitable result of reducing empirical realities—both human and otherwise—to "information that must be organized" as it is a matter of any specific content.[30] Nevertheless, one might begin to answer these questions by remarking that *JR* contains a multiplicity of *little* stories, some sad, some incredibly funny, some downright crazy. For the most part, these little stories have to do with the failure and wreckage of human lives, in obvious contrast to the amazing success of JR's financial enterprise. There are stories of lovers separating, families disintegrating, children being neglected, an artist driven to suicide. Not unexpectedly, venality and greed, madness and obsession define the characters, and their enterprisings are enlivened by a dark, satirical humor and air of desperate absurdity. One corporate executive is preoccupied with stocking American parks with game from Africa; another mismanages a sale of toy pistols, which are sent by mistake to an African tribe, with disasterous results. But inconspicuously set off against these stories are the activities of two serious characters, Jack Gibbs and Edward Bast, who elicit both interest and sympathy.

Gibbs, cynical and destitute after wasting most of his life, will snatch a few days of happiness in a lyrically brief love affair with Amy Joubert, a fellow part-time schoolteacher who is being coldly manipulated by her husband for custody of their son and by her uncle, Governor Cates, for her share in the family-owned investment firm. When Gibbs and Amy are pulled apart by forces beyond their control, Gibbs will try to give meaning to his life by completing a study begun sixteen years before of "mechanization and the arts, the destructive element." Unfortunately, he falls victim to the very same loss of energy and organization that he is attempting to analyze. Edward Bast, the novel's naive and romantic artist figure, provides a study in contrast. He is sentimentally obsessed with and thus easily duped by his cousin Stella, who though married, is willing to go to bed with him as part of her scheme to gain control of his shares in their family company. Penniless and unable to say no, Bast is subsequently sucked into the morass of "JR Corp" as JR's "Business Representative." In a chaos-ridden apartment on East 96th Street, Bast finally manages to finish the piece of music he is composing, only to see it become the unlikely and degraded score for a pornographic film.

Such ironies, both comic and catastrophic, inevitably raise the question of how we are to view the novel's achievement of a victory it denies its most serious characters. In a perceptive early review, George Stade, having characterized *JR* as a "chaos of disconnection, a blizzard of noise" and sketched several of its "epicenters of disorder," among them the East 96th Street apartment, has this to say:

> But if you stand back from the wild and whirling words to where you can see the novel as a structure, as a system of relations among its parts rather than as an assemblage of referents to what is outside it, you see something other

than the centrifugal forces of disruption at work. You see the equal if opposite
centripetal forces of recurrence, reflection and analogy, of interlocking motifs
and linked images, of buried puns and covert allusions, connecting the fragments. The esthetic order within the work is experienced as a compensation
of sorts for the disorder without to which it refers.[31]

Stade's assertion that the chaos of *JR*'s fragmented surface is held in check
and compensated for by an equal assertion of meaningful pattern amounts
essentially to reading the novel in modernist terms. No doubt *JR* will
often support such a reading: the introduction of Wagner's *Ring of the
Nibelungen* as intertexual analogy and motif early in the novel would be
one important instance of this aesthetic order. But a postmodern reading
might want to question this opposition, insofar as it predisposes us to
grasp aesthetic order as existing only *in* the novel, as something imposed
from without, rather than as a means of presentation elicited and even
discovered within the material itself. Following Bakhtin's argument (in
"Discourse in the Novel") that a tension between centripetal and centrifugal forces always exists within language itself, we might want to ask
what forces are acting on the language in *JR*.[32] The answer lies not in
the novel's artistry, which may even deflect our attention from the problem
toward a modernist "aesthetic" solution; if anywhere, we must look more
closely at the source of the chaos.

    JR opens with a conversation in which the elderly Bast sisters, Julia
and Anne, recall their first experience of paper money:

    —Money . . . ? in a voice that rustled.
    —Paper, yes.
    —And we'd never seen it. Paper money.
    —We never saw paper money till we came east.
    —It looked so strange the first time we saw it. Lifeless.
    —You couldn't believe it was worth a thing.
    —Not after Father jingling his change.
    —Those were silver dollars. (1)

In a certain sense, this moment stands "outside" the chaos which the
novel will soon register, not as a privileged origin or state of youthful,
prelapsarian happiness, but simply as the "time before" of another mode
of representation, both in the culture generally and for this novel in
particular. Yet even in this initial scene, we are not yet fully immersed
in the novel's present, for what is crucial is not the change from metal
to paper currency but rather the change from cash currency to the even

more abstract exchanges enabled by the extention of credit and the whole credit system.

The growth of JR's financial empire parodically illustrates what this evolutionary change makes possible. JR begins by scouring the mail order catalogues, collecting free samples and the penny stock his class invests in a Wall Street firm in a demonstration visit. His "break" comes when, working from a phone booth and disguising his adolescent voice with a "snot rag," he buys a large quantity of surplus picnic forks from the U.S. Navy on credit and then unloads them on the Army for a huge profit. He then acquires an assortment of bankrupt companies and near-worthless vested interests which include an upstate New England mill and brewery, a publishing house, a shipping line (its only vessel capsized), a chain of nursing homes and funeral parlors, pork bellies, sheep-gut condoms, plastic flowers—all of which, through tax write-offs and wheeling and dealing, he consolidates into a corporate "family of companies" that perilously threatens the stability of the stock market.

Though it does not really strain credibility, there is an unmistakably fabulous and parable-like quality to JR's story.[33] But what engages our interest is not so much *how* it all comes about as how well the novel conveys what one critic, adopting a term applied from information theory, calls a "run-away system."[34] Such a system extracts more and more from its environment without any equitable return ("the more you have, the more you get"); thus, in all likelihood, social or economic systems that are run-away finally result in social revolution or self-extinction. In this respect, the "run-away" system depicted in *JR* is strikingly similar to the technological and bureaucratic world order that Thomas Pynchon depicts in *Gravity's Rainbow,* which is also centrally concerned with the reduction of human reality to cybernetically codable "information." What is remarkable about *JR* is that it doesn't so much represent such a system in action as render it vividly present in the speech of its characters. Here is a sample of JR directing operations in a telephone call to Bast:

Bast? Listen I . . . no I know but . . . no I know but I was just coming to that where I was telling you where this here General Haight can help us out see this here Ray-X company it's getting screwed on all these dumb fixed-price contracts see where what we want is these here cost-plus ones where you get to . . . no I know it but . . . no but listen hey . . . No but look just let me tell you how it works okay? See you get this here contract to supply something to the government like and then you . . . how do I know, I mean just something

they want to buy off you like that's where this here General can help us out
see so what's neat about these cost-plus ones is you get to add this here percent
of how much it costs you to fill this here contract so I mean the more you
spend the more you get, see? I mean that's the whole . . . no well sure but . . .
No I know I was always yelling about low-cost operations see but . . . no but
listen a second hey I mean how do you think the telephone company works
where they're always yelling how they have to spend all this here money so
they need to raise the rates I mean the more money they can think of how to
spend it someplace they get to take this here percent where they keep raising
the rates till they're almost bigger than the gover . . . no but wait, see the . . .
No I know you don't I mean I'm just coming to that hey . . . no I know I said
that but I mean it won't take much longer see we just . . . no well I just mean
we like we the company, like not really anybody see so . . . No but see that's
the whole thing Bast see it's not money anyway it's just exchanging this here
stock around in like this merging it with this here X-L subsiderary which it's
worth like twenty times as much as, you know? See we just give these here
Ray-X stockholders one share of X-L's preferred for their share of Ray-X only
this here X-L's common stock capitalization is real low see so we have this
here tremendous leverage see and . . . no well I don't exactly either but that's
what this Mister Wiles said see he . . . No but . . . no I know but . . . . (465–466)

The "conversation" from which the above is excerpted—and it is not at
all untypical—runs on for almost five pages. Such passages make several
things clear at once. First, that there can be no adequate human response:
no dialogue is possible simply because this is not a human being talking,
but money itself. And second, it is not just the language of money but
the speech of money, the flux of capital as it enters into and becomes part
of verbal communication. Significantly, Bast will soon find himself speaking in a similar manner, as he becomes more and more deliriously en-
meshed in JR's schemes. In this way we see human speech itself taken
up and thoroughly "deterritorialized"—to borrow Gilles Deleuze and
Félix Guattari's useful term—as part of the capitalist exchange process.[35]

Like the speech which attempts to order and control it, finance capital
has a "life" of its own that exceeds all attempts to organize it for a
meaningful purpose: both speech and capital thus become part of the
same runaway system. For Governor Cates, at the helm of a "legitimate"
financial empire which is also threatening to go out of control, it's all a
game without rules in which you do what you can get away with. The
point is emphasized as several of his statements are picked up and then
repeated by JR: "—You can't just play to play because the rules are only
for if you're playing to win which that's the only rules there are" (301).

And later: "—Okay so with these here futures I'm not telling you to do something illegal see I'm telling you what I'm doing and you find out how to do it that's all" (470). To a certain extent, these "players" are as victimized by the system as are the less rich and powerful. Indeed, the cumulative evidence of the novel is that the profit motive has now attained such a hypertrophied state, feeding and being fed by the runaway and entropic system, that human love and goodness are literally no longer able to hold people together.

The victory the novel attains may now be described in somewhat different terms. What Gaddis has done is to take information theory and the communication model as the means by which the flux and disorder of finance capital can be made to pass into and take palpable form within a work of fiction. (In Deleuzian terms, he has created a novelistic assemblage.) Since the reduction of human reality in all its manifold complexity to the organization of information in communication theory is itself already a symptom of the furthest abstraction and deterritorialization of a language or sign system, such a strategy enables Gaddis to depict the destabilizing and entropic effects of capitalism at *its* point of greatest deterritorialization. The most extensive surface of contact between these two systems is, of course, human speech. Thus, by simply recording the speech acts of the characters in all their fluidity and flux, noise and redundancy, the novel has no difficulty showing that capitalism as an informational and communicational system has ceased to be either "economic" or "social" in the basic sense of these words. From this perspective, *JR* intends neither compensation nor redemption; it is simply a demonstration, in the most rigorous terms imaginable, of one aspect of the "postmodern condition" in which we now live.

Carpenter's Gothic: Gaddis's House of Fiction(s)

At first glance, Gaddis's third and most recent novel, *Carpenter's Gothic,* which appeared in 1984, looks like a highly wrought fragment of *JR,* a coda to its maelstrom, as it were—as if Gaddis had decided to treat in lingering detail one of the many domestic tragedies we only catch a glimpse of in *JR,* by focusing his attention on only one "epicenter of disorder" instead of several at once. Moreover, at least one of the central characters and several of the minor ones could easily have walked off the pages of *JR.* And, as in *JR,* the fractured surface of broken and delirious speech provides the novel's primary medium of presentation, although in *Carpenter's Gothic* the authorial "connecting passages" are more extended and less neutrally descriptive. Finally, questions raised about the futility and waste of contemporary life, about what is really "worth doing" provide thematic links with the previous novels. Yet, for all these similarities, the net effect of the novel is entirely different. In its maintenance of temporal and spatial unities, in its careful elaboration of poetic resonances relatively free of satiric deflation, in its manner of unraveling the patterns of expectation it so deftly articulates, *Carpenter's Gothic* projects a somber, tragic intensity.

The main outlines of the narrative situation are easily recounted. A couple, Paul and Elizabeth Booth, both about thirty-five, have rented an imitation Gothic-styled house above New York along the Hudson River. The husband is an energetic Vietnam veteran now trying desperately to make it as a publicity agent and media consultant for a Reverend Ude, a southern evangelist preacher who first attracted public attention when he accidentally drowned one of his parishioners during baptism, and who is now attempting to inaugurate a crusade against "evil powers" infiltrating the country. Paul's wife Elizabeth, a rather passive, red-haired beauty, is heiress to a trust set up, but also effectively tied up, by corporate interests after her father, owner of Vorakers Consolidated Reserve, a large mining company, committed suicide. Visitors to the house are few but crucial for what unfolds there. Most important are Elizabeth's brother Billy, whose unexpected and usually brief visits are indicative of his nomadic, hippie life-style, and Mr. McCandless, the mysterious owner of the house who becomes sexually involved with Elizabeth during one of Paul's frequent absences. It turns out that both Ude and Vorakers Consolidated Reserve are interested in the Great Rift Valley area in Africa: the one wants to build a mission for "harvesting souls," the other seeks a possibly rich mineral deposit; it also turns out that this particular stretch of land has been extensively surveyed by McCandless, a former geologist who knows its geopolitical history in exact and profuse detail.

But while such a sketch may begin to suggest how what happens at the house, which is where the author as recording apparatus stations the reader, is always intricated with events in the world "outside," it hardly conveys the extent to which they must be pieced together from bits of detail conveyed within the exchanges between characters, mostly in Paul's futile attempt to "see how all the God damn pieces fit together" or

McCandless's fulminations against the exploitative collusions and conspiracies of government and big business. In fact, the further we penetrate
into the novel, the more we learn about the characters and their situations,
but the less we understand of the plots—both in the sense of connected
events and conspiracies—that are wheeling just beyond our grasp. At the
same time, an inner logic of events seems to be developing that, as in a
traditional novel, will finally yield some meaningful pattern predicated
on the self-determined efforts of the characters to initiate change in their
lives.

The problem with the Booth's marriage is signaled early on. From the
minute Paul walks in the door, Liz (which is what he calls her) must
contend with the obvious fact that what he needs and what she is not
is a secretary:

> —Liz it was an hour, one solid God damn hour I couldn't reach you nobody
> could, that whole list I gave you? These calls I've been waiting for? State
> Department calling about this spade with his prisons and chicken factories
> did they call? And these pigs? Drug company bringing in these nutritionists
> for a look at these pigs did they call?[. . .] You're on the phone for an hour
> with Edie, somebody calls they get a busy . . . Liz I'm trying to get something
> going here, line up these clients tell them to check with my home office and
> you're talking to Edie.[36]

Paul also involves her in a scam to defraud an insurance company by
claiming that, as a result of an airplane crash, she is unable to perform
her "conjugal duties"; he continually harasses her about her brother and
misses no opportunity to intervene in family affairs in an attempt to
obtain access to the trust fund. Though callous and sometimes brutal,
Paul is less a monster, however, than a victim of the same world depicted
in *JR*.

Elizabeth's relationship with her husband is partly illuminated when
her brother Billy (he calls her Bibbs) accuses her of having always gone
with "these real inferior types" (90) in order to protect "a secret self":

> —Man like wait Bibbs, I mean wait! That's not what I, I mean it's like you've
> got this real secret self hidden someplace you don't want anybody to get near
> it, you don't even want them to know about it like you're afraid if some
> superior person shows up he'll like wipe you out so you protect it by these
> inferior types they're the only ones you'll let near you because they don't even
> know it's there. I mean they think they've taken over they never even like
> suspect you've always got the upper hand because that's your strength Bibbs,
> that's like how you survive [. . .] (193–194)

However, when McCandless—clearly a "superior person"—shows up (the rental agreement allows him access to a small room in the house where he stores old books and papers), Elizabeth is drawn immediately into a love affair with him that recalls the lyrical interlude Gibbs and Amy Joubert pass together in *JR*.

McCandless is older, worldly, knowledgeable about many things, and an ex-novelist. Many reviewers have taken him to be an author-surrogate, and with some reason. When an ominous intelligence agent named Lester comes seeking the survey data of the area in Africa mentioned above, the two fall into conversation about McCandless's first and only novel:

> —You looked better then, didn't you [Lester says]. Like this Frank Kinkead [the hero of the novel], that's what he's supposed to look like isn't it, this cool unwavering glance where he says from now on he's going to live deliberately? (139)

Here Gaddis the novelist may be subtly engaged in self-parody, since the words "to live deliberately" which Lester cites echo *verbatim* Wyatt's last words in *The Recognitions*. In the exchange that follows, however, McCandless's remarks appear to reflect more seriously upon the novel we are reading:

> —You saw how it ends.
> —I know how it ends. It doesn't end it just falls to pieces, it's mean and empty like everybody in it is that why you wrote it?
> —I told you why I wrote it, it's just an afterthought why are you so damned put out by it. This novel's just a footnote, a postscript, look for happy endings I come out mixed up with people like you and Klinger. (139)

Many other examples of this kind of self-reflexivity can be found, most notably in McCandless's conversations with Elizabeth (who is secretly writing a romantic novel).[37] The most apparently significant instance occurs when McCandless's remarks upon the construction of the house:

> —Oh the house yes, the house. It was built that way, yes, it was built to be seen from the outside it was, that was the style, he came on, abruptly rescued from uncertainty, raised to the surface—yes, they had style books, these country architects and the carpenters it was all derivative wasn't it, those grand Victorian mansions with their rooms and rooms and towering heights and cupolas and the marvelous intricate ironwork. The whole inspiration of medieval Gothic but these poor fellows didn't have it, the stonework and the wrought iron. All they had were the simple dependable old materials, the wood and their hammers and saws and their own clumsy ingenuity bringing those grandiose visions the old masters had left behind down to a human scale

with their own little inventions, those vertical darts coming down from the eaves? and that row of bull's eyes underneath? He was kicking leaves aside, gesturing, both arms raised embracing—a patchwork of conceits, borrowings, deceptions, the inside's a hodgepodge of good intentions like one last ridiculous effort at something worth doing even on this small a scale, because it's stood here, hasn't it, foolish inventions and all it's stood here for ninety years.... (227–228)

Again, the temptation to read these remarks as reflections on the novel we are reading and on the difficulties that afflict the postmodern novelist is nearly irresistible. Taken in this self-reflexive sense, they hint at a convergence between the problems confronting the writer and the problems the characters themselves must somehow resolve. Indeed, it is the recurrent problem in all of Gaddis's novels, the problem posed by despair itself: what is meaningfully worth doing in a world hell-bent on the destruction of all human values? In Elizabeth's final confrontation with McCandless, however, we hear a voice seeking to resist this despair; furthermore, in the complications which this confrontation entails for the novel, we witness something like the reemergence of a dialogic.

After spending an idyllic day and a half with Elizabeth, McCandless had left rather abruptly with Billy who once again passes unexpectedly on his way to New York. A week later, having heard nothing from him in the interval, Elizabeth returns from a morning in New York to discover McCandless there waiting for her in the house which has just been burglarized. McCandless soon reveals that he has come back to take her away "for good." But it has been a calamitous week and Elizabeth's feelings are no longer certain. One night, Paul had returned home with a serious knife wound inflicted by a mugger (or an assassin). In self-defense, Paul had killed the young black man, in what seems to have been a flashback in Paul's mind to an experience in Vietnam. Furthermore, it has become apparent that Paul's plans are falling apart as an already complicated situation grows out of his reach and understanding. It turns out that Ude is using him, or rather that Ude is being used by Grimes, the corporate head of Vorakers Consolidated Reserve, in a complicated scheme to force U.S. government intervention in Africa. What's more, when Senator Teakell, seemingly in collusion with Grimes—although his real interest is to sell Africans food and farm products, not mine their mineral resources—departs on a "fact-finding" mission to Africa, his plane is shot down. Though it is by no means clear who is responsible, the incident threatens to blow up into an international confrontation as the

United States prepares for a full-scale miltary intervention off the African coast. But the most devastating event for Elizabeth is that her brother Billy was aboard the senator's plane.

It is against this complex background of events that the final confrontation between Elizabeth and McCandless unfolds. Elizabeth blames McCandless for Billy's death, since it was his impassioned account of Western exploitation and wickedness in Africa that had set Billy in his determination to go there in order to find out what was going on. McCandless's motive, she says, was "to give him [Billy] some dumb kind of strength that wasn't real to try to destroy Paul" (242). Earlier, they had quarreled over the extent to which Paul had been set up and used. In the course of what becomes a complex, multitracked dialogue, Elizabeth begins to cast doubt on McCandless's previously convincing grasp of the situation. To McCandless's accusation that her husband is a killer, she retorts: "All your grand words about the truth and what really happened that don't mean anything because it was one of his own men that's the truth, that's what really happened. He was fragged. Do you know what that means?" To this new knowledge that Paul was not wounded in combat but the victim of an assassination attempt by one of his own men, McCandless can only respond: "It's madness then isn't it, it's just madness . . . " (240).

In her own faltering way, Elizabeth persistently argues for a more human meaning to events, or one which makes them more amenable to human responsibility. The most significant example occurs when she discovers that The Great Rift Valley in Africa—the area for which various interests are contending—may even be worthless, and that McCandless, who surveyed it earlier, knows this and refuses to do anything about it. His defense, he keeps repeating, is that no one will listen: "I told you, try to prove anything to them the clearer the proof and the harder they'll fight it, they . . . " (246). McCandless now simply wants to abandon the situation, with "madness coming one way and stupidity the other" (233), and take Elizabeth with him to South America. But in a further turn, Elizabeth detects another motive behind this refusal to intervene:

> —And it's why you've done nothing . . . She put down the glass,—to see them all go up like that smoke in the furnace all the stupid, ignorant, blown up in the clouds and there's nobody there, there's no rapture no anything just to see them wiped away for good it's really you, isn't it. That you're the one who

wants apocalypse, Armageddon all the sun going out and the sea turned to blood you can't wait no, you're the one who can't wait! The brimstone and fire and your Rift like the day it really happened because they, because you despise their, not their stupidity no, their hopes because you haven't any, because you haven't any left. (244)

For this reason, Elizabeth seems to have decided to stay with Paul, who, for whatever his faults, has not succumbed to this kind of despair. Yet we are not at all certain what she will finally decide, since McCandless suddenly agrees to do what he can to stop a possible war over the worthless strip of land in Africa, and hurries off to New York. But here, the drama ends abruptly, in an anguishing denial of any final resolution, for that very night Elizabeth is murdered, apparently struck by a burglar. The novel concludes in a blackly ironic denouement, as Paul, now in control of the family fortune, drives off with Elizabeth's childhood friend Edie.

As I have tried to show, in her confrontations with McCandless Elizabeth intimates that there is another logic to human events in addition to the public and historical one and, specifically, that McCandless's conspiratorial view of history is as much motivated by his own personal despair as it is by an apprehension of the way things really are. Without denying the calamitous nature of historical reality, she argues for a perspectival view, a view of the world that must include the participants. An unexpected visit from McCandless's wife, Elizabeth's last visitor before she is murdered, adds another twist to this view. When Mrs. McCandless alludes to a period when McCandless spent time in a hospital, possibly a mental hospital, and to his son Jack and to his experiences as a teacher, Elizabeth (and the reader) is suddenly forced to consider another facet of McCandless's identity. Surprisingly, Mrs. McCandless even hints that the version of McCandless's experiences in Africa and his earlier life that we have taken to be a factual account may be merely "stories" he made up. McCandless's credibility is not thereby destroyed, however, for his version of events in the novel (and the history with which it is imbricated) not only makes sense but would seem to compel at least a qualified assent; furthermore, his conversation with Lester, although centering on his own literal fictionalizing (and certain mysterious papers), would seem to bestow some authenticity on the account he provides of his earlier life.

Carpenter's Gothic thus concludes with a series of reversals and incongruent perspectives which do not cancel each other out but instead suggest a complex, dialogic interplay between different orders of fictional sense-making. In fact, the theme that much of life is a tissue of fictions is insistently present throughout the novel. We are often reminded that the newspapers and other media distort and misrepresent events and, even worse, "take a picture and make a story out of it." Moreover, the characters themselves are all guilty of making up at least a part of their lives. Paul maintains the fiction that his roots are genteel Southern stock when, in fact, he is an adopted Jew. Even Elizabeth lies to McCandless about her father's death. When he catches her out—he has seen the movie on which her lie is patterned—her simple response is that "when people stop lying you know they've stopped caring" (226). Looking back through the novel, we cannot help but be struck by the number and diversity of fictions interwoven into its texture. Elizabeth and Paul converse by means of little fictions—a telescope on a star that will allow you to look back at your past, the story that children choose their parents just so they can be born, the belief of the African Masai that all the cattle in the world belong to them—"a good serviceable fiction," (121) McCandless remarks. Bible stories, the adventure stories Elizabeth's father read her and which she later realizes are all about himself, novels by Faulkner and Conrad, in fact everything in their conversation turns on one "fiction" or another. Added to which McCandless fulminates deliriously against the "cheap entertainment, anything to fill the emptiness any invention to make them part of some grand design anything, the more absurd the better" (144), while also acknowledging the human necessity of "any lunatic fiction to get through the night and the more far-fetched the better, any evasion of the one thing that's inevitable" (157). But what upsets him most are "the desperate fictions like the immortal soul" (157). Evangelists like the Reverend Ude "talk about their religious convictions and that's what they are, they're convicts locked up in some shabby fiction doing life without parole and they want everybody else in prison with them" (186). And then there are the "paranoid sentimental fictions" about the South (224), not to mention the various scams, plots, and conspiracies in motion throughout the novel. As McCandless remarks:

> Paul thinks he's been using Ude but Ude's been using him and Lester's been using them both because he wrote the scenario, set up that site get a few missionaries killed and then that plane gets shot down, Cruikshank pulls out

the scenario dusts it off and we're back in the sixteenth century copper, gold, slavery sanitized in what they call the homelands and the cross of Jesus going before. (236)

Yet the one thing *Carpenter's Gothic* asserts unmistakeably, as it unravels our expectations and refuses answers to even basic plot questions, is that these various fictions will not be and could not be set against some absolute and ultimate truth. But by the same token, the novel also refuses the antithetical extreme of a totally relativistic universe where all fictions are equally valid and, hence, equally worthless. To be sure, as a manipulator of various kinds and levels of fiction, Gaddis takes pains to display them for us in all their detailed incongruity and variety of consequence. But finally, if his house of fiction is indeed carpenter gothic in style—a "patchwork of conceits, borrowings, [and] deceptions" (227)—it does not differ significantly in this respect from the fabric of much of contemporary American life. As we see these fictions resonating through the characters' lives, fictions played off and against one another, we are enjoined to take the measure of each one in relation to those lives, to what it makes possible and to what it inhibits. In this most Nietzschean of novels, then, the sense and value of a fiction provide its only measure; the truth itself is "unpresentable."

Counterfeit, copy, simulacrum, paper fiction, "a good serviceable fiction" as opposed to a desperate one—the terms suggest that, from *The Recognitions* to *JR* and *Carpenter's Gothic*, Gaddis's novels undergo less a progression or evolution than a constant redefinition. What gets redefined are the terms by which the novels can compellingly assert their pertinence to contemporary experience. For Gaddis this entails redefining the very form of the novel, which, as Bahktin reminds us, is a form without fixed rules or categories by which it can be judged, except in relation to its own contemporaneity.

How is art's contemporaneity in turn to be determined? For the last two hundred years, it has been conceived in relation to a theory of modernity. Lyotard's theory of postmodernism now suggests a new turn in this history. The modern work, he states, "allows the unpresentable to be put forward only as the missing contents; but the form, because of its recognizable consistency, continues to offer to the reader or the viewer matter for solace or pleasure."[38] In a postmodern work, on the other hand, the form does not allow this solace or pleasure, but seeks "to impart a stronger sense of the unpresentable." In Kantian terms, it maintains the breach between the concept and the sensible. For Lyotard, therefore, postmodern form is like the Kantian sublime, with its intrinsic combination of pleasure and pain: "the pleasure that reason should exceed all presentation, the pain that imagination or sensibility should not be equal to the concept." For Deleuze, who approaches this Kantian theme with the limits of representation in view, it is in this breach between the concept and the sensible that recognition and common sense are shattered, as the self dissolves and singularities are released like spores. For what is unthinkable and unimaginable ("unpresentable") in the Kantian sublime is the phantasm itself.[39] From this (Deleuzian) perspective, a postmodern form would be one in which the work of art's disjunctive parts communicate in and through the logic of the phantasm.

While readers may disagree about how exactly these terms apply to *The Recognitions, JR,* and *Carpenter's Gothic,* it is undeniable that these novels offer neither the solace of good form nor a shareable nostalgia for what is no longer presentable. Unlike the great modernist novels, armed with what George Stade calls their compensatory aesthetic, they provide no refuge in art but counter this impulse with unremitting black humor and satire. For in Gaddis's novels "form" is as much a specific "expression of content" with its own phantasmatic logic of proliferation as it is a means of containing and shaping experience—of making it recognizable. In allowing themselves no other ground to sustain them than a need to mark out and multiply differences within the fictions that both order and disorder our lives, Gaddis's novels not only demonstrate why traditional forms can no longer provide critical access to contemporary experience, they also render the "new contents" of that experience. In this sense, perhaps, they can indeed be said to present the "unpresentable."

Notes

INTRODUCTION

1. An exception is Stephen Moore's *A Reader's Guide to William Gaddis's The Recognitions* (Lincoln and London: University of Nebraska Press, 1982). Also noteworthy are the essays devoted to Gaddis published in *The Review of Contemporary Fiction,* Vol. II, No. 2 (summer 1982). Several of these have been republished, with the addition of new essays, in *In Recognition of William Gaddis,* ed. by John Kuehl and Steven Moore (Syracuse: Syracuse University Press, 1984). Kuehl and Moore's introduction to this volume provides a useful biographical sketch of William Gaddis as well as a brief summary of critical reception to his work.

2. See, for example, Richard Poirier's *The Performing Self* (New York: Oxford University Press, 1971) and Raymond M. Olderman's *Beyond the Waste Land* (New Haven: Yale University Press, 1972).

3. See my essay "Postmodern Theory/Postmodern Fiction" in *Clio,* Vol. 16, No. 2 (winter 1987), pp. 139–158, for a discussion of some recent fiction (including Gaddis's *JR*) in this context.

4. Lionel Trilling, to cite one example, registers an acute discomfort with this discovery in *Beyond Culture* (New York: Viking, 1965), p. 26.

5. Mikhail Bakhtin, *Problems in Dostoevsky's Poetics,* ed. and trans. by Caryl Emerson (Minneapolis: University of Minnesota Press, 1984), p. 6.

6. Mikhail Bakhtin, *The Dialogic Imagination,* ed. by Michael Holquist, trans. by Caryl Emerson and Michael Holquist (Austin and London: University of Texas Press, 1981), p. 427.

7. Julia Kristeva, "Word, Dialogue, and Novel," in *Desire in Language,* ed. by Leon S. Roudiez (New York: Columbia University Press, 1980), pp. 71–72.

8. Unfortunately, there are no summaries of Deleuze's work, in either French or English. The best general introduction is undoubtedly Michel Foucault's "Theatrum Philosophicum," in *Language, Counter-memory, Practice,* ed. and trans. by Donald F. Bouchard (Ithaca and New York: Cornell University Press, 1977), pp. 165–196.

CHAPTER ONE

1. The critic is George Stade, in his review of Gaddis's second novel, *JR,* for *The New York Times Book Review,* Nov. 9, 1975, p. 1.

2. See P. M. Palmer and R. P. More, *The Sources of the Faust Tradition* (New York: Octagon Books, 1978), pp. 9–41. The *Clementine Recognitions* is available in English in the *Ante-Nicene Christian Library,* Vol. 3, trans. by Rev. Thomas Smith (Edinburgh: T. & T. Clark, 1868), pp. 143–471. One character in Gaddis's

The Recognitions (New York: Harcourt, Brace, 1955) summarizes the plot very briefly as follows:

> Yes. The what? The Recognitions? No, it's Clement of Rome. Mostly talk, talk, talk. The young man's deepest concern is for the immortality of his soul, he goes to Egypt to find the magicians and learn their secrets. It's been referred to as the first Christian novel. What? Yes, it's really the beginning of the whole Faust legend. (p. 373)

All further references to Gaddis's *The Recognitions* will be to the edition cited above, with page numbers indicated in the text in parentheses. All ellipses are Gaddis's, unless otherwise indicated.

3. In "Presupposition and Intertextuality," a chapter in *The Pursuit of Signs* (Ithaca: Cornell University Press, 1981), Jonathan Culler discusses intertextuality as "the discursive space of a culture" and notes that in "all these cases [of intertextualtiy] there are no moments of authority and points of origin except those which are retrospectively designated as origins and which, therefore, can be shown to derive from the series for which they are constituted as origin." In this sense, the problematizing of authority and origin in *The Recognitions* is an essential effect of its structure. I consider the issue of intertextuality in more detail in Chapter Four.

4. Gaddis as much as admitted a debt to Joyce (at least for his method) when he revealed to Peter Koenig that he had begun *The Recognitions* as a parody of Goethe's *Faust*, but that it began to change after he read Frazer's *The Golden Bough*, the latter having led him to discover that beneath the Faust story the *Clementine Recognitions* lay as a subtext. See William Peter Koenig, "Recognizing Gaddis's *Recognitions*," *Contemporary Literature*, 16 (winter 1975), p. 64. For Benstock's account of Gaddis's borrowings from Joyce, see Bernard Benstock, "On William Gaddis: In Recognition of James Joyce," *Wisconsin Studies in Contemporary Literature*, 6 (summer 1965), pp. 177–189.

5. This is a condensed summary of an argument put forward by Jean Baudrillard in *For a Critique of the Political Economy of the Sign*, trans. by Charles Lerin (St. Louis: Telos Press, 1981), Chapters 4 and 5. Oddly, Baudrillard does not consider the problem of copying in relation to mechanical reproduction, which I discuss in Chapter Two.

6. In Borges's story an exact repetition of Cervantes's novel produces a radical difference. Quoting identical passages (one from the text of Cervantes, the other from that of Menard), the author of this "review essay" then points out "differences" in content and style. See "Pierre Menard, Author of Don Quixote," in *Ficciones* (New York: Grove Press, 1962), pp. 52–53.

7. Joseph S. Salemi, "To Soar in Atonement: Art as Expiation in Gaddis's *The Recognitions*," *Novel*, 10 (winter 1977), p. 127. Salemi fails to realize that this commutability subverts his argument that art is a transcendent power or authority.

8. Jean-Joseph Goux, *Économie et symbolique* (Paris: Editions du Seuil, 1973), p. 54. My translation, as are all passages from French sources cited hereafter unless otherwise indicated.

9. Joel Dana Black, "The Paper Empires and Empirical Fictions of William

Gaddis," *The Review of Contemporary Fiction,* Vol. II, No. 2 (summer 1982), p. 27.

10. Jacques Derrida, "Plato's Pharmacy," in *Dissemination,* trans. by Barbara Johnson (Chicago: University of Chicago Press, 1981), pp. 63–172.

11. Plato, *The Sophist,* 236b, 264c.

12. See Gilles Deleuze, *Logique du sens* (Paris: Minuit, 1969), pp. 292–307, and *Différence et répétition* (Paris: P.U.F., 1968), pp. 91–95. Martin Heidegger offers a similar reading of Plato in his *Nietzsche,* Vol. 4 (New York: Harper and Row, 1982). For a judicious "rehabilitation" of the Sophists as well as a brief history of similar efforts, from Hegel to Mario Untersteiner, see G. B. Kerferd's *The Sophistic Movement* (Cambridge: Cambridge University Press, 1981).

13. Deleuze, *Logique du sens,* p. 302.

14. See Deleuze, *Différence et répétition,* Chapters 1 and 2 (particularly pp. 164–165). Nietzsche's doctrine of the "eternal return" is discussed more fully as it applies to *The Recognitions* in Chapter Three.

15. Ibid., p. 1.

16. Given that the novel contains a long religio-aesthetic debate or a modern Platonic dialogue conducted between two of the major characters, Wyatt and Valentine, this is less surprising than it might at first appear. Bakhtin emphasizes the importance of the Socratic dialogues in the evolution of the novel and to the formation of dialogic fiction in particular. In this context one should also note Nietzsche's remarks in *The Birth of Tragedy,* trans. by Walter Kaufman (New York: Vintage, 1967), pp. 90–91:

> If tragedy has absorbed into itself all the earlier types of art, the same might also be said in an eccentric sense of the Platonic dialogue which, a mixture of all extant styles and forms, hovers midway between narrative, lyric and drama, between prose and poetry, and so has broken the strict old law of the unity of stylistic form. . . . Indeed, Plato has given to all posterity the model of a new art form, the model of the novel—which may be described as an infinitely enhanced Aesopian fable in which poetry holds the same rank in relation to dialectical philosophy as the same philosophy held for many centuries in relation to theology; namely, the rank of ancilla.

17. The dissolution of the Platonic paradigm spells the end of certain modernist assumptions as well, insofar as the latter valorize iconic revelation (as both Joyce and Woolf do, for instance, in *A Portrait of the Artist* and *To the Lighthouse,* respectively). For an extended discussion of how postmodernist fiction constitutes a rupture with iconic and visionary structures and the expressive theories of language that subtend them, see Allen Thiher, *Words in Reflection: Modern Language Theory and Postmodern Fiction* (Chicago: University of Chicago Press, 1984).

18. Deleuze, *Différence et répétition,* p. 168.

19. See Deleuze, *Logique du sens,* pp. 190–197, for a fuller account of this notion of time, which is contrasted with the time of Chronos, or an eternal present.

20. See, for example, Nietzsche's "On Truth and Lie in an Extra-Moral Sense," where these themes are elaborated. The essay can be found in *The Portable*

Nietzsche, ed. and trans. by Walter Kaufman (New York: The Viking Press, 1954), pp. 42–47. In *Le même et l'autre* (Paris: Editions de Minuit, 1979), Vincent Descombes discusses these themes in relation to contemporary French philosophy and its radical interpretation of Nietzsche.

21. At this point Deleuze's critique of Plato and his own "overturning of Platonism" converge with Jacques Derrida's deconstructive reading of Plato as elaborated in his essay "Plato's Pharmacy," which Deleuze cites.

22. See Lucien Dallenbach, *Le récit spéculaire: essai sur la mise en abyme* (Paris: Editions du Seuil, 1977) for extended discussion of the *mise en abyme* structure in modern French fiction.

23. See Freud's *Jokes and Their Relation to the Unconscious,* trans. by James Strachey (New York: W. W. Norton, 1960), especially Chapter 4, "The Mechanism of Pleasure and the Psychogenesis of Jokes." The entire study is pertinent to the textual peculiarities found in *The Recognitions.*

24. Here I am roughly following the distinction Deleuze makes between simple and complex repetition in *Différence et répétition.*

25. Deleuze, *Logique du sens,* p. 63. Deleuze draws upon Lévi-Strauss's discussion of "floating signifiers and signifieds," which is found in the latter's "Introduction" to Marcel Mauss's *Sociologie et Anthropologie* (Paris, P.U.F., 1950), pp. 48–49. The quotations below are taken from these pages. Jeffrey Mehlman discusses the entire problematic in "The 'Floating Signifier': From Lévi-Strauss to Lacan," *Yale French Studies,* 48 (1972), pp. 10–26.

26. Deleuze, *Logique du sens,* p. 65.

27. Deleuze, *Différence et répétition,* pp. 154–155.

28. Ibid., p. 155.

29. Deleuze himself employed an earlier version of this "intensive system" in his analysis of Proust's *À la recherche du temps perdu.* See his *Proust and Signs,* trans. by Richard Howard (New York: George Braziller, 1972), especially Chapter 8, entitled "Antilogos, or the Literary Machine," where the literary work is seen as a machine that produces certain kinds of effects. Also pertinent to Deleuze's formulation of this theory is the "machinic" aspect of Malcolm Lowry's fiction. In the Proust study Deleuze quotes this passage from the letter Lowry wrote to explain how *Under the Volcano* functions:

> It can be regarded as a kind of symphony, or in another way as a kind of opera—or even a horse opera. It is hot music, a poem, a song, a tragedy, a comedy, a farce, and so forth. It is superficial, profound, entertaining and boring, according to taste. It is a prophecy, and political warning, a cryptogram, a preposterous movie, and a writing on the wall. It can even be regarded as a sort of machine: it works too, believe me, as I have found out.

Needless to add, Lowry's description also fits *The Recognitions.*

30. Timothy Hilton, *Picasso* (New York and Toronto: Oxford University Press, 1975), p. 250.

31. Most important in this regard are Wyatt's comments on the Flemish painters of the early Northern Renaissance. According to Moore's *A Reader's Guide,* Gaddis drew extensively from Sir Martin Conway's *The Van Eycks and*

Their Followers (New York: Dutton, 1921). As I show in Chapter Two, however, Wyatt's statements are ambiguous and shifting.

CHAPTER TWO

1. See Bakhtin, *Problems of Dostoevsky's Poetics,* pp. 106–137, for an extended discussion of the distinguishing features of carnivalesque fiction.

2. For example, her carriage passes up a hill, "renovated like that remontant goddess who annually clambered forth from the pool with her virginity renewed" (14–15), an obvious reference to Artemis, who is described in these terms in *The White Goddess* (New York: Farrar, Straus and Giroux, 1948), p. 217. Graves's study supplies many incidental details, such as Gwyon's name, and refers to *The Recognitions* (Clementine's, of course) as a "novel" popularizing the religious theories of the Clementine Gnostics.

3. For Bakhtin, "carnivalization" is an essential feature of Menippean satire and dialogic fiction. It "makes possible the transfer of ultimate questions from the abstractly philosophical sphere, through a carnival sense of the world, to the concretely sensuous plane of images and events" (*Problems of Dostoevsky's Poetics,* p. 134). A "carnivalization of knowledge" therefore would be a heterogeneous mixture that breaks down hierarchies and principles of separation.

4. Steven Weisenburger discusses Wyatt's name in these terms in "Paper Currencies: Reading William Gaddis," *The Review of Contemporary Fiction,* Vol. II, No. 2 (summer 1982), p. 14.

5. See Francis A. Yates, "The Art of Ramon Lull," *Journal of the Warburg and Courtald Institutes,* Vol. XVII (1954), pp. 115–173, for a full account. Yates maintains however that Lully was not an alchemist.

6. See Anne Bergman's "The Original Confidence Man," *American Quarterly,* Vol. XXI (fall 1969), pp. 560–577, for the lineage of this figure who pervades American literature.

7. A number of passages, like the following, insist on this debased economy of exchange:

> Tragedy was foresworn, in the ritual denial of the ripe knowledge that we are drawing away from one another, that we share only one thing, share the fear of belonging to one another, or to others, or to God; love or money, tender equated in advertising and the world, where only money is currency, and under dead trees and brittle ornaments prehensile hands exchange forgeries of what the heart dare not surrender. (p. 103)

8. Stephen Moore, in the introduction to his *A Reader's Guide to William Gaddis's The Recognitions,* pp. 1–28, emphasizes this aspect of the novel. Moore's textual annotations, which comprise the major portion of the book, are extremely valuable, but his introductory reading is basically "monological" : "At its most basic level, *The Recognitions* is an account of personal integration amid collective disintegration, of an individual's finding himself in a society losing itself. And just as Gaddis drew upon the apocalyptic tradition to chronicle collective disintegration, he chose alchemy as the closest parallel to individual re-integration."

Moore thus privileges what I argue is only one strand of the novel's polyphonic discourse.

9. Walter Benjamin, "The Work of Art in the Age of Mechanical Reproduction," in *Illuminations*, trans. by Harry Zohn (New York: Schocken Books, 1969), pp. 223–224.

10. In his discussion of the Vermeer forgeries of Hans van Meegeren, who was one of the "models" on which Wyatt is based, Otto Kurz argues for their value as works of art. He asserts, for example, that van Meegeren "will always be remembered as the creator of one of the very few forgeries which can count as a work of art in its own right" (p. 334). See also Chapter XVII, "Fakes without Models," in Kurz, *Fakes*, 2nd enlarged ed. (New York: Dover Publications, 1967), pp. 302–313. Though differing considerably from my own view of Wyatt's relationship to van Meegeren (see Chapter Four), Tom Sawyer's essay "False Gold to Forge: The Forger Behind Wyatt Gwyon," *The Review of Contemporary Fiction*, Vol. 2, No. 2 (summer 1982), pp. 50–54, summarizes the similarities between the two.

11. "The vanity of time" is of course a familiar topos in seventeenth-century sermons. Otto discovers the phrase on a scrap of paper he finds at Wyatt's apartment. Wyatt had copied it from one of his father's sermons. Gwyon, in turn, had taken it from William Law, the seventeenth-century English theologian whom he quotes on p. 41. The example thus illustrates how various phrases circulate through the novel.

12. "Syncrisis" and "anacrisis" are Bakhtin's terms and refer specifically to features characteristic of Platonic dialogues. Syncrisis means the juxtaposition of various points of view toward a given object or topic; anacrisis means to provoke or elicit the words of others. See Bakhtin, *Problems of Dostoevsky's Poetics*, pp. 101–102.

13. The passage is quoted in part in note 2 to Chapter One.

14. See Bakhtin's discussion in *Problems of Dostoevsky's Poetics*, p. 116.

15. Jean-Paul Sartre, *Critique de la raison dialectique* (Paris: Gallimard, 1960), pp. 306–377.

16. According to Laurence Dwight Smith, whose *Counterfeiting: Crime against the People* (New York: W. W. Norton, 1944) was probably one of Gaddis's "source" texts, "Jim the Penman" "was one of the most remarkable counterfeiters in the history of the craft. . . . So remarkable and artistic were his notes considered to be at the time that there was a public protest after his arrest, subsequent to his passing a $100 bill in New York. Collectors paid high rates for specimens of his work" (pp. 87–88). Gaddis also probably intends a buried or double reference to James Joyce, for whom "Jim the Penman" was also important.

17. Elliot Braha, "Menippean Form in *Gravity's Rainbow* and in Other Contemporary American Novels," Ph.D. diss., Columbia University, 1979, p. 59. Braha seems to have been the first to recognize the importance of Bakhtin and Menippean satire in general to Gaddis's *The Recognitions*. Curiously, however, he fails to consider the relevance of Bakhtin's notion of the dialogic to the novel, which leads to a rather one-sided reading. He states, for example, that *The Recognitions* "delineates in cultural-historical terms the profanation of the sacred, the demystification of religion and the degradation of traditional values" (p. 48).

This would account for much of the novel's obvious satire, but not for the book as a whole, which includes, of course, both Anselm's and Valentine's counter-arguments to this idea.

18. Braha, p. 45.

19. See Nathalie Sarraute, "Conversation and Sub-conversation," in *The Age of Suspicion*, trans. by Maria Jolas (New York: George Braziller, 1963), pp. 77–117. Sarraute is probably the leading contemporary practitioner of the dialogic novel in France.

20. In these terms one could argue, without falling victim to a naive mimeticism or crude sociology, that *The Recognitions* insists that questions about authenticity, originality, and textuality ought not to be dissociated from questions about mechanical reproduction, simulation, the mass media, and mass culture; in short, that questions posed by the "text" have as their inevitable ground the simple fact of post–World War II consumer society. Unlike much contemporary theory, then, *The Recognitions* refuses to allow the question of the text to be extirpated from the larger cultural matrix out of which the text as text emerges. For a discussion of some of these issues (though not in relation to *The Recognitions*), see Fredric Jameson's "The Ideology of Text," *Salmagundi*, No. 31–32 (fall 1975/winter 1976), pp. 204–246, and "Reification and Utopia in Mass Culture," *Social Text*, 1 (winter 1979), pp. 130–148.

21. See *Beyond the Waste Land*, where Raymond Olderman considers a number of contemporary American novels as prose fiction versions of Eliot's poem. Unfortunately, he fails to mention *The Recognitions*.

22. Actually, these chapter titles (the only ones in the novel) apply as much to Sinisterra as they do to Wyatt. In the first chapter Sinisterra himself repeats the old adage that the first turn of the screw pays all debts, and it is his death that brings Chapter III (Part III) to a close.

23. The distinction Wyatt draws between El Greco and the painters of the Northern Renaissance has been widely known among art historians at least since Heinrich Wölfflin formulated it in terms of the "painterly" or "pictorial" (*Der Malerisch*) and "linear" styles. In Wölfflin's terms, Wyatt is advocating the "linear style," but his own language corresponds to the "pictorial." What is interesting in this context is that Bakhtin also appropriated Wölfflin's terms to categorize the dynamic relationships between authorial speech or discourse and the reported speech of characters. He distinguishes them in *Marxism and the Philosophy of Language*, which appeared under the name of (or perhaps was co-authored with) V. N. Volosinov, trans. by L. Matejka and I. R. Titunik (New York and London: Seminar Press, 1973), as follows:

> The basic tendency of the linear style is to construct clear-cut, external contours for reported speech, whose own internal individuality is minimized. Wherever the entire content displays a complete stylistic homogeneity (in which the author and his characters all speak exactly the same language), the grammatical and compositional manipulation of reported speech achieves a maximal compactness and plastic relief.

At the other pole, in the "pictorial" style,

Language devised means for infiltrating reported speech with authorial retort and commentary in deft and subtle ways. The reporting (i.e., authorial) context strives to break down the self-contained compactness of the reported speech, to resolve it, to obliterate its boundaries. We may call this style of speech reporting pictorial. Its tendency is to obliterate the precise, external contours of reported speech; at the same time, the reported speech is individualized to a much greater degree—the tangibility of the various facets of an utterance may be subtly differentiated. (pp. 120–121)

Bakhtin takes up these categories in order to mark out a historical progression of tendencies: from the authoritarian discourse of the Middle Ages to the rationalistic dogmatism of the seventeenth and eighteenth centuries, in which the linear style characterized reported speech transmission, then to the realistic and critical individualism of the nineteenth century, with its pictorial style and its tendency to permeate reported speech with authorial retort and commentary, and finally to the relativistic individualism of the present period, with its decomposition of the "authorial context." Particularly important is the increasing role of indirect discourse and *style indirect libre,* which produce a double articulation of subjectivity (author's and character's) not easily analyzable in linguistic terms. Moreover, reported speech in general is fundamental to Bakhtin's theory of language, since it illustrates most directly the fact that language is always permeated with the language of others, that it is by nature heterogeneous. Paradoxically, it is the presence of "speech within speech, utterance within utterance," that insures the continual openness of language. See Bakhtin, especially pp. 115–119, for discussion of these ideas.

24. An adequate analysis of Wyatt's deliria in *The Recognitions* would entail a study in itself, or at least a digression too lengthy to be attempted here. Verbal delirium is likewise important in Gaddis's second novel, *JR,* as well as in much postmodern literature. Deleuze and Félix Guattari provide a fruitful starting point for work in this neglected area in their notion that delirium represents a particular investment of the social field, which is why it is always expressed in world-historical, political, economic, religious, and racial terms, and thus transcends the familial order of the individual. In their terms Wyatt's delirium represents a "molecular schizophrenic line of escape" rather than a "paranoic molar investment." See their *Anti-Oedipus,* trans. by Robert Hurley, Mark Seem, and Helen R. Lane (New York: The Viking Press, 1977), especially pp. 84–90.

25. Bakhtin's theory of the grotesque (and his critique of Wolfgang Kayser's theory) in the "Introduction" to his *Rabelais and His World,* trans. by Helene Iswolsky (Cambridge: M.I.T. Press, 1968), pp. 1–58, raises the problem of whether any of the varieties of the grotesque in *The Recognitions* transcend the modernist form that evolves out of the Romantic tradition under the influence of existentialism. Kayser's limitation, from Bakhtin's viewpoint, is that his analysis is based only on the modern and Romantic forms, and fails to consider earlier folk and carnival forms in which there is nothing of the "hostile, alien, and inhuman." In "folk grotesque," in contrast, the emphasis is on the body not separate from the world, but growing with offshoots and ramifications, and on madness as a "gay parody of official reason." While the grotesque in Gaddis is

obviously linked to this kind of parody, the lack of associations of fecundity and rebirth makes it seem closer to black humor.

26. Bernard Benstock, "On William Gaddis: In Recognition of James Joyce," pp. 181–182.

27. For example, Joseph S. Salemi, "To Soar in Atonement: Art as Expiation in Gaddis's *The Recognitions*"; Susan Strehle Klemtner, " 'For a Very Small Audience': The Fiction of William Gaddis," *Critique: Studies in Modern Fiction*, Vol. XIX, No. 3, pp. 61–73; and William Koenig, "Recognizing Gaddis' *Recognitions.*" Steven Moore, in his *Reader's Guide*, waffles on this point.

28. Tony Tanner, "Conclusion," *City of Words*, p. 399.

29. Rauschenberg exhibited the "Erased de Kooning Drawing" in 1953. For a brief account, see Michele Cone, *The Roots and Routes of Art in the 20th Century* (New York: Horizon Press, 1975), p. 204.

30. This sense of "decoding" (rather than simply "deciphering") as a dissolving of previous cultural codings is developed by Deleuze and Guattari in *Anti-Oedipus*.

31. Tanner, p. 398.

CHAPTER THREE

1. See in particular Althusser's "Ideology and Ideological State Apparatuses" and "Freud and Lacan," in *Lenin and Philosophy*, trans. by Ben Brewster (New York and London: Monthly Review Press, 1971), pp. 127–186, 190–219; and Lacan's *Four Fundamental Concepts of Psycho-Analysis*, trans. by Alan Sheridan (New York: W. W. Norton, 1978), pp. 203–229.

2. Distinguishing between monological and dialogic fiction, with Tolstoi and Dostoevsky, respectively, representing these two modes, Bakhtin states that the former "contains but one cognitive subject, all else being merely the object of its cognition." Thus, in the first type the reader identifies with a presumed author, who as a cognitive subject transcends and synthesizes conflicting viewpoints, attitudes, and values. In polyphonic fiction, on the other hand, there is no possible synthesis of the conflicting polyphony of voices, and the author remains immanent to the divisions and dialogic relationships that rift the novel's discourse. As a result the cognitive subject of dialogical fiction is split and pluralized, and answers to no transcendent unity or organic synthesis. Furthermore, in Julia Kristeva's reading of Bakhtin, this authorial splitting can be correlated with the Freudian *Spaltung*. Dialogic discourse may then be described in terms of a dream logic belonging doubly to an "I" and to the "other" or to a textual unconscious. See Bakhtin, *Problems of Dostoevsky's Poetics*, pp. 69–75, for the Dostoevsky-Tolstoi comparison, and Kristeva, "Word, Dialogue, Novel."

3. In his discussion of the relation of Dostoevsky's polyphonic fiction to the earlier genre of Menippean satire, Bakhtin stresses the importance of certain themes bearing on "abnormal moral and psychic states" and the formal, genre-related nature of these themes. According to Bakhtin, "moral-psychological experimentation" appears for the first time in Menippean satire. Insanity of all sorts, split personalities, unrestrained daydreaming, unusual dreams, passions bordering on insanity, and suicide are all represented. These themes are genre-specific be-

cause they articulate the "underside" of the epic, or those aspects of human experience that the epic cannot accommodate. See Bakhtin, pp. 116–117.

4. Cf. E. M. Forster, *Aspects of the Novel* (New York: Harcourt, Brace and World, 1927), p. 71, as well as T. S. Eliot's comments in "Wilkie Collins and Dickens," *Selected Essays* (London: Faber and Faber, 1951), p. 410.

5. Mikhail Bakhtin, *Rabelais and His World*, pp. 26–27.

6. See Masao Miyoshi's *The Divided Self: A Perspective on the Literature of the Victorians* (New York: New York University Press, 1969) for an extended discussion of the split-self theme in nineteenth-century English literature, particularly pp. 265–178 on Dickens's *Our Mutual Friend*.

7. Bakhtin, *Problems of Dostoevsky's Poetics*, p. 28.

8. Ibid., p. 30.

9. Joseph Frank, "Spatial Form in Modern Literature," reprinted in *The Widening Gyre* (Bloomington: Indiana University Press, 1968), pp. 3–62.

10. See T. S. Eliot, "Ulysses, Order and Myth," *The Dial* (1923), reprinted in *Forms of Modern Fiction*, ed. by William Van O'Connor (Bloomington: Indiana University Press, 1948), pp. 120–124. Eliot's review, published after he had already used the mythic method himself, might be read in part as a defense against the possible charge of plagiarism. For an extended and judicious account of Eliot's "borrowings" from Joyce, consult Stanley Sultan's *Ulysses, The Waste Land, and Modernism* (Port Washington, N.Y.: Kennikat Press, 1977).

11. Umberto Eco, *L'oeuvre ouverte*, trans. from Italian by Chantal Roux de Bezieu (Paris: Editions du Seuil, 1965), p. 239. Since the Italian edition was not available, I have used a French one.

12. Something similar is accomplished by Alain Robbe-Grillet in relation to the Oedipus myth in his first novel *Les Gommes (The Erasers)*, published in 1953. Cf. the commentary by David Grossvogel in his *Mystery and its Fictions: From Oedipus to Agatha Christie* (Baltimore: The Johns Hopkins University Press, 1979), p. 174:

> Within its disjointed fragments . . . the Oedipal myth subsists as echo but disappears as meaning; in a similar way, the fragments of the myth surface throughout the story, but with too much coyness and too little reason to construe meaning. If those fragments instanced only a failure to mean, the story would indeed be parody, and purposeless. But to read *The Erasers* as only parody is to neglect the purpose and the effect of their surfacing.

The same can be said of *The Recognitions*, but instead of one myth several are involved. Here, we should also note the distance separating *The Recognitions* from *Doctor Faustus*, where Thomas Mann also employs the Faust myth to construct a portrait of the modern artist. In Mann's use of myth, as in Joyce's, myth retains its integrity: it never becomes the object of interrogation, parody, or fragmentation.

13. Fredric Jameson, *Fables of Aggression: Wyndham Lewis, The Modernist as Fascist* (Berkeley: University of California Press, 1979), p. 57.

14. Ibid., p. 20.

15. Obviously the terms "imaginary" and "symbolic" are not used here in a rigorously Lacanian sense. For precise definitions, see J. Laplanche and J. B.

Pontalis, *The Language of Psycho-Analysis*, trans. by Donald Nicholson-Smith (New York: W. W. Norton, 1973), pp. 210, 439–441. The important distinction lies between the older sense of the symbolic, according to which the relation of symbol to symbolized is based on resemblance and analogy (thus, the symbol is really an imaginary entity), and the symbolic in the more recent sense of a set of laws and relations constitutive of an order or system that is not reducible to any forms taken in the real or the imaginary. No doubt, there is a certain overlap between the two senses, particularly in literary works, where the distinction made by Edmond Ortigues in *Le Discours et le symbole* (Paris: Aubier, 1962), p. 194, would seem to be the most relevant one: "The same term may be considered imaginary if taken absolutely [i.e., for itself] and symbolic if taken as a differential value correlative with other terms which limit it reciprocally." Lacan has demonstrated how the symbolic in this second sense structures a literary work in his "Seminar on the Purloined Letter" in *Écrits* (Paris: Editions du Seuil, 1966), pp. 11–41.

16. In *Words in Reflection: Modern Language Theory and Postmodern Fiction*, Allen Thiher argues that Joyce's language in *Ulysses* embodies a modernist fullness and plenitude that must be distinguished from the language of "fallen logos or alienated otherness" that typifies must post–World War II fiction. See pp. 236–237 in particular for a discussion of a passage cited from *Ulysses*.

17. That Joyce's *Ulysses* effects a synthesis of the naturalistic and the symbolic has been a commonplace of Joyce criticism since Edmund Wilson's *Axel's Castle*. The shift in focus from the symbol to the symbolic function is discussed extensively by Anthony Wilden in his *The Language of the Self* (New York: Delta Books, 1968), pp. 229–284, and in his *System and Structure* (London: Tavistock Publications, 1972), pp. 1–34. Claude Lévi-Strauss's writing on Marcel Mauss's theory of symbolic exchange and studies of primitive kinship systems are the key texts, as are those of Lacan. Wilden also finds both notions of the symbolic operative in Freud. For a critical but relevant study, see Dan Sperber, *Rethinking Symbolism* (Cambridge: Cambridge University Press, 1975).

18. Bakhtin, *Problems of Dostoevsky's Poetics*, p. 125.

19. Edward W. Said, *Beginnings: Intention and Method* (New York: Basic Books, 1975), pp. 81–188.

20. See Steven Moore, *A Reader's Guide to William Gaddis's The Recognitions*, pp. 7–9, for a brief discussion of this imagery.

21. See, in particular, Lacan's "The Function and Field of Speech and Language in Psychoanalysis" (1953), reprinted in *Écrits: A Selection*, trans. by Alan Sheridan (New York: W. W. Norton, 1977), pp. 30–113.

22. William Gaddis, unpublished notes quoted by William Peter Koenig, " 'Splinters from the Yew Tree': A Critical Study of William Gaddis' *The Recognitions*" (Ph.D. diss., New York University, 1971), pp. 99–100.

23. Koenig reports that, in fact, while reworking *The Recognitions* Gaddis decided to make Wyatt more "vague" and his identity less explicit.

24. Bakhtin, *Problems of Dostoevsky's Poetics*, p. 79.

25. Gilles Deleuze, "À quoi reconnait-on le structuralism?" in *Le Philosophie au XXe siècle*, ed. by François Chatelet (Verviers, Belgium: Librarie Hachette, n.d.), p. 327.

26. Erich Auerbach, *Mimesis: The Representation of Reality in Western Literature*, trans. by Willard Trask (Princeton: Princeton University Press, 1953), p. 472.

27. Susan Isaacs makes the case for this translation in her study, "The Nature and Function of Phantasy," *The International Journal of Psycho-Analysis*, Vol. XXIX Part 2 (1948), pp. 73–97.

28. Freud discusses this significant "reversal" in many places. See, for example, *An Autobiographical Study*, trans. by James Strachey (New York: W. W. Norton, 1963), p. 58.

29. Deleuze, *Différence et répétition*, p. 163.

30. See Deleuze, *Différence et répétition*, p. 139, and *Logique du sens*, p. 54, as well as Lacan's "The Neurotic's Individual Myth," *Psychoanalytic Quarterly*, Vol. XLVIII, No. 3 (1979), pp. 405–425, for a discussion of the Rat Man in these terms.

31. See Friedrich Nietzsche, *Thus Spake Zarathustra*, "On Redemption" (Part II) and "The Convalescent" (Part III) as well as *The Will to Power*, Book Four, Part III.

32. Deleuze, *Différence et répétition*, p. 19.

33. Edward W. Said, "Response" [to Ihab Hassan], *Diacritics*, Vol. III, No. 1 (spring 1973), p. 55.

34. Deleuze, *Logique du sens*, p. 53.

35. See John Godley, *Van Meegeren: Master Art Forger* (New York: Wilfred Funk, 1951) for an extended account of van Meegeren. One textual peculiarity worthy of note: in an earlier version of Chapter II (Part I), published in *New World Writing* (New York: NAL, 1952), there is more emphasis on Wyatt's student friend Han, an apparent homosexual who tries to seduce Wyatt. Wyatt will later tell Ludy that he shot Han in self-defense in Oran. This Han seems to be a buried reference (the only one I have found) to Hans van Meegeren. That Gaddis should insert a fictional stand-in for one of Wyatt's "sources" and then have Wyatt kill him is again suggestive of the kind of self-reflexive compositional "play" evident throughout *The Recognitions*.

36. Cf. Deleuze and Guattari: "There is no Nietzsche-the-self, professor of philology, who suddenly loses his mind and supposedly identifies with all sorts of strange people; rather, there is the Nietzschean subject who passes through a series of states, and who identifies these states with the names of history: 'every name in history is I . . .'." *Anti-Oedipus* (New York: Viking, 1977), p. 21. See also *Selected Letters of Friedrich Nietzsche*, particularly the letter to Jakob Burckhard, Jan. 5, 1889 (Chicago: University of Chicago Press, 1969), p. 347.

37. Both Koenig's and Moore's readings may be fairly described as Platonic. The former asserts that "the total act of recognition for Gaddis would be to see what is counterfeit in contemporary life, but to believe that life has a spiritual design" ("Splinters from the Yew Tree," pp. 12–13), while the latter's reading assumes unquestioningly the existence of eternal archetypes. Both argue for a "symbolist" reading of the novel in the sense adumbrated by Edmund Wilson in *Axel's Castle* (New York: Charles Scribner's Sons, 1959). The reading of *The Recognitions* proposed here is symbolic, but in a structuralist (or postmodern) sense.

38. Deleuze, *Différence et répétition,* p. 155.

39. Stephen-Paul Martin, "Vulnerability and Aggression: Characters and Objects in *The Recognitions,*" *The Review of Contemporary Fiction,* Vol. II, No. 2 (summer 1982), pp. 45–50.

40. Cf. Roland Barthes, *S/Z,* trans. by Richard Miller (New York: Hill and Wang, 1974), pp. 67–68, 191, for a discussion of the role of the proper name in relation to the constellations of *semes* that constitute a fictional character.

41. Deleuze, *Logique du sens,* p. 249. The passage continues:

> It [the phantasm] literally releases them [singularities] like spores, and explodes in this unballasting. The expression "neutral energy" must be interpreted in this sense: neutral thus signifies pre-individual and impersonal, but does not describe a state of energy that would return to the bottomless depths; on the contrary it refers to singularities liberated from the ego by a narcissistic wound. This neutrality, that is, this movement by which singularities are emitted or rather restored by an ego that is dissolved or absorbed at the surface, belongs essentially to the phantasm. . . . Thus the ego's individuality is inseparable from the event of the phantasm itself, even if it means that the event represented in the phantasm is grasped as another individual, or rather as a series of other individuals through which the dissolved ego passes.

The point of this rather difficult passage (made even more difficult by extracting it from its context) is that the ego's individuality is produced by a distribution of singularities in the movement of the phantasm and that this is most clearly revealed in the ego's dissolution.

42. Propp and Greimas are cited as two representative structuralists who have analyzed narrative. See Vladimir Propp, *Morphology of the Folk Tale,* trans. by L. Scott (Austin: University of Texas Press, 1968), and A. J. Greimas, *Sémantique structurale* (Paris: Larousse, 1966), pp. 171–221.

43. For example, by Kenneth Burke in *Attitudes Toward History* (Los Altos, Calif.: Hermes Publications, 1959), p. 49.

CHAPTER FOUR

1. In the "Singed Phoenix and Gift of Tongues: William Gaddis's *The Recognitions*" (*Diacritics,* 16, 1986, p. 34), Dominick LaCapra notes in passing that Gaddis's novel

> might even be taken as the epitome of Mikhail Bakhtin's notion of the significant novel as the polyphonic orchestration of the heterogeneous, fragmentary, often chaotic, at times cacophonous discourses of the times into a seriocomic, provocatively ambivalent *agon* or carnival of contending "voices" and dissonant possibilities in society and culture. For any given element— event, character, development—is never simply univocal or one-sided but generally has two or more valences: it is serious and ironic, pathos-charged and parodic, apocalyptic and farcical, critical and self-critical.

My own study seeks to account for this "dialogic," as well as describe its various effects and manifestations.

2. Cf. Bakhtin's definition of the novel in "Discourse in the Novel," in *The Dialogic Imagination,* ed. by Michael Holquist, trans. by Caryl Emerson and Michael Holquist (Austin and London: University of Texas Press, 1981), p. 263:

> The novel can be defined as a diversity of social speech types (sometimes even diversity of languages) and a diversity of individual voices, artistically organized. The internal stratification of any single national language into social dialects, characteristic group behavior, professional jargons, generic languages, languages of generations and age groups, tendentious languages, languages of the authorities, of various circles and of passing fashions, languages that serve the specific sociopolitical purposes of the day, even of the hour (each day has its own slogan, its own vocabulary, its own emphases)—this internal stratification present in every language at any given moment of its historical existence is the indispensable prerequisite for the novel as a genre. The novel orchestrates all its themes, the totality of the world of objects and ideas depicted and expressed in it, by means of the social diversity of speech types (*raznorecie*) and by the differing individual voices that flourish under such conditions. Authorial speech, the speeches of narrators, inserted genres, the speech of characters are merely those fundamental compositional unities with whose help heteroglossia (*raznorecie*) can enter the novel; each of them permits a multiplicity of social voices and a wide variety of their links and interrelationships (always more or less dialogized). These distinctive links and interrelationships between utterances and languages, this movement of the theme through different languages and speech types, its dispersion into the rivulets and droplets of social heteroglossia, its dialogization—this is the basic distinguishing feature of the stylistics of the novel.

3. Bakhtin, *Problems of Dostoevsky's Poetics,* p. 189.

4. Koenig, " 'Splinters from the Yew Tree': A Critical Study of William Gaddis's *The Recognitions,*" p. 49.

5. Ibid., p. 70.

6. See Roland Barthes, "From Work to Text," in *Image–Music–Text,* trans. by Stephen Heath (New York: Hill and Wang, 1977), pp. 155–164.

7. See W. J. Phythian-Adams, *Mithraism* (London: Constable & Co., 1915), p. 94, and J. Huizinga's *The Waning of the Middle Ages* (New York: Doubleday Anchor Books, 1954), especially pp. 242–264.

8. F. C. Conybeare, *Myth, Magic and Morals: A Study of Christian Origins* (Boston: Beacon Press, 1910), p. 321.

9. George P. Marsh, *Mediaeval and Modern Saints and Miracles* (1876; reprint, New York: Harper and Row, 1969), pp. 40–43. Moore also cites this passage in his *Reader's Guide,* pp. 192–193.

10. According to Moore's textual annotations, there are about thirty references to Frazer and eleven to Lang in *The Recognitions,* and in at least three instances, these references bring to light a contradiction between them. See Moore, pp. 66, 150, and 179. The first, for example, has to do with the relationship between magic and religion and is set off by Gwyon's attempt to "summon back, a time before death entered the world, before accident, before magic, and before magic despaired, to become religion" (pp. 11–12).

11. See Chapter Two, note 3 for a definition of carnivalization.

12. Moore, *A Reader's Guide*, p. 53.

13. See Ronald T. Swigger's discussion of Flaubert, Borges, and Raymond Queneau in this light in his "Fictional Encyclopedism and the Cognitive Value of Literature," *Comparative Literature Studies*, 12 (December 1975), pp. 351–366.

14. Edward W. Said, *The World, the Text and the Critic* (Cambridge, Mass.: Harvard University Press, 1983), p. 139.

15. Michel Foucault, "The Fantasia of the Library," in *Language, Counter-Memory, Practice*, p. 91.

16. In an unsympathetic (and ignorant) review in *The Saturday Review* (March 12, 1955), Maxwell Geismar noted that the plot of *The Recognitions* was "reminiscent of Rex Warner's *Wild Goose Chase*." Gaddis takes revenge in *JR*, where he has a Public Relations man cite "M Axswilla Gummer's review" of *O! Chittering Ones* from a publisher's trade list. The seven titles he reads are all anagrams of *The Recognitions*, and the blurbs are comments from its reviews.

17. See David Madden, "On William Gaddis's *The Recognitions*," in *Rediscoveries*, ed. by David Madden (New York: Crown, 1971), p. 298.

18. The term and definition are usually credited to Julia Kristeva, who develops the concept in *Semiotikè* (Paris: Editions du Seuil, 1969).

19. Jonathan Culler, *In Pursuit of Signs*, p. 103.

20. Jacques Derrida, "Outwork," in *Dissemination*, trans. by Barbara Johnson (Chicago: University of Chicago Press, 1981), pp. 41–42.

21. Gregory Bateson, *Steps to an Ecology of Mind* (New York: Ballantine Books, 1972), pp. 3–58.

22. Roland Barthes, "L'effet du réel," *Communications*, 11 (1968), pp. 84–89.

23. See Jean Ricardou, *Pour une théorie du nouveau roman* (Paris: Editions du Seuil, 1971) and Paul De Man, *Allegories of Reading* (New Haven: Yale University Press, 1979).

24. See Derrida, "Structure, Sign, and Play," in *Writing and Difference*, trans. by Alan Bass (Chicago: University of Chicago Press, 1978), p. 289.

25. Such a reading would constitute an updating of the kind of "homological" reading of the *nouveau roman* that Lucien Goldman performs in *Pour une sociologie du roman* (Paris: Gallimard, 1964). Jean Baudrillard gives many such readings (though from a "post-Marxist" perspective) of various contemporary cultural phenomena in *Pour une critique de l'économie politique du signe, L'échange symbolique et la mort*, and *Simulacres et simulation*. In the second book mentioned, Baudrillard develops a historical analysis of three "order of simulacra" —the counterfeit, reproduction, and simulation—which in fact correspond to the different kinds of fakes found in *The Recognitions*, though of course on a much smaller scale. At the same time, and similarly pertinent to Gaddis's novel, Baudrillard seeks to unmask textuality as obeying the very logic of consumer society. His analysis of the latter as a complex of sign systems predicated on a "logic of the simulacrum" —by which he means the reproduction of copies without originals—argues therefore for a perspective different from Deleuze's, but one that may be seen as a useful (dare I say, dialogic?) complement. By pinpointing a logic of reversibility

"haunting" today's conceptual systems and by demonstrating how everyday experience is dominated by simulacra and strategies of simulation, Baudrillard provides the basis for a historical analysis of matters which have been considered here from a literary and philosophical perspective. As I point out in Chapter Five, however, Baudrillard's theory is perhaps more directly applicable to the postmodern fiction of the 1980s.

26. Joseph Riddel, "The 'Crypt' of Edgar Poe," *Boundary 2*, Vol. VII, No. 3 (spring 1979), p. 141. Riddel makes it clear that an obsession with "originality" and especially the fiction of an "original author" is indigenous to an important strain of American literature. For an excellent reading of Melville's *Pierre* in just these terms, see Edgar A. Dryden's essay "The Entangled Text: Melville's *Pierre* and the Problem of Reading" in the same issue of *Boundary 2*.

27. Jean-Paul Sartre, preface to Nathalie Sarraute's *Portrait d'un inconnu* (Paris: Gallimard, 1948). The quotation is taken from Maria Jolas's translation (New York: Braziller, 1958), p. viii.

28. From "Sartre par Sartre," *Nouvel Observateur*, No. 272 (Jan. 27, 1970).

29. In *Words in Reflection* Allen Thiher has shown how Sartre adumbrates a postmodern position in his novel *La Nausée*, first published in 1938, and then backs down from this position in his later writings. See Thiher, pp. 93–97.

30. Deleuze, *Différence et répétition*, p. 161.

31. See Mathew Winston, "*Humour noir* and Black Humor," in *Harvard English Studies 3: Veins of Humor*, ed. by Harry Levin (Cambridge, Mass.: Harvard University Press, 1972), p. 282.

32. Bakhtin, "Epic and Novel," *The Dialogic Imagination*, p. 7.

33. Cf. Deleuze, *Logique du sens*, p. 298. Deleuze quotes X. Audouard's essay "Le Simulacre" (in *Cahiers pour l'analyse*, No. 3), which demonstrates that "simulacra are constructions which include the angle of the observer, in order that the illusion be produced at the very point where the observer is located."

34. Kathleen L. Lathrop, "Comic-Ironic Parallels in William Gaddis's *The Recognitions*," *The Review of Contemporary Fiction*, Vol. II, No. 2 (summer 1982), p. 32.

35. Deleuze, *Différence et répétition*, p. 375.

CHAPTER FIVE

1. For a useful history of the term, see Hans Bertens, "The Postmodern *Weltanschauung* and Its Relation with Modernism," in *Approaching Postmodernism*, ed. by Douwe Fokkema and Hans Bertens (Amsterdam and Philadelphia: John Benjamins Publishing Company, 1986), pp. 9–51.

2. The last chapter of Michel Foucault's *The Order of Things*, originally published in 1966, would seem to support just such a claim. Another detailed account of the modernist epistēmē is provided by Timothy Reiss in *The Discourse of Modernism* (Ithaca: Cornell University Press, 1982). Reiss, in the wake of Foucault, renames the modernist epistēmē "analytico-referential discourse"; it involves

such notions as those of truth and valid experiment (in science), of referential language and representation (in all types of discourse), of possessive individualism (in political and economic theory), of contract (in sociopolitical and legal history), of taste (in aesthetic theory), of commonsense and the corresponding notion of concept (in philosophy), all of which are hypostatizations of a particular discursive system. (pp. 13–14)

3. In a recent survey of the period, Malcolm Bradbury makes a strong case for the term "neo-realism," having quite correctly pointed out that this fiction does not simply return (after the period of high modernist experimentation) to any nineteenth- or early twentieth-century kind of realism. The problem with the term is that one could make an analogous argument for the "realism" that reappears in American fiction in the 1980s. See Bradbury, "Neo-realist Fiction," in *The Columbia Literary History of the United States,* ed. by Emory Elliott (New York: Columbia University Press, 1988).

4. Cf. Michel Foucault's statements on the (French) reorientation of philosophical thought since the 1950s:

We have experienced Sartre's generation as a generation certainly courageous and generous, which had a passion for life, politics, existence. . . . But we, we have discovered something else, another passion: the passion for concepts and for what I will call 'system.' . . . By system it is necessary to understand an ensemble of relations which maintain themselves and transform themselves independently of the things they connect . . . an anonymous system without subjects. . . . The "I" has exploded (look at modern literature).

In "Entretien: Michel Foucault" by Madeleine Chapsal, *La Quinzaine litteraire,* 5 (May 15, 1966), pp. 15–16.

5. For Hawks's statement on character and plot, see "John Hawks: An Interview," *Wisconsin Studies in Contemporary Literature* (summer 1964), p. 146. Burroughs expresses his belief in the impossibility of direct representation in a passage in *Naked Lunch* (New York: Grove Press, 1966, orig. pub. 1955): "The word cannot be expressed direct. . . . It can perhaps be indicated by mosaic of juxtaposition like articles abandoned in a hotel drawer, defined by negatives and absence . . . " (p. 116).

6. Ricardo J. Quinones convincingly argues this point in *Mapping Literary Modernism* (Princeton: Princeton University Press, 1985). Irving Howe's description is taken from his introduction to *The Idea of the Modern,* ed. by Irving Howe (New York: Horizon Press, 1967), p. 34.

7. For a discussion of this problematic in the theoretical context of postmodernism, see my article, "Ideology, Representation, Schizophrenia: Toward a Theory of the Postmodern Subject," in *Postmodernism,* ed. by Gary Shapiro (New York: SUNY Press, 1989).

8. In *City of Words: American Fiction 1950–1970,* Tony Tanner emphasizes the recurrent American fear of systems, structures, and organizations, but without establishing any systematic connection between this fear and the subject in contemporary fiction as fluid, mobile, partial, or deliberately schizoid (as opposed to the fragmented or alienated self).

9. Bruce Jay Friedman, "Introduction," *Black Humor* (New York: Bantam Books, 1965), p. x.

10. Philip Roth, "Writing American Fiction," reprinted in *The Novel Today,* ed. by Malcolm Bradbury (Glasgow: Fontana Paperbacks, 1977). Roth states: "The American writer in the middle of the twentieth century has his hands full in trying to understand, describe, and then make *credible* much of American reality. It stupifies, it sickens, it infuriates, and finally it is even a kind of embarrassment to one's own meagre imagination. The actuality is continually outdoing our talents, and the culture tosses up figures almost daily that are the envy of any novelist" (p. 34, emphasis in original).

11. See Hans Bertens, "The Postmodern *Weltanschuung* and Its Relation with Modernism" for a discussion of this point.

12. Robert Scholes, in *The Fabulators* (New York: Oxford University Press, 1967), is to be credited for introducing this term into literary criticism. In the enlarged edition, *Fabulation and Metafiction* (Urbana: University of Illinois Press, 1979), Scholes moves toward a flexible, inclusive definition through discussions of romance (Durrell and Fowles), allegory (Murdock and Barth), metafiction (Barth, Barthelme, Coover, Gass, *et al.*), black humor (Vonnegut, Hawks, Southern), and historical fabulation (Pynchon, García Márquez, Coover, *et al.*).

13. Hugh Kenner, *The Counterfeiters* (New York: Doubleday Anchor Book, 1973), p. xiii.

14. I would take issue therefore with Andreas Huyssen's statement in *After the Great Divide: Modernism, Mass Culture, Postmodernism* (Bloomington: Indiana University Press, 1986) that "French [poststructuralist] theory provides us primarily with an *archeology of modernity,* a theory of modernism at its state of exhaustion" rather than a *"theory of postmodernity"* (p. 209, emphasis in original). First, because there is not as great a distance between these two projects as Huyssen indicates. Second, while it is true that, with the exception of Lyotard, French poststructuralism does not expressly provide a theory of postmodernity, it has been of enormous influence in the recent formulation of such theories. I might also point out that the term "archeology," while clearly applicable to such modernist works as Joyce's *Ulysses* and Eliot's *The Waste Land,* is used by Huyssen himself in a postmodern sense, since it explicitly assumes a critical and historical distance from modernism.

15. Jean-François Lyotard, "What Is Postmodernism," in *The Postmodern Condition,* trans. by Geoff Bennington and Brian Massumi (Minneapolis: University of Minnesota Press, 1984, orig. pub. 1979), p. 79.

16. This use of the German term *Nachträglichkeit,* meaning "deferred action," derives from Freud, who employed it repeatedly in connection with his view of psychical temporality and causality. For a useful discussion of the term, see the entry under "Deferred Action" in J. Laplanche and J.-B. Pontalis's *The Language of Psychoanalysis* (New York: W. W. Norton, 1973).

17. Of course, Gaddis was not the only writer of the period to refuse the modernist use of myth. Richard Wasson, in "Notes on a New Sensibility" (*Partisan Review,* Vol. 36, No. 3, 1969), shows that contemporary novelists like Robbe-Grillet, Murdock, Barth, and Pynchon all rejected the "mythical method" as a way of integrating self and history into a timeless order.

18. In an essay entitled "Periodizing the 60s" in *The 60s Without Apology* (Minneapolis: University of Minnesota Press, 1984), Fredric Jameson has re-

ferred to postmodernism as a "culture of the simulacrum (an idea developed out of Plato by Deleuze and Baudrillard to convey some specificity of a reproducible object world, not of copies or reproductions marked as such, but a proliferation of trompe-l'oeil copies *without originals*)" (p. 195, author's emphasis). Unfortunately, Jameson does not develop the idea any further.

19. By the four aspects of representation (its "quadruple links"), Deleuze means identity in the concept, opposition in the predicate, analogy in judgment, and resemblance in perception. See *Différence et répétition,* especially pp. 44ff.

20. See Alice A. Jardin's *Gynesis: Configurations of Woman and Modernity* (Ithaca: Cornell University Press, 1985) for an attempt to link the concern with "difference" evident in both poststructuralism and feminism.

21. See in particular Derrida's essay "Differance" in *Margins,* trans. by Alan Bass (Chicago: University of Chicago Press, 1982, orig. pub. 1972).

22. See Jean Baudrillard, *Simulations* (New York: Foreign Agents Series, 1983). Page numbers to further references to this book, which is comprised of sections extracted from *L'échange symbolic et la mort* and *Simulacres et simulation,* will be inserted in the text.

23. See, in particular, Gilles Deleuze and Félix Guattari, *A Thousand Plateaus,* trans. by Brian Massumi (Minneapolis: University of Minnesota Press, 1987, orig. pub. 1982), pp. 111–148 and 208–231, as well as my article "Ideology, Representation, Schizophrenia: Toward a Theory of the Postmodern Subject."

24. For a specific illustration of the theory, see Deleuze and Guattari's study *Kafka: Toward a Minor Literature,* trans. by Dana Polan (Minneapolis: University of Minnesota Press, 1986, orig. pub. 1975).

25. Joel Dana Black, "The Paper Empires and Empirical Fictions of William Gaddis," p. 24.

26. In this respect *JR* bears certain affinities with what Fredric Jameson calls the satire-collage, which is "the form taken by artificial epic in the degraded world of commodity production and of the mass media: it is artificial epic whose raw materials have become spurious and inauthentic, monumental gesture now replaced by the cultural junk of industrial capitalism." See *Fables of Aggression,* p. 80.

27. Frederick R. Karl, *American Fictions 1940–1980* (New York: Harper and Row, 1983), p. 190. Karl is to be greatly commended for giving Gaddis pride of place in his detailed but overarching survey of contemporary American fiction.

28. William Gaddis, *JR* (New York: Knopf, 1975), p. 20. Page numbers for all subsequent quotations will be inserted in the text.

29. Carl D. Malgren, "William Gaddis's *JR:* The Novel of Babel," *The Review of Contemporary Fiction,* Vol. II, No. 2 (summer 1982), p. 10.

30. In this subversion of an overarching narrative structure amidst a fragmentation of speech, *JR* illustrates Lyotard's contention in *The Postmodern Condition* that today "the narrative function ... is being dispersed in clouds of narrative language elements—narrative, but also denotative, prescriptive, descriptive, and so on. Conveyed within each cloud are pragmatic valencies specific to its kind. Each of us lives at the intersection of many of these. However, we do not necessarily establish stable language combinations, and the properties of the ones we do establish are not necessarily communicable" (p. xxiv). While it would

be going too far to see the disintegration of speech forms in *JR* exclusively in these terms, the relevance of the passage to the novel should be obvious.

31. George Stade, "JR," *New York Times Book Review,* November 9, 1975, p. 50.

32. The centripetal and centrifugal forces within language are discussed by Mikhail Bakhtin in "Discourse in the Novel," pp. 270ff.

33. Insofar as its recorded speech acts all refer only to other speech acts, *JR* corresponds in its structure to the definition of fabulation offered earlier. In most postmodern fiction, however, fabulation is achieved through embedded or nested acts of narration or alternative sources of information.

34. Thomas LeClair, "William Gaddis, *JR* and the Art of Excess" in *Modern Fiction Studies,* Vol. 27, No. 4 (winter 1981–1982), pp. 592–593. The term was coined by Gregory Bateson in *Steps to an Ecology of Mind* and developed by Anthony Wilden in *System and Structure.*

35. "Deterritorialization" is a term developed by Deleuze and Guattari in *Anti-Oedipus* (New York: Viking Press, 1977) to describe the inevitable dismantling or destruction of all traditional codes in the growth and expansion of capitalism into all aspects of life. Greatly simplified, their theory proposes that the primordial flux of desire is produced and coded (given meaning and significance) by means of and in relation to a semiotic regime and a territory. In primitive regimes, this primary coding is inscribed on the body, in dance, ritual, and myth in multiple and nonhierarchical forms, and takes as its ultimate referential territory the body of the earth itself. In barbaric regimes, signs undergo a paranoid reorganization and are overcoded, through constant (re)interpretation by a priest class, as certain signifiers are centered and become privileged over others, and the ultimate territory becomes the body of the despot or monarch himself. In civilized or capitalist society, these traditional and archaic codings are progressively undone or decoded, in a process of release and abstraction in which everything of value is such only because of its relation to capital. Compared to the previous regimes, capitalism is both more cynical (or nihilistic) and more productive. First of all, capitalism decodes and deterritorializes all previous traditional value systems, since it recognizes only those values that can be made equivalent to its own (re)production, as Marx has shown in great detail. Thus, in the capitalist regime, there is no longer any corresponding territory except for the deterritorialized body of capital itself. However, in axiomatizing all values in the exchange process—in reducing all human values to the cash nexus—capitalism also releases a tremendous amount of energy and expands productive capacity beyond all former limits. In order to control and regulate this release of energy and productive potential, Deleuze and Guattari argue, capitalism must defer and displace its own limits and re-inscribe (or re-territorialize) them in repressive channels, structures, and inhibitions. In short, by its very nature, capitalism breaks down older social structures and identities which it then must artificially shore up in order to continue to operate.

36. William Gaddis, *Carpenter's Gothic* (New York: Viking, 1984), p. 39. Page numbers to all subsequent quotations will be inserted in the text.

37. For two examples in *Carpenter's Gothic* which refer to *JR*, see the quoted passage on p. 150 containing the phrase "my vision of a disorder which it was

beyond any one man to put right" and Elizabeth's summary of Adolph's statement that Paul knows "as much about finance as some snot nosed sixth grader" on p. 209.

38. Lyotard, *The Postmodern Condition*, p. 81.

39. For Deleuze on the Kantian sublime, see *Différence et répétition*, pp. 187ff.

Index